Classwork

INTELLASTIC
SUCCESS READING PROGRAM
FOR OLDER STUDENTS

Learn To Read English With Directions In Korean
Classwork
Color Edition

Classwork

ISBN 978-1-945738-65-4
© 2022 – Wendy A. Charles & Alexander J. Charles
All Rights Reserved
Baldwin, New York
www.intellastic.com

All rights reserved. No portion of this book may be reproduced, stored in a retrieval system, or transmitted in any form or by any means – electronic, mechanical, photocopy, recording, video presentation, private instruction, scanning or other – except for brief quotations in critical reviews or articles, without the prior written permission of the writers.

All Rights Reserved. Printed in the USA.

Classwork

Table of Contents

Unit A

Lesson 1.1	Reading Words with the Letter A/a	1
Lesson 1.2	Reading Words with the Short Vowel "a" Sound	2
Lesson 1.2	Reading & Writing Words with the Short Vowel "a" Sound	3
Lesson 1.3	Reading Words with the Long Vowel "a" Sound	4
Lesson 1.3	Reading & Writing Words with the Long Vowel "a" Sound	5
Lessons 1.2 & 1.3	Reading Short Vowel and Long Vowel Words	6
Lesson 1.4	Reading Words with the "age" Letter Combination	7
Lesson 1.5	Reading Words with the "ai" Vowel Pair	8
Lesson 1.6	Reading Letter "a" Words with the Schwa Sound	9
Lesson 1.7	Reading Words with the "ar" Letter Combination	10
Lesson 1.7	Reading Words with the "ar" Letter Combination	11
Lesson 1.8	Reading Words with a Silent Letter "a"	12
Unit Review	Reading Words with Vowel "a" Sounds: /ă/, /ā/, /ə/ & Silent	13
Lesson 1.9	Reading Multisyllable Words	14
Lesson 1.9	Reading Multisyllable Words	15
Lesson 1.10	Proper and Common Nouns and Adjectives	16

Unit B

Lesson 2.1	Reading Words with the Letter B/b	17
Lesson 2.2	Reading Words with the "br" Letter Combination	18
Lesson 2.3	Reading Words with the "bl" Letter Combination	19
Lesson 2.3	Reading Words with the "ble" Letter Combination	20
Lesson 2.4	Reading Words with the "mb" Letter Combination	21
Lesson 2.4	Reading Words with the "bt" Letter Combination	22
Lesson 2.5	Reading Words with a Silent Letter "b"	23
Lesson 2.6	Reading Multisyllable Words	24
Lesson 2.6	Reading Multisyllable Words	25
Lesson 2.7	Proper and Common Nouns and Adjectives	26

Classwork

Unit C

Lesson 3.1	Reading Words with the Letter C/c	27
Lesson 3.1	Reading Words with the Hard Letter "c"	28
Lesson 3.2	Reading Words with the Soft Letter "c"	29
Lessons 3.1 & 3.2	Reading Hard Letter "c" and Soft Letter "c" Words	30
Lesson 3.3	Reading Words with the "cr" Letter Combination	31
Lesson 3.4	Reading Words with the "cl" Letter Combination	32
Lesson 3.4	Reading Words with the "cle" Letter Combination	33
Lesson 3.5	Reading Words with the "ct" Letter Combination	34
Lesson 3.6	Reading Soft Letter "c" Words	35
Lesson 3.6	Reading Soft Letter "c" Words	36
Lesson 3.7	Reading Words with the "ch" Letter Combination	37
Lesson 3.8	Reading Words with the "cc" Letter Combination	38
Lesson 3.9	Reading Words with a Silent Letter "c"	39
Lesson 3.10	Reading Multisyllable Words	40
Lesson 3.10	Reading Multisyllable Words	41
Lesson 3.11	Proper and Common Nouns and Adjectives	42

Unit D

Lesson 4.1	Reading Words with the Letter D/d	43
Lesson 4.2	Reading Letter "d" Words with the /d/ Sound & /j/ Sound	44
Lesson 4.2	Reading Words with the "dr" Letter Combination	45
Lesson 4.3	Reading Words with the "ed" Suffix/ Past Tense Verbs	46
Lesson 4.4	Reading Words with a Silent Letter "d"	47
Lesson 4.5	Reading Multisyllable Words	48
Lesson 4.5	Reading Multisyllable Words	49
Lesson 4.6	Proper and Common Nouns and Adjectives	50

Unit E

Lesson 5.1	Reading Words with the Letter E/e	51
Lesson 5.2	Reading Words with the Short Vowel "e" Sound	52
Lesson 5.2	Reading & Writing Words with the Short Vowel "e" Sound	53

Classwork

Lesson 5.3	Reading Words with the Long Vowel "e" Sound	54
Lesson 5.3	Reading & Writing Words with the Long Vowel "e" Sound	55
Lessons 5.2 & 5.3	Reading Short Vowel and Long Vowel Words	56
Lesson 5.4	Reading Words with Letter "e" Vowel Pairs	57
Lesson 5.5	Reading Words with the Final Letter "e"	58
Lesson 5.6	Reading Letter "e" Words with the Schwa Vowel Sound	59
Lesson 5.7	Reading Words with the "er" Letter Combination	60
Lesson 5.8	Reading Words with the "eu" and "ew" Letter Combinations	61
Lesson 5.9	Reading Words with the "ey" Letter Combination	62
Lesson 5.10	Reading Words with a Silent Letter "e"	63
Unit Review	Reading Words with Vowel "e" Sounds: /ĕ/, /ē/, /ə/ & Silent	64
Lesson 5.11	Reading Multisyllable Words	65
Lesson 5.11	Reading Multisyllable Words	66
Lesson 5.12	Proper and Common Nouns and Adjectives	67

Unit F

Lesson 6.1	Reading Words with the Letter F/f	68
Lesson 6.2	Reading Words with the "fr" Letter Combination	69
Lesson 6.3	Reading Words with the "fl" Letter Combination	70
Lesson 6.3	Reading Words with the "fle" Letter Combination	71
Lesson 6.4	Reading Words with the "ft," "lf" and "ff" Letter Combinations	72
Lesson 6.5	Reading Words with a Silent Letter "f"	73
Lesson 6.6	Reading Singular and Plural forms of Words Ending in "-f" & "-fe"	74
Lesson 6.7	Reading Multisyllable Words	75
Lesson 6.7	Reading Multisyllable Words	76
Lesson 6.8	Proper and Common Nouns and Adjectives	77

Unit G

Lesson 7.1	Reading Words with the Letter G/g	78
Lesson 7.1	Reading Words with the Hard Letter "g"	79
Lesson 7.2	Reading Words with the Soft Letter G/g	80
Lessons 7.1 & 7.2	Reading Hard Letter "g" and Soft Letter "g" Words	81

Classwork

Lessons 7.1 & 7.2	Reading Hard Letter "g" and Soft Letter "g" Words	82
Lesson 7.3	Reading Words with the "gr" Letter Combination	83
Lesson 7.4	Reading Words with the "gl" Letter Combination	84
Lesson 7.4	Reading Words with the "gle" Letter Combination	85
Lesson 7.5	Reading Words with the "gh" Letter Combination	86
Lesson 7.6	Reading Words with the "gn" Letter Combination	87
Lesson 7.7	Reading Words with a Silent Letter "g"	88
Lesson 7.8	Reading Multisyllable Words	89
Lesson 7.8	Reading Multisyllable Words	90
Lesson 7.9	Proper and Common Nouns and Adjectives	91

Unit H

Lesson 8.1	Reading Words with the Letter H/h	92
Lesson 8.2	Reading Words with the Letter "h" Combinations: "sh," "wh," "ch," "th," "rh," "ph" and "gh"	93
Lesson 8.2	Reading Words with the Letter "h" Combinations: "sh," "wh," "ch," "th," "rh," "ph," "gh" and "sch"	94
Lesson 8.3	Reading Words with a Silent Letter "h"	95
Lesson 8.4	Reading Multisyllable Words	96
Lesson 8.4	Reading Multisyllable Words	97
Lesson 8.5	Proper and Common Nouns and Adjectives	98

Unit I

Lesson 9.1	Reading Words with the Letter I/i	99
Lesson 9.2	Reading Words with the Short Vowel "i" Sound	100
Lesson 9.2	Reading & Writing Words with the Short Vowel "i" Sound	101
Lesson 9.3	Reading Words with the Long Vowel "i" Sound	102
Lesson 9.3	Reading & Writing Words with the Long Vowel "i" Sound	103
Lessons 9.2 & 9.3	Reading Short Vowel and Long Vowel Words	104
Lesson 9.4	Reading Words with Letter "i" Vowel Pairs	105
Lesson 9.5	Reading Words with the Final Letter "i"	106
Lesson 9.6	Reading Letter "i" Words with the Schwa Vowel Sound	107

Classwork

Lesson 9.7	Reading Words with the "ir" Letter Combination	108
Lesson 9.8	Reading Letter "i" Words with the Long Vowel "e" Sound	109
Lesson 9.9	Reading Words with a Silent Letter "i"	110
Unit Review	Reading Words with Vowel "i" Sounds: /ĭ/, /ī/, /ə/ & Silent	111
Lesson 9.10	Reading Multisyllable Words	112
Lesson 9.10	Reading Multisyllable Words	113
Lesson 9.11	Proper and Common Nouns and Adjectives	114

Unit J

Lesson 10.1	Reading Words with the Letter J/j	115
Lesson 10.2	Reading Multisyllable Words	116
Lesson 10.2	Reading Multisyllable Words	117
Lesson 10.3	Proper and Common Nouns and Adjectives	118

Unit K

Lesson 11.1	Reading Words with the Letter K/k	119
Lesson 11.2	Reading Words with the Letter "k" and "ck" Letter Combination	120
Lesson 11.3	Reading Words with the "kle" Letter Combination	121
Lesson 11.4	Reading Words with a Silent Letter "k"	122
Lesson 11.5	Reading Multisyllable Words	123
Lesson 11.5	Reading Multisyllable Words	124
Lesson 11.6	Proper and Common Nouns and Adjectives	125

Unit L

Lesson 12.1	Reading Words with the Letter L/l	126
Lesson 12.2	Reading Words with the Letter "l" Combinations: "fl," "pl" & "sl"	127
Lesson 12.3	Reading Words with a Silent Letter "l"	128
Lesson 12.4	Reading Multisyllable Words	129
Lesson 12.4	Reading Multisyllable Words	130
Lesson 12.5	Proper and Common Nouns and Adjectives	131

Classwork

Unit M
Lesson 13.1	Reading Words with the Letter M/m	132
Lesson 13.2	Reading Words with a Silent Letter "m"	133
Lesson 13.3	Reading Multisyllable Words	134
Lesson 13.3	Reading Multisyllable Words	135
Lesson 13.4	Proper and Common Nouns and Adjectives	136

Unit N
Lesson 14.1	Reading Words with the Letter N/n	137
Lesson 14.2	Reading Words with the "ng" Letter Combination	138
Lesson 14.3	Reading Words with a Silent Letter "n"	139
Lesson 14.4	Reading Multisyllable Words	140
Lesson 14.4	Reading Multisyllable Words	141
Lesson 14.5	Proper and Common Nouns and Adjectives	142

Unit O
Lesson 15.1	Reading Words with the Letter O/o	143
Lesson 15.2	Reading Words with the Short Vowel "o" Sound	144
Lesson 15.2	Reading & Writing Words with the Short Vowel "o" Sound	145
Lesson 15.3	Reading Words with the Long Vowel "o" Sound	146
Lesson 15.3	Reading & Writing Words with the Long Vowel "o" Sound	147
Lessons 15.2 & 15.3	Reading Short Vowel and Long Vowel Words	148
Lesson 15.4	Reading Words with Letter "o" Vowel Pairs	149
Lesson 15.5	Reading Words with the Final Letter "o"	150
Lesson 15.6	Reading Letter "o" Words with the Schwa Vowel Sound	151
Lesson 15.7	Reading Words with Vowel "o" Sounds: /ŏ/, /ō/ & /$\overline{oo}$/	152
Lesson 15.8	Reading Words with the "or" Letter Combination	153
Lesson 15.8	Reading Words with the "or" Letter Combination	154
Lesson 15.9	Reading Words with a Silent Letter "o"	155
Unit Review	Reading Words with Vowel "o" Sounds: /ŏ/, /ō/, /ə/ & Silent	156
Lesson 15.10	Reading Multisyllable Words	157
Lesson 15.10	Reading Multisyllable Words	158

Classwork

Lesson 15.11	Proper and Common Nouns and Adjectives	159
Unit P		
Lesson 16.1	Reading Words with the Letter P/p	160
Lesson 16.2	Reading Words with the "ph" Letter Combination	161
Lesson 16.3	Reading Words with the "pr" Letter Combination	162
Lesson 16.4	Reading Words with the "pl" Letter Combination	163
Lesson 16.4	Reading Words with the "ple" Letter Combination	164
Lesson 16.5	Reading Words with a Silent Letter "p"	165
Lesson 16.6	Reading Multisyllable Words	166
Lesson 16.6	Reading Multisyllable Words	167
Lesson 16.7	Proper and Common Nouns and Adjectives	168
Unit Q		
Lesson 17.1	Reading Words with the Letter Q/q	169
Lesson 17.2	Reading Words with the Letter "q" and "qu" Letter Combination	170
Lesson 17.2	Reading Words with the "qu" Letter Combination	171
Lesson 17.3	Reading Multisyllable Words	172
Lesson 17.3	Reading Multisyllable Words	173
Lesson 17.4	Proper and Common Nouns and Adjectives	174
Unit R		
Lesson 18.1	Reading Words with the Letter R/r	175
Lesson 18.2	Reading Words with the Letter "r" Combinations: "br," "cr," "dr," "fr," "gr," "pr" and "tr"	176
Lesson 18.3	Reading Multisyllable Words	177
Lesson 18.3	Reading Multisyllable Words	178
Lesson 18.4	Proper and Common Nouns and Adjectives	179
Unit S		
Lesson 19.1	Reading Words with the Letter S/s	180
Lesson 19.1	Reading Words with the Letter S/s	181

Classwork

Lesson 19.2	Reading Words with the "sion," "sial" & "scious" Suffixes	182
Lesson 19.3	Reading Words with the "sch" Letter Combination	183
Lesson 19.4	Reading Words with the "scr," "shr," "spr" & "str" Letter Combinations	184
Lesson 19.5	Reading Words with the "sl" & "sle" Letter Combinations	185
Lesson 19.5	Reading Words with the "sle" Letter Combination	186
Lesson 19.6	Reading Words with the "sm" Letter Combination	187
Lesson 19.7	Reading Words with the "ss" Letter Combination	188
Lesson 19.8	Reading Words with a Silent Letter "s"	189
Lesson 19.9	Reading Multisyllable Words	190
Lesson 19.9	Reading Multisyllable Words	191
Lesson 19.10	Proper and Common Nouns and Adjectives	192

Unit T

Lesson 20.1	Reading Words with the Letter T/t	193
Lesson 20.2	Reading Words with the "thm" Letter Combination	194
Lesson 20.3	Reading Words with the "tion," "tial" & "tious" Suffixes	195
Lesson 20.4	Reading Words with the "tr" Letter Combination	196
Lesson 20.5	Reading Words with the "tle" Letter Combination	197
Lesson 20.6	Reading Words with the Letter "t" Sounds	198
Lesson 20.7	Reading Words with a Silent Letter "t"	199
Lesson 20.8	Reading Multisyllable Words	200
Lesson 20.8	Reading Multisyllable Words	201
Lesson 20.9	Proper and Common Nouns and Adjectives	202

Unit U

Lesson 21.1	Reading Words with the Letter U/u	203
Lesson 21.2	Reading Words with the Short Vowel "u" Sound	204
Lesson 21.2	Reading & Writing Words with the Short Vowel "u" Sound	205
Lesson 21.3	Reading Words with the Long Vowel "u" Sound	206
Lesson 21.3	Reading & Writing Words with the Long Vowel "u" Sound	207
Lessons 21.2 & 21.3	Reading Short Vowel and Long Vowel Words	208
Lesson 21.4	Reading Words with Letter "u" Vowel Pairs	209

Classwork

Lesson 21.5	Reading Words with the Final Letter "u"	210
Lesson 21.6	Reading Letter "u" Words with the Schwa Vowel Sound	211
Lesson 21.7	Reading Words with the "ur" Letter Combination	212
Lesson 21.8	Reading Words with a Silent Letter "u"	213
Unit Review	Reading Words with Vowel "u" Sounds: /ŭ/, /o͞o/, /ə/ & Silent	214
Lesson 21.9	Reading Multisyllable Words	215
Lesson 21.9	Reading Multisyllable Words	216
Lesson 21.10	Proper and Common Nouns and Adjectives	217

Unit V

Lesson 22.1	Reading Words with the Letter V/v	218
Lesson 22.2	Reading Multisyllable Words	219
Lesson 22.2	Reading Multisyllable Words	220
Lesson 22.3	Proper and Common Nouns and Adjectives	221

Unit W

Lesson 23.1	Reading Words with the Letter W/w	222
Lesson 23.2	Reading Words with a Vowel before the Letter "w"	223
Lesson 23.3	Reading Words with a Silent "w" and "wr" Letter Combination	224
Lesson 23.3	Reading Words with a Silent Letter "w"	225
Lesson 23.4	Reading Multisyllable Words	226
Lesson 23.4	Reading Multisyllable Words	227
Lesson 23.5	Proper and Common Nouns and Adjectives	228

Unit X

Lesson 24.1	Reading Words with the Letter X/x	229
Lesson 24.1	Reading Words with the Letter X/x	230
Lesson 24.2	Reading Multisyllable Words	231
Lesson 24.2	Reading Multisyllable Words	232
Lesson 24.3	Proper and Common Nouns and Adjectives	233

Classwork

Unit Y

Lesson 25.1	Reading Words with the Letter Y/y	234
Lesson 25.1	Reading Words with the Letter Y/y	235
Lesson 25.2	Reading Words with a Vowel before the Letter "y"	236
Lesson 25.3	Reading Words with the "cy" Letter Combination	237
Lesson 25.4	Reading Words with the Final Letter "y"	238
Lesson 25.5	Reading Words with the "yr" Letter Combination	239
Lesson 25.6	Reading Letter "y" Words with the Schwa Sound	240
Lesson 25.7	Reading Words with a Silent Letter "y"	241
Lesson 25.8	Reading Multisyllable Words	242
Lesson 25.8	Reading Multisyllable Words	243
Lesson 25.9	Proper and Common Nouns and Adjectives	244

Unit Z

Lesson 26.1	Reading Words with the Letter Z/z	245
Lesson 26.1	Reading Words with the Letter Z/z	246
Lesson 26.2	Reading Words with a Silent Letter "z"	247
Lesson 26.3	Reading Multisyllable Words	248
Lesson 26.3	Reading Multisyllable Words	249
Lesson 26.4	Proper and Common Nouns and Adjectives	250

Appendix

Appendix 1.0	Introduction of the Letter A/a	251
Appendix 2.0	Introduction of the Letter B/b	252
Appendix 2.0	Letter Recognition B/b	253
Appendix 3.0	Introduction of the Letter C/c	254
Appendix 3.0	Letter Recognition C/c	255
Appendix 4.0	Introduction of the Letter D/d	256
Appendix 4.0	Letter Recognition D/d	257
Appendix 5.0	Introduction of the Letter E/e	258
Appendix 6.0	Introduction of the Letter F/f	259
Appendix 6.0	Letter Recognition F/f	260

Appendix 7.0	Introduction of the Letter G/g	261
Appendix 7.0	Letter Recognition G/g	262
Appendix 8.0	Introduction of the Letter H/h	263
Appendix 8.0	Letter Recognition H/h	264
Appendix 9.0	Introduction of the Letter I/i	265
Appendix 10.0	Introduction of the Letter J/j	266
Appendix 10.0	Letter Recognition J/j	267
Appendix 11.0	Introduction of the Letter K/k	268
Appendix 11.0	Letter Recognition K/k	269
Appendix 12.0	Introduction of the Letter L/l	270
Appendix 12.0	Letter Recognition L/l	271
Appendix 13.0	Introduction of the Letter M/m	272
Appendix 13.0	Letter Recognition M/m	273
Appendix 14.0	Introduction of the Letter N/n	274
Appendix 14.0	Letter Recognition N/n	275
Appendix 15.0	Introduction of the Letter O/o	276
Appendix 16.0	Introduction of the Letter P/p	277
Appendix 16.0	Letter Recognition P/p	278
Appendix 17.0	Introduction of the Letter Q/q	279
Appendix 17.0	Letter Recognition Q/q	280
Appendix 18.0	Introduction of the Letter R/r	281
Appendix 18.0	Letter Recognition R/r	282
Appendix 19.0	Introduction of the Letter S/s	283
Appendix 19.0	Letter Recognition S/s	284
Appendix 20.0	Introduction of the Letter T/t	285
Appendix 20.0	Letter Recognition T/t	286
Appendix 21.0	Introduction of the Letter U/u	287
Appendix 22.0	Introduction of the Letter V/v	288
Appendix 22.0	Letter Recognition V/v	289
Appendix 23.0	Introduction of the Letter W/w	290
Appendix 23.0	Letter Recognition W/w	291

Classwork

Appendix 24.0	Introduction of the Letter X/x	292
Appendix 24.0	Letter Recognition X/x	293
Appendix 25.0	Introduction of the Letter Y/y	294
Appendix 25.0	Letter Recognition Y/y	295
Appendix 26.0	Introduction of the Letter Z/z	296
Appendix 26.0	Letter Recognition Z/z	297

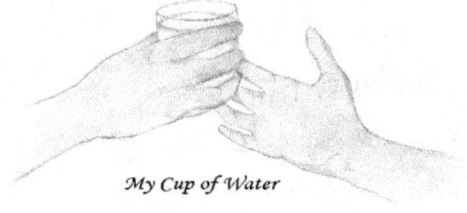

My Cup of Water

Classwork

 Name: _____ Date:___/___/_____ Score: _____

Lesson 1.1

Reading Words with the Letter A/a

✓ Lesson Check Point

 **Directions:** Read each target word. Find the letter "a" and put a check (✓) in the column that identifies its position: beginning, within or end.
지도: 각 대상 단어를 읽으십시오. 문자 "a"를 찾아 해당 위치를 나타내는 열에 확인 표시(✓)를 하십시오: 시작, 내부 또는 끝.

Target Words	Beginning (First Letter)	Within	End (Last Letter)
1. taxicab			
2. black			
3. anklet			
4. opera			
5. above			

 Directions: Read each target word. Read the words in the row and circle the word that has a different vowel "a" sound.
지도: 각 대상 단어를 읽으십시오. 행에 있는 단어를 읽고 모음 "a" 소리가 다른 단어에 동그라미를 치십시오.

Target Words				
6. am	cat	sand	pail	bank
7. apple	cab	sofa	back	sad
8. happy	band	ant	sank	cake
9. pants	zebra	sat	cap	man
10. thanks	cash	bake	map	pan

Learn To Read English With Directions In Korean

Classwork

 Name: _____ Date:___/___/_____ Score:_____

Lesson 1.2

Reading Words with the Short Vowel "a" Sound

✓ **Lesson Check Point**

Directions: Read the words in the four boxes. Circle two words with the short vowel /ă/ sound. The anchor word for the short vowel /ă/ sound is <u>apple</u>.

지도: 네 개의 상자에 있는 단어를 읽으십시오. 짧은 모음 /ă/ 소리로 두 단어에 동그라미를 치십시오. 단모음 /ă/ 소리의 앵커 워드는 apple입니다.

day	hat
cap	sofa

grass	nap
tuna	lake

agree	yam
sand	paint

Asia	pad
ago	back

walk	father
flap	map

flag	man
grape	bake

Directions: Read the words in the four boxes. Circle two words that rhyme. Rhyming words have the same ending sound, such as <u>tap</u> and <u>map</u>.

지도: 네 개의 상자에 있는 단어를 읽으십시오. 운이 맞는 두 단어에 동그라미를 치십시오. 운율이 있는 단어는 tap 및 map과 같이 끝 소리가 같습니다.

had	tax
dad	zap

nap	cake
cape	map

camp	lamp
spa	alike

away	plane
ran	man

game	cat
sat	lane

take	tan
ate	ran

Classwork

L Name: _____ Date: ___/___/_____ Score: _____

Lesson 1.2

Reading & Writing Words with the Short Vowel "a" Sound

✓ **Lesson Check Point**

Directions: Read each sentence and underline three words with the short vowel /ă/ sound. Then, write the underlined words on the lines below. The anchor word for the short vowel /ă/ sound is apple.

지도: 각 문장을 읽고 세 단어에 짧은 모음 /ă/ 소리에 밑줄을 긋습니다. 그런 다음 밑줄 친 단어를 아래 줄에 쓰십시오. 단모음 /ă/ 소리의 기준어는 appple입니다.

Model

<u>Ann</u> raised her <u>hand</u> in <u>class</u>.

    Ann   hand   class
  _____   _____   _____

1. Pam's tan hat is faded.

　　_____　　_____　　_____

2. My father asked for apples and grapes.

　　_____　　_____　　_____

3. Sam and Dan walked by the lake.

　　_____　　_____　　_____

4. David planted the flag in the sand.

　　_____　　_____　　_____

5. My music teacher plays the sax in a large jazz band.

　　_____　　_____　　_____

Classwork

 Name: _____ Date: ___/___/_____ Score: _____

Lesson 1.3

Reading Words with the Long Vowel "a" Sound

✓ **Lesson Check Point**

 **Directions:** Read the words in the four boxes. Circle two words with the long vowel /ā/ sound. The anchor word for the long vowel /ā/ sound is ape.

지도: 네 개의 상자에 있는 단어를 읽으십시오. 장모음 /ā/ 소리로 두 단어에 동그라미를 치십시오. 장모음 /ā/ 소리의 기준어는 ape입니다.

cap	sale		alike	cat		ate	sofa
talk	nail		gain	pace		wave	tap

rat	lake		page	mate		stay	above
male	ago		pan	about		alone	sail

 Directions: Read the words in the four boxes. Circle two words that rhyme. Rhyming words have the same ending sound, such as wait and date.

지도: 네 개의 상자에 있는 단어를 읽으십시오. 운이 맞는 두 단어에 동그라미를 치십시오. 운율이 있는 단어는 wait 및 date와 같이 끝 소리가 같습니다.

mama	wake		tuna	lane		land	puma
take	ban		dad	cane		rate	late

came	man		tale	Asia		pave	gave
same	panda		bran	mail		villa	have

Classwork

L Name: _____ Date: ___/___/_____ Score: _____

Lesson 1.3

Reading & Writing Words with the Long Vowel "a" Sound

✓ **Lesson Check Point**

Directions: Read each sentence and underline three words with the long vowel /ā/ sound. Then, write the underlined words on the lines below. The anchor word for the long vowel /ā/ sound is ape.

지도: 각 문장을 읽고 장모음 /ā/ 소리로 세 단어에 밑줄을 긋습니다. 그런 다음 밑줄 친 단어를 아래 줄에 쓰십시오. 장모음 /ā/ 소리의 기준어는 ape입니다.

Model

Ann has grapes and cake on her plate.

    grapes   cake   plate
   _____   _____   _____

1. Dain can't wait to paint the chair.

   _____   _____   _____

2. The skates and sails are packed in the basement.

   _____   _____   _____

3. Alvin did not take the large slice of cake from the plate.

   _____   _____   _____

4. Dale Anderson said, "Beware of garter snakes by the lake."

   _____   _____   _____

5. Jackson and Andrew sold chocolate cupcakes at Annie's bake sale.

   _____   _____   _____

Unit A Lesson 1.3

L Learn To Read English With Directions In Korean   Copyrighted Material

Classwork

Name: _____ Date:___/___/_____ Score:_____

Review Lessons 1.2 & 1.3
Reading Short Vowel and Long Vowel Words

Directions: Read the target words in the word box. In the first column, write the words that have the short vowel /ă/ sound, as in the word <u>apple</u>. In the second column, write the words that have the long vowel /ā/ sound, as in the word <u>ape</u>.

지도: 단어 상자에 있는 대상 단어를 읽습니다. 첫 번째 열에는 apple이라는 단어에서와 같이 단모음 /ă/ 소리가 나는 단어를 씁니다. 두 번째 열에는 장모음이 포함된 단어를 쓰십시오 /ā/ 소리, 단어 ape에서와 같이.

Target Word Box				
bagel	grass	glad	clan	basic
trap	came	taken	grapes	hat
fame	maps	sand	stay	gain
slaps	bake	train	flag	brand

Letter "a" has the /ă/ sound as in the word <u>apple</u>

Letter "a" has the /ā/ sound as in the word <u>ape</u>

Classwork

 Name: _____ Date:___/___/_____ Score:_____

Lesson 1.4

Reading Words with the "age" Letter Combination

✓ Lesson Check Point

 Directions: Read each target word. Find the "age" letter combination and put a check (✓) in the column that correctly identifies its sounds.
지도: 각 대상 단어를 읽으십시오. "age" 문자 조합을 찾아 해당 소리를 올바르게 식별하는 열에 체크(✓)를 하십시오.

Target Words	"age" has the /ā/ + /j/ sounds as in the word stage	"age" has the /ĭ/ + /j/ sounds as in the word package	"age" has the /ä/ + /j/ or /ä/ + /zh/ sounds as in the word massage
1. camouflage			
2. Anchorage			
3. enrage			
4. baggage			
5. teenagers			

 Directions: Read each sentence and underline the word that has an "age" letter combination that has the /ĭ/ + /j/ sounds, as in the word package.
지도: 각 문장을 읽고 단어 package에서와 같이 /ĭ/ + /j/ 소리가 나는 "age" 문자 조합이 있는 단어에 밑줄을 긋습니다.

6. The teenager's albums and books are in the cottage.

7. The teenager's luggage set was stolen from the airport.

8. My large boxes from Anchorage, Alaska are on the stage.

9. The backstage manager ate apple pie and drank lemonade.

10. Everyone in the entourage had massages after their long voyage.

Classwork

Name: _____ Date: ___/___/_____ Score: _____

Lesson 1.5

Reading Words with the "ai" Vowel Pair

✓ **Lesson Check Point**

Directions: Read each target word. Circle the word in the column that has the same "ai" sound as the target word.

지도: 각 대상 단어를 읽으십시오. 목표 단어와 같은 "ai" 소리가 나는 열의 단어에 동그라미를 치십시오.

mail	a. said
	b. male

wait	a. basic
	b. land

paid	a. change
	b. salt

aim	a. plant
	b. page

Directions: Read each target word. Put a check (✓) under the correct column heading.

지도: 각 대상 단어를 읽으십시오. 올바른 열 제목 아래에 체크(✓)를 하십시오.

Target Words	Words have the long "a" sound as in the word <u>sail</u>	Words do not have the long "a" sound
1. tail		
2. trait		
3. plaid		
4. pain		

Classwork

 Name: _____ Date:___/___/_____ Score:_____

Lesson 1.6

Reading Letter "a" Words with the Schwa Vowel Sound

✓ Lesson Check Point

 **Directions:** Read each target word. Circle the word in the column that has the same "a" sound as the target word.
지도: 각 대상 단어를 읽으십시오. 대상 단어와 동일한"a"소리가 나는 열의 단어에 동그라미를 치십시오.

hang<u>a</u>r	a. zebra
	b. carpet

banana	a. relative
	b. place

ahead	a. admit
	b. separate

sofa	a. static
	b. alone

 Directions: Read each sentence and underline the letter "a" word that has the schwa vowel /ə/ sound. The anchor word for the letter "a" schwa vowel sound is <u>sofa</u>.
지도: 각 문장을 읽고 슈와 모음 /ə/ 소리가 있는 문자"a" 단어에 밑줄을 긋습니다. 문자"a" 슈와 모음 소리의 앵커 단어는 sofa입니다.

1. The class is going to the opera.

2. The Erie Canal is an awesome place.

3. On Saturday, Ann ate two large bananas.

4. This year, I have an amazing math teacher.

5. Dr. Anderson paid the cab driver three dollars.

6. Andrew ate whole wheat spaghetti with white sauce.

Classwork

 Name: _____   Date: ___/___/_____   Score: _____

Lesson 1.7

Reading Words with the "ar" Letter Combination

✓ **Lesson Check Point**

 Directions: Read each target word. Circle the word in the column that has the same "a" + "r" sounds as the target word.
지도: 각 대상 단어를 읽으십시오. 해당 열에 있는 단어에 동그라미를치십시오. 대상 단어와 동일한 "a" + "r" 소리가 있습니다.

| art | a. park |
| | b. carrot |

| marry | a. sharp |
| | b. marigold |

| lunar | a. calendar |
| | b. start |

| farm | a. sugar |
| | b. star |

 Directions: Read each target word. Put a check (✓) under the correct column heading.
지도: 각 대상 단어를 읽으십시오. 올바른 열 제목 아래에 체크(✓)를하십시오.

Target Words	"ar" has the /ă/ + /r/ sounds as in the word <u>baron</u>	"ar" has the /ə/ + /r/ sounds as in the word <u>dollar</u>	"ar" has the /ä/ + /r/ sounds as in the word <u>car</u>	"ar" has the /ô/ + /r/ sounds as in the word <u>war</u>
1. art				
2. marry				
3. lunar				
4. farm				

Classwork

 Name: _____   Date: ___/___/_____   Score: _____

Lesson 1.7

Reading Words with the "ar" Letter Combination

Dictionary Skills/ Vocabulary

✓ Lesson Check Point

 Directions: Read each target word and its definition. Write the target word on the line in front of its meaning. Use a dictionary or the Internet to check your answers.
지도: 각 대상 단어와 그 정의를 읽으십시오. 의미 앞 줄에 대상단어를 쓰십시오. 사전이나 인터넷을 사용하여 답을 확인하십시오.

Target Word Box				
Oscar	narrator	party	paramedics	garlic

1. _____ a fun gathering where people socialize
2. _____ medical professionals
3. _____ a boy or man's name
4. _____ an edible plant that looks like a bulb
5. _____ a person who tells the events of the story

 Directions: Read each sentence and write the target word that correctly completes the sentence.
지도: 각 문장을 읽고 다음과 같은 목표 단어를 쓰십시오. 장을 올바르게 완성합니다.

6. Baroness invited all her friends to the _____.

7. _____ registered for classes at the registrar's office.

8. The dynamic _____ dramatically read the play's stage directions.

9. I enhanced the flavor of the soup by adding vinegar and _____.

10. The skilled _____ saved Arty's life by administering CPR.

Classwork

Name: _____   Date: ___/___/_____   Score: _____

Lesson 1.8

Reading Words with a Silent Letter "a"

✓ **Lesson Check Point**

Directions: Read the target words in the word box. Write the words that have a silent letter "a" in the first column. Write the words that do not have a silent letter "a" in the second column.

지도: 단어 상자에 있는 대상 단어를 읽습니다. 첫 번째 열에 묵음 문자"a"가 있는 단어를 쓰십시오. 두 번째 열에 묵음 문자"a"가 없는 단어를 쓰십시오.

Target Word Box				
floats	pain	dragon	aisle	goats
games	broad	oasis	sandy	anthills
beauty	oats	days	raining	crash
central	gloating	bread	bureau	boating

Letter "a" is silent

Letter "a" has a letter "a" sound

Unit A Lesson 1.8

Learn To Read English With Directions In Korean

Classwork

Name: _____ Date: ___/___/_____ Score: _____

Unit Review - A/a

Reading Words with Vowel "a" Sounds: /ă/, /ā/, /ə/ & Silent

✓ **Lesson Check Point**

Directions: Read each target word. Circle the word in the column that has the same "a" sound as the target word.
지도: 각 대상 단어를 읽으십시오. 대상 단어와 동일한"a" 소리가 나는 열의 단어에 동그라미를 치십시오.

lake	a. plate
	b. flag

plant	a. grass
	b. gorilla

pasta	a. away
	b. hallway

algebra	a. rake
	b. cobra

Directions: Read each target word. Put a check (✓) under the correct column heading.
지도: 각 대상 단어를 읽으십시오. 올바른 열 제목 아래에 체크(✓)를하십 시오.

Target Words	"a" has the /ă/ sound as in the word apple	"a" has the /ā/ sound as in the word ate	"a" has the /ə/ sound as in the word sofa	"a" is silent as in the word boat
1. lake				
2. plant				
3. pasta				
4. algebra				

Learn To Read English With Directions In Korean

Classwork

 Name: _____ Date: ___/___/_____ Score: _____

The Reading Challenge

Lesson 1.9

Reading Multisyllable Words

✓ Lesson Check Point

 Directions: Read and divide each target word into syllables. Write each word and place a hyphen (-) between the syllables in the second column. Write the number of syllables in the third column. Use a dictionary or the Internet to check your answers.

지도: 각 대상 단어를 읽고 음절로 나눕니다. 각 단어를 쓰고 두 번째 열의 음절 사이에 하이픈(-)을 넣습니다. 세 번째 열에 음절 수를 쓰십시오. 사전이나 인터넷을 사용하여 답을 확인하십시오.

Target Words	Words Divided into Syllables	Number of Syllables
1. payback	_____	_____
2. slogan	_____	_____
3. turban	_____	_____
4. abdomen	_____	_____
5. batman	_____	_____
6. husband	_____	_____
7. Alaskan	_____	_____
8. Scotland	_____	_____
9. embanking	_____	_____
10. migrated	_____	_____

Unit A Lesson 1.9

Classwork

Name: _____ Date: ___/___/_____ Score: _____

The Reading Challenge

Lesson 1.9

Reading Multisyllable Words

✓ **Lesson Check Point**

Directions: Read each target word. Circle the word in the row that is divided correctly into syllables. Use a dictionary or the Internet to check your answers.

지도: 각 대상 단어를 읽으십시오. 음절로 올바르게 나누어진 행에 있는 단어에 동그라미를 치십시오. 사전이나 인터넷을 사용하여 답을 확인하십시오.

Model

| important | a. im-por-tant ⃝ | b. im-port-ant | c. im-porta-nt |

1. diploma	a. di-plo-ma	b. di-plom-a	c. dip-lom-a
2. absolute	a. a-bso-lute	b. a-bsol-ute	c. ab-so-lute
3. admonish	a. adm-o-nish	b. a-dmon-ish	c. ad-mon-ish
4. magistrate	a. mag-is-trate	b. mag-i-strate	c. ma-gis-trate
5. kilogram	a. ki-lo-gram	b. ki-log-ram	c. kil-o-gram
6. caravan	a. ca-rav-an	b. car-a-van	c. car-av-an
7. admiral	a. ad-mir-al	b. ad-mi-ral	c. a-dmir-al
8. monogram	a. mo-no-gram	b. mo-nog-ram	c. mon-o-gram

Learn To Read English With Directions In Korean

Classwork

Name: _____ Date: ___/___/_____ Score: _____

Lesson 1.10

Reading and Writing

Proper and Common Nouns and Adjectives

✓ **Lesson Check Point**

Directions: Read the words in the word box. Put an (X) on the line next to each word that is written incorrectly. Remember that all proper nouns and proper adjectives are capitalized. Use a dictionary or the Internet to check your answers.

지도: 단어 상자에 있는 단어를 읽으십시오. 잘못 쓰여진 각 단어 옆의 줄에 (X)를 표시하십시오. 모든 고유 명사와 고유 형용사는 대문자임을 기억하십시오. 사전이나 인터넷을 사용하여 답을 확인하십시오.

Word Box					
__	August	__	Argentina	__	Author
__	Achievers	__	advanced	__	adventure
__	apollo	__	athens	__	America
__	airmail	__	alaska	__	ArubA

Directions: Read each unedited sentence and underline the word that is written incorrectly. Write each sentence correctly on the line.

지도: 편집되지 않은 각 문장을 읽고 잘못 쓰여진 단어에 밑줄을긋습 니다. 각 문장을 줄에 올바르게 쓰십시오.

Model
Andrew has a view of the <u>atlantic</u> Ocean from his apartment.
<u>Andrew has a view of the Atlantic Ocean from his apartment.</u>

1. Anne and <u>alex</u> are from Australia.
_____

2. The <u>Author's</u> article, "Awaken," is amazing.
_____

3. Mr. <u>aaron</u> got a lot of cash from the ATM.
_____

4. In <u>august</u>, Ashley will attend Ace Academy.
_____

Classwork

 Name: _____ Date:___/___/_____ Score:_____

Lesson 2.1

Reading Words with the Letter B/b

✓ Lesson Check Point

 Directions: Read each target word. Find the letter "b" and put a check (✓) in the column that identifies its position: beginning, within or end.
지도: 각 대상 단어를 읽으십시오. 문자"b"를 찾아 위치를 나타내는열: 시작, 내부 또는 끝에 체크(✓)를 하십시오.

Target Words	Beginning (First Letter)	Within	End (Last Letter)
1. cab			
2. bit			
3. table			
4. tab			
5. bottom			

 Directions: Read each sentence and underline the words that begin with the letter "b." Write all the underlined words in alphabetical order on the lines below.
지도: 각 문장을 읽고"b"로 시작하는 단어에 밑줄을 긋습니다. 밑줄친모든단어를 아래 줄에 알파벳 순서로 쓰십시오.

6. Andy's bat is black.

7. He has a belt and a billfold.

8. There is a cat on the baby's bib.

9. Abe and Andy are in the big band.

10. Annie and Aaron have the best books.

_____   _____   _____
_____   _____   _____
_____   _____   _____
                 _____

Classwork

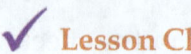 Name: _____ Date: ___/___/_____ Score: _____

Lesson 2.2

Reading Words with the "br" Letter Combination

Dictionary Skills/ Vocabulary

✓ **Lesson Check Point**

 Directions: Read each target word and its definition. Write the letter of the definition on the line of each target word. Use a dictionary or the Internet to check your answers.
지도: 각 대상 단어와 그 정의를 읽으십시오. 각 대상 단어의 행에 정의의 문자를 씁니다. 사전이나 인터넷을 사용하여 답을 확인하십시오.

Target Words	Definitions
1. __ brags	a. a large country on the South American continent
2. __ Brazil	b. a physical injury without an open cut
3. __ broccoli	c. to say something in a boastful way
4. __ bridal	d. a green vegetable with densely clustered flower buds
5. __ bruise	e. something or someone pertaining to a wedding

 Directions: Read each sentence. Underline the word in the parentheses that correctly completes each sentence. Then, write the underlined word on the line.
지도: 각 문장을 읽으십시오. 각 문장을 올바르게 완성하는 괄호 안에 있는 단어에 밑줄을 긋습니다. 그런 다음 밑줄 친 단어를 줄에 쓰십시오.

6. The bride has a nice _____ dress. (bridal, brags)

7. The _____ on Betsy's back is black. (Brazil, bruise)

8. I ate _____ and bread for breakfast. (bruise, broccoli)

9. Brenda _____ about her brand new boat. (brags, broccoli)

10. Do you know that _____ is a big country? (bruise, Brazil)

Classwork

 Name: _____ Date:___/___/_____ Score:_____

Lesson 2.3

Reading Words with the "bl" Letter Combination

Dictionary Skills/ Vocabulary

✓ Lesson Check Point

 Directions: Read each target word and its definition. Write the target word on the line in front of its meaning. Use a dictionary or the Internet to check your answers.
지도: 각 대상 단어와 그 정의를 읽으십시오. 의미 앞 줄에 대상 단어를 쓰십시오. 사전이나 인터넷을 사용하여 답을 확인하십시오.

Target Word Box				
blanket	blasted	bleed	blender	blinks

1. _____ the flow of blood out of a blood vessel
2. _____ a machine that mixes things together
3. _____ the quick closing and opening movement of eyes
4. _____ to have shot something out with great force
5. _____ a large cloth covering used to cover a bed

 Directions: Read each sentence. Underline the word in the parentheses that correctly completes each sentence. Then, write the underlined word on the line.
지도: 각 문장을 읽으십시오. 각 문장을 올바르게 완성하는 괄호 안에 있는 단어에 밑줄을 긋습니다. 그런 다음 밑줄 친 단어를 줄에 쓰십시오.

6. My big rocket _____ off. (blinks, blasted)

7. Bill blends bananas in his _____. (blanket, blender)

8. Bethany _____ her big, brown eyes. (bleed, blinks)

9. Betty puts a big, blue _____ on her bed. (blanket, blender)

10. The big blade cut Bill and made him _____. (bleed, blasted)

Classwork

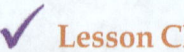 Name: _____ Date: ___/ ___/ _____ Score: _____

Lesson 2.3

Reading Words with the "ble" Letter Combination

✓ Lesson Check Point

 Directions: Read each target word. Find the "ble" letter combination and put a check (✓) in the column that identifies its position: beginning, within or end.

지도: 각 대상 단어를 읽으십시오. "ble" 문자 조합을 찾아 위치를 식별하는 열에 체크(✓)를 하십시오: 시작, 내부 또는 끝.

Target Words	Beginning (First 3 Letters)	Within	End (Last 3 Letters)
1. table			
2. problem			
3. bleach			
4. adorable			
5. scribbler			

 Directions: Read each target word. Put a check (✓) in the "yes" column if the "ble" letter combination has the /b/ + /ə/ + /l/ sounds. Put a check (✓) in the "no" column if the "ble" letter combination does not have the /b/ + /ə/ + /l/ sounds.

지도: 각 대상 단어를 읽으십시오. "ble" 문자 조합에 /b/ + /ə/ + /l/ 소리가 있는 경우 "yes" 열에 체크(✓)를 하십시오. "ble" 문자 조합에 /b/ + /ə/ + /l/ 소리가 없으면 "no" 열에 체크(✓)를 하십시오.

Target Words	Yes	No
6. bleed		
7. bleach		
8. babble		
9. agreeable		
10. collectible		

Classwork

 Name: _____ Date: ___/___/_____ Score: _____

Lesson 2.4

Reading Words with the "mb" Letter Combination

✓ Lesson Check Point

 Directions: Read each target word. Circle the word in the column that has the same "mb" sound(s) as the target word.
지도: 각 대상 단어를 읽으십시오. 대상 단어와 동일한 "mb" 소리가 있는 열의 단어에 동그라미를 치십시오.

| honeycomb | a. lumber |
| | b. breadcrumbs |

| humble | a. ambulance |
| | b. lamb |

| womb | a. bombard |
| | b. entomb |

| slumber | a. crumble |
| | b. womb |

 Directions: Read each target word. In the second column, write the number of letters in the word. In the third column, write the number of letters heard in the word.
지도: 각 대상 단어를 읽으십시오. 두 번째 열에는 단어의 글자 수를 씁니다. 세 번째 열에는 단어에서 들리는 글자 수를 쓰십시오.

Target Words	Number of letters in the word	Number of letters heard
1. combat		
2. climber		
3. limbs		
4. lumber		

Classwork

 Name: _____ Date:___/___/_____ Score:_____

Lesson 2.4

Reading Words with the "bt" Letter Combination

✓ **Lesson Check Point**

 Directions: Read each target word. Circle the word in the column that has the same "bt" sound(s) as the target word.
지도: 각 대상 단어를 읽으십시오. 대상 단어와 동일한 "bt" 소리가 있는 열의 단어에 동그라미를 치십시오.

| doubt | a. subtle |
| | b. subtitle |

| subtext | a. debtor |
| | b. obtuse |

| debt | a. subtend |
| | b. doubting |

| subtract | a. obtain |
| | b. subtle |

 Directions: Read each target word. In the second column, write the number of letters in the word. In the third column, write the number of letters heard in the word.
지도: 각 대상 단어를 읽으십시오. 두 번째 열에는 단어의 글자 수를 씁니다. 세 번째 열에는 단어에서 들리는 글자 수를 쓰십시오.

Target Words	Number of letters in the word	Number of letters heard
1. doubt		
2. subtext		
3. debt		
4. subtract		

Classwork

 Name: _____ Date: ___/___/_____ Score: _____

Lesson 2.5

Reading Words with a Silent "b"

✓ Lesson Check Point

 Directions: Read the target words in the word box. Write the words that have a silent letter "b" in the first column. Write the words that do not have a silent letter "b" in the second column.

지도: 단어 상자에 있는 대상 단어를 읽습니다. 첫 번째 열에 묵음 문자"b"가 있는 단어를 쓰십시오. 두 번째 열에 묵음 문자"b"가 없는 단어를 쓰십시오.

Target Word Box				
labels	climbing	bread	zebra	subpoena
thumbs	bugs	debt	crumb	lamb
abandon	plumbers	basement	ability	bedroom
combs	brother	entomb	books	limbs

Letter "b" is silent	Letter "b" has the /b/ sound
_____	_____
_____	_____
_____	_____
_____	_____
_____	_____
_____	_____
_____	_____
_____	_____

Classwork

Name: _____ Date: ___/___/_____ Score: _____

The Reading Challenge

Lesson 2.6

Reading Multisyllable Words

✓ **Lesson Check Point**

Directions: Read and divide each target word into syllables. Write each word and place a hyphen (-) between the syllables in the second column. Write the number of syllables in the third column. Use a dictionary or the Internet to check your answers.

지도: 각 대상 단어를 읽고 음절로 나눕니다. 각 단어를 쓰고 두 번째 열의 음절 사이에 하이픈(-)을 넣습니다. 세 번째 열에 음절 수를 쓰십시오. 사전이나 인터넷을 사용하여 답을 확인하십시오.

Target Words	Words Divided into Syllables	Number of Syllables
1. balance	_____	_____
2. submit	_____	_____
3. sublet	_____	_____
4. bigwig	_____	_____
5. banana	_____	_____
6. obstacle	_____	_____
7. biceps	_____	_____
8. tablet	_____	_____
9. beckon	_____	_____
10. blanket	_____	_____

Classwork

Name: _____ Date: ___/___/_____ Score: _____

The Reading Challenge

Lesson 2.6

Reading Multisyllable Words

✓ **Lesson Check Point**

Directions: Read each target word. Circle the word in the row that is divided correctly into syllables. Use a dictionary or the Internet to check your answers.

지도: 각 대상 단어를 읽으십시오. 음절로 올바르게 나누어진 행에 있는 단어에 동그라미를 치십시오. 사전이나 인터넷을 사용하여 답을 확인하십시오.

Model

| because | a. be-cause (circled) | b. beca-use | c. b-ecause |

1. bachelor	a. bac-he-lor	b. bach-e-lor	c. ba-ch-elor
2. backpack	a. back-pack	b. ba-ckpa-ck	c. ba-ckp-ack
3. bellboy	a. be-llboy	b. bellb-oy	c. bell-boy
4. blackout	a. bla-ckout	b. black-out	c. bl-ackout
5. bicycle	a. bi-cycle	b. bi-cy-cle	c. bicy-cle
6. baritone	a. ba-ri-tone	b. ba-rit-one	c. bar-i-tone
7. bracelet	a. bracel-et	b. bra-celet	c. brace-let
8. bumblebee	a. bum-ble-bee	b. bumb-le-bee	c. bu-mbleb-ee

Learn To Read English With Directions In Korean   25   Copyrighted Material

Classwork

👤 Name: _____ Date: ___/___/_____ Score: _____

Lesson 2.7

Reading and Writing

Proper and Common Nouns and Adjectives

✓ **Lesson Check Point**

Directions: Read the words in the word box. Put an (X) on the line next to each word that is written incorrectly. Remember that all proper nouns and proper adjectives are capitalized. Use a dictionary or the Internet to check your answers.

지도: 단어 상자에 있는 단어를 읽으십시오. 잘못 쓰여진 각 단어 옆의 줄에 (X)를 표시하십시오. 모든 고유 명사와 고유 형용사는 대문자임을 기억하십시오. 사전이나 인터넷을 사용하여 답을 확인하십시오.

Word Box		
__ Bolivia	__ BuBBle	__ absent
__ barber	__ bottom	__ BarBados
__ Bread	__ bread	__ bridges
__ buckingham	__ bulB	__ bahamas

Directions: Read each unedited sentence and underline the word that is written incorrectly. Write each sentence correctly on the line.

지도: 편집되지 않은 각 문장을 읽고 잘못 쓰여진 단어에 밑줄을긋습 니다. 각 문장을 줄에 올바르게 쓰십시오.

Model
<u>brandon's</u> books are about big boats.
<u>Brandon's books are about big boats.</u>

1. The black <u>Bat</u> is really big.
   _____

2. <u>bob</u> has a brown bag.
   _____

3. The blue <u>taBle</u> is too big.
   _____

4. <u>benjamin's</u> baked bread is in his bag.
   _____

Classwork

Name: _____ Date: ___/___/_____ Score: _____

Lesson 3.1

Reading Words with the Letter C/c

✓ **Lesson Check Point**

Directions: Read each target word. Find the letter "c" and put a check (✓) in the column that identifies its position: beginning, within or end.
지도: 각 대상 단어를 읽으십시오. 문자"c"를 찾아 위치를 나타내는 열: 시작, 내부 또는 끝에 체크(✓)를 하십시오.

Target Words	Beginning (First Letter)	Within	End (Last Letter)
1. clog			
2. toxic			
3. tackle			
4. basic			
5. picture			

Directions: Read each sentence and underline the words that begin with the letter "c." Write all the underlined words in alphabetical order on the lines below.
지도: 각 문장을 읽고"c"로 시작하는 단어에 밑줄을 긋습니다. 밑줄 친 모든 단어를 아래 줄에 알파벳 순서로 쓰십시오.

6. The big cows are cute.

7. The black car is very clean.

8. The child is in the blue crib.

9. Bobby has a cap and a big coat.

10. The boys are chasing the chicken.

_____ _____ _____

_____ _____ _____

_____ _____ _____

_____

Learn To Read English With Directions In Korean

Classwork

Name: _____ Date: ___/___/_____ Score: _____

Lesson 3.1

Reading Words with the Hard Letter "c"

✓ Lesson Check Point

Directions: Read each target word. Put a check (✓) under the correct column heading.

지도: 각 대상 단어를 읽으십시오. 올바른 열 제목 아래에 체크(·)를 하십시오.

Target Words	Hard "c" has the /k/ sound as in the word cat	Soft "c" has the /s/ sound as in the word cell
1. school		
2. cleaning		
3. cement		
4. civilized		
5. character		

Directions: Read each sentence and underline the words that have the hard "c" sound, as in the word cat. Write all the underlined words in alphabetical order on the lines below.

지도: 각 문장을 읽고 단어 cat에서와 같이 단단한"c" 소리가 나는 단어에 밑줄을 긋습니다. 아래 줄에 밑줄 친 단어를 알파벳 순서로 모두 쓰십시오.

6. Ms. Clarke's big chips are crunchy.

7. The cake has a caramel apple center.

8. Andrew is chewing cranberry candy.

9. Cindy is counting the crabs in the bowl.

10. Everyone in my class had a bowl of ice cream.

_____   _____   _____

_____   _____   _____

_____   _____   _____

_____

Unit C Lesson 3.1

Classwork

Name: _____ Date: ___/___/_____ Score: _____

Lesson 3.2

Reading Words with the Soft Letter "c"

Directions: Read each target word. Put a check (✓) under the correct column heading.
지도: 각 대상 단어를 읽으십시오. 올바른 열 제목 아래에 체크(✓)를 하십시오.

Target Words	Hard "c" has the /k/ sound as in the word cat	Soft "c" has the /s/ sound as in the word cell
1. face		
2. curl		
3. cast		
4. city		
5. clue		

Directions: Read each sentence and underline the words that have the soft "c" sound, as in the word cell. Write all the underlined words in alphabetical order on the lines below.
지도: 각 문장을 읽고 cell이라는 단어에서처럼 부드러운 "c" 소리가 나는 단어에 밑줄을 긋습니다. 아래 줄에 밑줄 친 단어를 알파벳 순서로 모두 쓰십시오.

6. City Hall is in the center of Clarkston.

7. Lucy said, "The comedian is a cynic."

8. Caleb said, "We live in a civilized society."

9. The baby in the crib ate cranberry and cinnamon cereal.

10. I stored my bicycles and ceramic casserole dishes in the den.

_____   _____   _____

_____   _____   _____

_____   _____   _____

_____

Learn To Read English With Directions In Korean

Classwork

Name: _____ Date: ___/___/_____ Score: _____

Review Lessons 3.1 & 3.2

Reading Hard Letter "c" and Soft Letter "c" Words

Directions: Read the target words in the word box. In the first column, write the words with the letter "c" that have the /k/ sound, as in the word <u>cat</u>. In the second column, write the words with the letter "c" that have the /s/ sound, as in the word <u>cell</u>.

지도: 단어 상자에 있는 대상 단어를 읽으십시오. 첫 번째 열에는 cat라는 단어에서와 같이 /k/ 소리가 나는 문자"c"가 있는 단어를 씁니다. 두 번째 열에는 cell이라는 단어에서와 같이 /s/ 소리가 나는 문자"c"가 있는 단어를 씁니다.

Target Word Box				
cause	cook	citizen	city	curb
curve	mice	cute	code	citrus
cedar	cube	cake	call	spicy
coil	cysts	place	cease	cent

Hard letter "c" has the /k/ sound as in the word <u>cat</u>

Soft letter "c" has the /s/ sound as in the word <u>cell</u>

Classwork

Name: _____ Date:___/___/_____ Score:_____

Lesson 3.3

Reading Words with the "cr" Letter Combination

Dictionary Skills/ Vocabulary

✓ **Lesson Check Point**

Directions: Read each target word and its definition. Write the letter of the definition on the line of each target word. Use a dictionary or the Internet to check your answers.
지도: 각 대상 단어와 그 정의를 읽으십시오. 각 대상 단어의 행에 정의의 문자를 씁니다. 사전이나 인터넷을 사용하여 답을 확인하십시오.

Target Words	Definitions
1. __ cranberry	a. to really want something, such as food
2. __ craving	b. to move along the ground on hands and knees
3. __ crawls	c. a thick dairy product made from milk
4. __ cream	d. a small, tart, red berry-like fruit
5. __ crumbs	e. small pieces of bread or other baked goods

Directions: Read each sentence. Underline the word in the parentheses that correctly completes each sentence. Then, write the underlined word on the line.
지도: 각 문장을 읽으십시오. 각 문장을 올바르게 완성하는 괄호 안에 있는 단어에 밑줄을 긋습니다. 그런 다음 밑줄 친 단어를 줄에 쓰십시오.

6. The cats ate the cookie _____. (crawls, crumbs)

7. Cindy's ice _____ is very cold. (cream, craving)

8. The baby _____ on the carpet. (crawls, cream)

9. I have a _____ for cotton candy. (craving, cranberry)

10. Chad likes to drink _____ juice. (crumbs, cranberry)

Learn To Read English With Directions In Korean

Classwork

Name: _____ Date: ___/___/_____ Score: _____

Lesson 3.4

Reading Words with the "cl" Letter Combination

Dictionary Skills/ Vocabulary

✓ **Lesson Check Point**

Directions: Read each target word and its definition. Write the target word on the line in front of its meaning. Use a dictionary or the Internet to check your answers.
지도: 각 대상 단어와 그 정의를 읽으십시오. 의미 앞 줄에 대상 단어를 쓰십시오. 사전이나 인터넷을 사용하여 답을 확인하십시오.

Target Word Box				
cleared	cliff	clipped	clock	closet

1. _____ the overhanging of a mountain
2. _____ a device used to display time
3. _____ a small inner room used for clothing and storage
4. _____ to have moved something out of the way
5. _____ to fasten or grip with a firm metal or plastic clamp

Directions: Read each sentence. Underline the word in the parentheses that correctly completes each sentence. Then, write the underlined word on the line.
지도: 각 문장을 읽으십시오. 각 문장을 올바르게 완성하는 괄호 안에 있는 단어에 밑줄을 긋습니다. 그런 다음 밑줄 친 단어를 줄에 쓰십시오.

6. Chad cleaned out his bedroom _____. (closet, cliff)

7. Charles _____ the clogged drain. (cleared, closet)

8. Yesterday, we climbed up the steep _____. (clipped, cliff)

9. I _____ my index cards on the clipboard. (clipped, clock)

10. This morning, my alarm _____ woke me up. (clock, cleared)

Classwork

 Name: _____ Date: ___/___/_____ Score: _____

Lesson 3.4

Reading Words with the "cle" Letter Combination

✓ Lesson Check Point

 Directions: Read each target word. Find the "cle" letter combination and put a check (✓) in the column that identifies its position: beginning, within or end.

지도: 각대상 단어를 읽으십시오. "cle" 문자 조합을 찾아 위치를식별 하는 열에 체크(✓)를 하십시오: 시작, 내부 또는 끝.

Target Words	Beginning (First 3 Letters)	Within	End (Last 3 Letters)
1. article			
2. cleaning			
3. inclement			
4. particle			
5. cleverly			

 Directions: Read each target word. Put a check (✓) in the "yes" column if the "cle" letter combination has the /k/ + /ə/ + /l/ sounds. Put a check (✓) in the "no" column if the "cle" letter combination does not have the /k/ + /ə/ + /l/ sounds.

지도: 각 대상 단어를 읽으십시오. "cle" 문자 조합에/k/ + /ə/ + /l/소리가있으면 "yes" 열에 체크(✓)를 하십시오. "cle" 문자 조합에/k/ + /ə/ + /l/ 소리가없으면 "no" 열에 체크(✓)를 하십시오.

Target Words	Yes	No
6. article		
7. cleaning		
8. inclement		
9. particle		
10. cleverly		

Classwork

Name: _____ Date: ___/___/_____ Score: _____

Lesson 3.5

Reading Words with the "ct" Letter Combination

✓ **Lesson Check Point**

Directions: Read each target word. Circle the word in the column that has the same "ct" sound(s) as the target word.
지도: 각 대상단어를 읽으십시오. 대상 단어와 동일한 "ct" 소리가 있는 열의 단어에 동그라미를 치십시오.

conflict	a. impact
	b. benediction

predict	a. viaduct
	b. prediction

electric	a. inject
	b. victual

Connecticut	a. connection
	b. indict

Directions: Read each target word. Put a check (✓) under the correct column heading.
지도: 각 대상 단어를 읽으십시오. 올바른 열 제목 아래에 체크(✓)를하십시오.

Target Words	"ct" has the /k/ + /t/ sounds as in the word <u>fact</u>	"ct" has the silent "c" + /t/ sound as in the word <u>indict</u>
1. conflict		
2. predict		
3. electric		
4. Connecticut		

Classwork

 Name: _____   Date: ___/___/_____   Score: _____

Lesson 3.6

Reading Soft Letter "c" Words

✓ Lesson Check Point

 Directions: Read each target word. Circle the word in the column that has the same "cean," "cian," "cial," "cious," or "cient" sound as the target word.

지도: 각 대상 단어를 읽으십시오. 대상 단어와 동일한 "cean," "cian," "cial," "cious" 또는 "cient" 소리가 나는 열의 단어에 동그라미를 치십시오.

ferocious	a. judicious
	b. special

optician	a. pelican
	b. ocean

social	a. rascal
	b. racial

efficient	a. accent
	b. deficient

 Directions: Read each target word. Put a check (✓) in the column that identifies the same "cean," "cian," "cial," "cious," or "cient" sound within the target word.

지도: 각 대상 단어를 읽으십시오. 대상 단어 내에서 동일한 "cean," "cian," "cial," "cious" 또는 "cient" 소리를 식별하는 열에 체크(✓)를 하십시오.

Target Words	"cean" has the /sh/+/ə/+/n/ sounds as in the word <u>ocean</u>	"cial" has the /sh/+/ə/+/l/ sounds as in the word <u>special</u>	"cious" has the /sh/+/ə/+/s/ sounds as in the word <u>delicious</u>	"cient" has the /sh/+/ə/+/n/+/t/ sounds as in the word <u>ancient</u>
1. ferocious				
2. optician				
3. social				
4. efficient				

Classwork

Name: _____ Date: ___/___/_____ Score: _____

Lesson 3.6

Reading Soft Letter "c" Words

Directions: Read the target words in the word box. In the first column, write the words with the letter "c" that have the /s/ sound, as in the word <u>cell</u>. In the second column, write the words with the letter "c" that have the /sh/ sound, as in the word <u>ocean</u>.

지도: 단어 상자에 있는 대상 단어를 읽으십시오. 첫 번째 열에는 cell이라는 단어에서와 같이 /s/ 소리가 나는 문자"c"가 있는 단어를 씁니다. 두 번째 열에는 다음과 같은 문자"c"가 포함된 단어를 쓰십시오. /sh/ 소리, ocean 이라는 단어에서처럼.

Target Word Box				
commercial	delicious	office	place	lacy
technician	gallinacean	spices	cement	artificial
circus	proficient	prince	race	decided
omniscient	twice	optician	conscious	socialize

Soft letter "c" has the /s/ sound as in the word <u>cell</u>

Soft letter "c" has the /sh/ sound as in the word <u>ocean</u>

Classwork

 Name: _____ Date: ___/___/_____ Score: _____

Lesson 3.7

Reading Words with the "ch" Letter Combination

✓ Lesson Check Point

 Directions: Read each target word. Circle the word in the column that has the same "ch" sound as the target word.
지도: 각 대상 단어를 읽으십시오. 대상 단어와 같은 "ch" 소리가 나는 열의 단어에 동그라미를 치십시오.

chicken	a. chaos
	b. chance

fuchsia	a. yacht
	b. scholar

anchor	a. school
	b. change

parachute	a. couch
	b. chauvinist

 Directions: Read each target word. Put a check (✓) under the correct column heading.
지도: 각 대상 단어를 읽으십시오. 올바른 열 제목 아래에 체크(✓)를 하십시오.

Target Words	"ch" has the /ch/ sound as in the word chain	"ch" has the /sh/ sound as in the word chef	"ch" has the /k/ sound as in the word chaos	"ch" is silent as in the word yacht
1. chicken				
2. fuchsia				
3. anchor				
4. parachute				

Classwork

Name: _____ Date: ___/___/_____ Score: _____

Lesson 3.8

Reading Words with the "cc" Letter Combination

✓ Lesson Check Point

Directions: Read each target word. Circle the word in the column that has the same "cc" sound(s) as the target word.
지도: 각 대상 단어를 읽으십시오. 대상 단어와 동일한 "cc" 소리가 나는 열의 단어에 동그라미를 치십시오.

| access | a. hiccups |
| | b. accident |

| succeed | a. vaccine |
| | b. succumb |

| occupy | a. raccoon |
| | b. accept |

| accommodate | a. accuse |
| | b. accessory |

Directions: Read each target word. Put a check (✓) under the correct column heading.
지도: 각 대상 단어를 읽으십시오. 올바른 열 제목 아래에 체크(✓)를 하십시오.

Target Words	"cc" has the /k/ sound as in the word <u>soccer</u>	"cc" has the /k/ + /s/ sounds as in the word <u>accept</u>
1. access		
2. succeed		
3. occupy		
4. accommodate		

Classwork

Name: _____ Date: ___/___/_____ Score: _____

Lesson 3.9

Reading Words with a Silent Letter "c"

✓ Lesson Check Point

Directions: Read the target words in the word box. Write the words that have a silent letter "c" in the first column. Write the words that do not have a silent letter "c" in the second column.

지도: 단어 상자에 있는 대상 단어를 읽으십시오. 첫 번째 열에 묵음 문자"c"가 있는 단어를 쓰십시오. 두 번째 열에 묵음 문자"c"가 없는 단어를 쓰십시오.

Target Word Box				
czar	scent	scalp	cake	acquit
occupy	corpuscle	muscle	excited	scissors
citizens	produce	congress	scenery	ascend
classic	yacht	increase	court	scale

Letter "c" is silent

Letter "c" has the /k/, /s/ or /sh/ sound

Classwork

Name: _____ Date: ___/___/_____ Score: _____

The Reading Challenge

Lesson 3.10

Reading Multisyllable Words

✓ Lesson Check Point

Directions: Read and divide each target word into syllables. Write each word and place a hyphen (-) between the syllables in the second column. Write the number of syllables in the third column. Use a dictionary or the Internet to check your answers.

지도: 각 대상 단어를 읽고 음절로 나눕니다. 각 단어를 쓰고 두 번째 열의 음절 사이에 하이픈(-)을 넣습니다. 세 번째 열에 음절 수를 쓰십시오. 사전이나 인터넷을 사용하여 답을 확인하십시오.

Target Words	Words Divided into Syllables	Number of Syllables
1. climber	_____	_____
2. cleaner	_____	_____
3. climbing	_____	_____
4. crayons	_____	_____
5. construction	_____	_____
6. cereal	_____	_____
7. crocodile	_____	_____
8. creditors	_____	_____
9. crackers	_____	_____
10. camping	_____	_____

Unit C Lesson 3.10

Classwork

Name: _____ Date: ___/___/_____ Score: _____

The Reading Challenge

Lesson 3.10

Reading Multisyllable Words

✓ **Lesson Check Point**

Directions: Read each target word. Circle the word in the row that is divided correctly into syllables. Use a dictionary or the Internet to check your answers.

지도: 각 대상 단어를 읽으십시오. 음절로 올바르게 나누어진 행에 있는 단어에 동그라미를 치십시오. 사전이나 인터넷을 사용하여 답을 확인하십시오.

Model

| calculus | a. calcu-lus | b. cal-cu-lus (circled) | c. cal-culus |

1. chipmunk	a. chip-munk	b. chip-mu-nk	c. ch-ipmu-nk
2. calendar	a. ca-lend-ar	b. cal-en-dar	c. ca-le-ndar
3. circuit	a. cir-cu-it	b. circu-it	c. cir-cuit
4. compound	a. com-pound	b. co-mpou-nd	c. com-po-und
5. cereal	a. ce-re-al	b. cer-e-al	c. c-ere-al
6. charisma	a. char-isma	b. cha-rism-a	c. cha-ris-ma
7. cinema	a. cin-e-ma	b. cine-ma	c. ci-ne-ma
8. cylinder	a. cy-lin-der	b. cyl-in-der	c. cylin-der

Learn To Read English With Directions In Korean   41   Copyrighted Material

Classwork

Name: _____ Date: ___/___/_____ Score: _____

Lesson 3.11

Reading and Writing

Proper and Common Nouns and Adjectives

✓ Lesson Check Point

Directions: Read the words in the word box. Put an (X) on the line next to each word that is written incorrectly. Remember that all proper nouns and proper adjectives are capitalized. Use a dictionary or the Internet to check your answers.

지도: 단어 상자에 있는 단어를 읽으십시오. 잘못 쓰여진 각 단어 옆의 줄에 (X)를 표시하십시오. 모든 고유 명사와 고유 형용사는 대문자임을 기억하십시오. 사전이나 인터넷을 사용하여 답을 확인하십시오.

Word Box		
__ China	__ cliniC	__ camp
__ cleveland	__ College	__ Colombia
__ cities	__ castle	__ charles
__ chicago	__ chinese	__ cherry

Directions: Read each unedited sentence and underline the word that is written incorrectly. Write each sentence correctly on the line.

지도: 편집되지 않은 각 문장을 읽고 잘못 쓰여진 단어에 밑줄을 긋습 니다. 각 문장을 줄에 올바르게 쓰십시오.

Model
The <u>Camp</u> in Cleveland is closed.
<u>The camp in Cleveland is closed.</u>

1. The crickets chirp loudly on clement Cliff.
_____

2. Do you like cindy's corn and chili?
_____

3. The City of Chicago is cold and Chilly.
_____

4. The coyotes is the name of our chess team.
_____

Classwork

Name: _____   Date: ___/___/_____   Score: _____

Lesson 4.1

Reading Words with the Letter D/d

✓ Lesson Check Point

Directions: Read each target word. Find the letter "d" and put a check (✓) in the column that identifies its position: beginning, within or end.
지도: 각 대상 단어를 읽으십시오. 문자"d"를 찾아 위치를 나타내는 열에 체크(✓)를 하십시오: 시작, 내부 또는 끝.

Target Words	Beginning (First Letter)	Within	End (Last Letter)
1. calendar			
2. dusting			
3. garden			
4. hard			
5. dictionary			

Directions: Read each sentence and underline the words that begin with the letter "d." Write all the underlined words in alphabetical order on the lines below.
지도: 각 문장을 읽고 문자"d"로 시작하는 단어에 밑줄을 긋습니다. 아래 줄에 밑줄 친 단어를 알파벳 순서로 모두 쓰십시오.

6. Brandon has a dark blue drum.

7. The barking dogs are on the deck.

8. The driver is driving a big blue bus.

9. My daughter ate the biggest drumstick.

10. Candice designed a beautiful black dress.

_____   _____   _____
_____   _____   _____
              _____

Learn To Read English With Directions In Korean   Copyrighted Material

Classwork

Name: _____ Date: ___/___/_____ Score: _____

Lesson 4.2

Reading Letter "d" Words with the /d/ Sound & /j/ Sound

✓ **Lesson Check Point**

Directions: Read each target word. Circle the word in the column that has the same "d" sound as the target word.

지도: 각 대상 단어를 읽으십시오. 대상 단어와 "d" 소리가 같은 열의 단어에 동그라미를 치십시오.

London	a. handle
	b. nodule

golden	a. glandular
	b. field

education	a. explode
	b. schedule

modulate	a. soldier
	b. modify

Directions: Read each target word. Put a check (✓) under the correct column heading.

지도: 각 대상 단어를 읽으십시오. 올바른 열 제목 아래에 체크(✓)를 하십시오.

Target Words	"d" has the /d/ sound as in the word <u>doctor</u>	"d" has the /j/ sound as in the word <u>educate</u>
1. London		
2. golden		
3. education		
4. modulate		

Classwork

 Name: _____   Date:___/___/_____   Score: _____

Lesson 4.2

Reading Words with the "dr" Letter Combination

Dictionary Skills/ Vocabulary

✓ Lesson Check Point

Directions: Read each target word and its definition. Write the letter of the definition on the line of each target word. Use a dictionary or the Internet to check your answers.
지도: 각 대상 단어와 그 정의를 읽으십시오. 각 대상 단어의 행에 정의의 문자를 씁니다. 사전이나 인터넷을 사용하여 답을 확인하십시오.

Target Words	Definitions
1. __ dreams	a. to have fallen unintentionally
2. __ driveway	b. the cooked leg of a chicken, duck or turkey
3. __ driving	c. visualizing events that happen during sleep
4. __ dropped	d. a short path that leads to a house or garage
5. __ drumstick	e. the process of operating a vehicle

Directions: Read each sentence. Underline the word in the parentheses that correctly completes each sentence. Then, write the underlined word on the line.
지도: 각 문장을 읽으십시오. 각 문장을 올바르게 완성하는 괄호 안에 있는 단어에 밑줄을 긋습니다. 그런 다음 밑줄 친 단어를 줄에 쓰십시오.

6. I drove the blue car into the _____. (dreams, driveway)

7. The boy _____ his big chocolate donut. (dropped, driving)

8. At night, Dan _____ about big animals. (dreams, driveway)

9. I am _____ my car to Denver, Colorado. (driving, drumstick)

10. At dinner, David ate a delicious _____. (dropped, drumstick)

Classwork

Name: _____ Date: ___/__/_____ Score: _____

Lesson 4.3

Reading Words with the "ed" Suffix/ Past Tense Verbs

✓ **Lesson Check Point**

Directions: Read each target word. Circle the word in the column that has the same "ed" sound(s) as the target word.
지도: 각 대상 단어를 읽으십시오. 대상 단어와 동일한"ed" 소리(들)가있는열의 단어에 동그라미를 치십시오.

missed	a. ended
	b. trapped

burned	a. grabbed
	b. planted

named	a. snapped
	b. pulled

ended	a. signed
	b. traded

Directions: Read each target word. Put a check (✓) under the correct column heading.
지도: 각 대상 단어를 읽으십시오. 올바른 열 제목 아래에 체크(✓)를하십시오.

Target Words	"ed" has the /ĭ/ + /d/ sounds as in the word <u>rested</u>	"ed" has the /d/ sound as in the word <u>hugged</u>	"ed" has the /t/ sound as in the word <u>tipped</u>
1. missed			
2. burned			
3. named			
4. ended			

Name: _____ Date: ___/___/_____ Score: _____

Classwork

Lesson 4.4

Reading Words with a Silent Letter "d"

✓ Lesson Check Point

 Directions: Read the target words in the word box. Write the words that have a silent letter "d" in the first column. Write the words that do not have a silent letter "d" in the second column.

지도: 단어 상자에 있는 대상 단어를 읽으십시오. 첫 번째 열에 묵음문자 "d"가 있는 단어를 쓰십시오. 두 번째 열에 묵음 문자"d"가 없는 단어를 쓰십시오.

Target Word Box				
handicap	Cambridge	dock	Windsor	elder
does	conduct	handsome	adjourn	adjustment
judge	adjacent	director	handkerchief	discuss
padlock	doctor	footbridge	Wednesday	depend

Letter "d" is silent

_____
_____
_____
_____
_____
_____
_____
_____
_____
_____

Letter "d" has the /d/ sound

_____
_____
_____
_____
_____
_____
_____
_____
_____
_____

Classwork

Name: _____ Date: ___/___/_____ Score: _____

The Reading Challenge

Lesson 4.5

Reading Multisyllable Words

✓ **Lesson Check Point**

Directions: Read and divide each target word into syllables. Write each word and place a hyphen (-) between the syllables in the second column. Write the number of syllables in the third column. Use a dictionary or the Internet to check your answers.

지도: 각 대상 단어를 읽고 음절로 나눕니다. 각 단어를 쓰고 두 번째 열의 음절 사이에 하이픈(-)을 넣습니다. 세 번째 열에 음절 수를 쓰십시오. 사전이나 인터넷을 사용하여 답을 확인하십시오.

Target Words	Words Divided into Syllables	Number of Syllables
1. demonstrate	_____	_____
2. duplicate	_____	_____
3. diagram	_____	_____
4. decimal	_____	_____
5. descendent	_____	_____
6. digital	_____	_____
7. disengaged	_____	_____
8. doormat	_____	_____
9. discomfort	_____	_____
10. driver	_____	_____

Classwork

Name: _____ Date: ___/___/_____ Score: _____

The Reading Challenge

Lesson 4.5

Reading Multisyllable Words

✓ Lesson Check Point

Directions: Read each target word. Circle the word in the row that is divided correctly into syllables. Use a dictionary or the Internet to check your answers.

지도: 각 대상 단어를 읽으십시오. 음절로 올바르게 나누어진 행에 있는 단어에 동그라미를 치십시오. 사전이나 인터넷을 사용하여 답을 확인하십시오.

Model

| dictionary | a. di-ction-ary | b. dic-tion-ar-y (circled) | c. dic-tiona-ry |

| 1. disciple | a. di-sci-ple | b. dis-cip-le | c. dis-ci-ple |

| 2. deceptive | a. de-cep-tive | b. dec-ep-tive | c. de-cept-ive |

| 3. Dakota | a. Dako-ta | b. Da-kot-a | c. Da-ko-ta |

| 4. disgruntle | a. dis-grun-tle | b. di-sgrun-tle | c. dis-grunt-le |

| 5. dimension | a. dim-e-nsion | b. dim-en-sion | c. di-men-sion |

| 6. domino | a. dom-i-no | b. do-min-o | c. dom-in-o |

| 7. decelerate | a. decel-er-ate | b. dec-el-er-ate | c. de-cel-er-ate |

| 8. distribute | a. dist-rib-ute | b. dis-tri-bute | c. dis-trib-ute |

Learn To Read English With Directions In Korean

Classwork

Name: _____ Date: ___/___/_____ Score: _____

Lesson 4.6

Reading and Writing

Proper and Common Nouns and Adjectives

✓ **Lesson Check Point**

Directions: Read the words in the word box. Put an (X) on the line next to each word that is written incorrectly. Remember that all proper nouns and proper adjectives are capitalized. Use a dictionary or the Internet to check your answers.

지도: 단어 상자에 있는 단어를 읽으십시오. 잘못 쓰여진 각 단어 옆의 줄에 (X)를 표시하십시오. 모든 고유 명사와 고유 형용사는 대문자임을 기억하십시오. 사전이나 인터넷을 사용하여 답을 확인하십시오.

Word Box		
__ Daughter	__ denmark	__ Dutch
__ Dana	__ detroit	__ director
__ Denver	__ diner	__ danish
__ dakota	__ door	__ Detective

Directions: Read each unedited sentence and underline the word that is written incorrectly. Write each sentence correctly on the line.

지도: 편집되지 않은 각 문장을 읽고 잘못 쓰여진 단어에 밑줄을긋습 니다. 각 문장을 줄에 올바르게 쓰십시오.

Model
Dan said, "My daughter's name is <u>donna</u>."
<u>Dan said, "My daughter's name is Donna."</u>

1. Drake's Dictionary is not on his desk.
   _____

2. The dark blue Doormat has one big dot.
   _____

3. The diploma belongs to doctor Davis.
   _____

4. The danish pastries, pancakes, and donuts cost five dollars.
   _____

Classwork

 Name: _____ Date:___/___/_____ Score:_____

Lesson 5.1

Reading Words with the Letter E/e

✓ Lesson Check Point

 Directions: Read each target word. Find the letter "e" and put a check (✓) in the column that identifies its position: beginning, within or end.
지도: 각 대상 단어를 읽으십시오. 문자"e"를 찾아 체크 표시(✓)위치를식별하는 열에서 시작, 내부 또는 끝.

Target Words	Beginning (First Letter)	Within	End (Last Letter)
1. eating			
2. belong			
3. cake			
4. father			
5. embark			

 Directions: Read each target word. Read the words in the row and circle the word that has a different vowel "e" sound.
지도: 각 대상 단어를 읽으십시오. 줄에 있는 단어를 읽고 모음"e" 소리가 다른 단어에 동그라미를 치세요.

Target Words				
6. beds	leg	she	check	pet
7. men	be	ten	vet	hen
8. decks	yet	pen	we	set
9. stem	hem	me	net	fled
10. them	he	send	less	test

Classwork

 Name: _____ Date: ___/___/_____ Score: _____

Lesson 5.2

Reading Words with the Short Vowel "e" Sound

✓ **Lesson Check Point**

 Directions: Read the words in the four boxes. Circle two words with the short vowel /ĕ/ sound. The anchor word for the short vowel /ĕ/ sound is <u>egg</u>.

지도: 네 개의 상자에 있는 단어를 읽으십시오. 짧은 모음 /ĕ/ 소리로 두 단어에 동그라미를 치십시오. 단모음 /ĕ/ 소리의 앵커 워드는 egg입니다.

cake	web		bead	speck		ease	choose
check	theme		bee	fed		dwelt	hem

Fred	mean		well	them		sped	beat
eat	hedge		Pete	free		yell	mate

 Directions: Read the words in the four boxes. Circle two words that rhyme. Rhyming words have the same ending sound, such as <u>set</u> and <u>wet</u>.

지도: 네 개의 상자에 있는 단어를 읽으십시오. 운이 맞는 두 단어에동그라미를 치십시오. 운율이 있는 단어는 set 및 wet와 같이 끝 소리가같습 니다.

bean	neck		gem	stem		bell	each
wise	deck		deal	pie		true	spell

shoe	meat		toe	bed		edge	zeal
men	ten		red	heal		pledge	they

Classwork

Name: _____ Date: ___/___/_____ Score: _____

Lesson 5.2

Reading & Writing Words with the Short Vowel "e" Sound

✓ **Lesson Check Point**

Directions: Read each sentence and underline three words with the short vowel /ĕ/ sound. Then, write the underlined words on the lines below. The anchor word for the short vowel /ĕ/ sound is egg.

지도: 각 문장을 읽고 세 단어에 짧은 모음 /ĕ/ 소리에 밑줄을 긋습니다. 그런 다음 밑줄 친 단어를 아래 줄에 쓰십시오. 단모음 /ĕ/ 소리의 기준어는 egg입니다.

Model

She placed her <u>legs</u> on the <u>wet</u> <u>deck</u>.

  legs   wet   deck
 _____   _____   _____

1. She will not let us get a pet.

 _____   _____   _____

2. We smell the three wet hens.

 _____   _____   _____

3. Andre bent his leg and fell.

 _____   _____   _____

4. Eve went to Ed's summer wedding.

 _____   _____   _____

5. We have to go to bed by ten o'clock for a restful night's sleep.

 _____   _____   _____

Classwork

 Name: _____ Date: ___/___/_____ Score: _____

Lesson 5.3

Reading Words with the Long Vowel "e" Sound

✓ **Lesson Check Point**

 Directions: Read the words in the four boxes. Circle two words with the long vowel /ē/ sound. The anchor word for the long vowel /ē/ sound is <u>me</u>.

지도: 네 개의 상자에 있는 단어를 읽으십시오. 장모음 /ē/ 소리로두단어에 동그라미를 치십시오. 장모음 /ē/ 소리의 기준어는 <u>me</u>입니다.

break	east		cease	scene		chest	these
pea	spell		clever	here		cakes	zebra

zero	scent		east	next		heal	trend
believe	come		eating	beard		where	react

 Directions: Read the words in the four boxes. Circle two words that rhyme. Rhyming words have the same ending sound, such as <u>beep</u> and <u>reap</u>.

지도: 네 개의 상자에 있는 단어를 읽으십시오. 운이 맞는 두 단어에동그라미를 치십시오. 운율이 있는 단어는 <u>beep</u> 및 <u>reap</u>과 같이 끝 소리가같습니다.

speed	read		lead	eat		see	were
bread	felt		when	heat		held	tea

tease	fence		head	theme		realm	temp
lease	there		scheme	deck		leave	weave

Name: _____ Date: ___/___/_____ Score: _____

Lesson 5.3

Reading & Writing Words with the Long Vowel "e" Sound

✓ **Lesson Check Point**

Directions: Read each sentence and underline three words with the long vowel /ē/ sound. Then, write the underlined words on the lines below. The anchor word for the long vowel /ē/ sound is <u>me</u>.

지도: 각 문장을 읽고 장모음 /ē/ 소리로 세 단어에 밑줄을 긋습니다. 그런 다음 밑줄 친 단어를 아래 줄에 쓰십시오. 장모음 /ē/ 소리의 기준어는 me 입니다.

Model

<u>We</u> are <u>reading</u> an article entitled, "<u>Eagles</u> Bird of Prey."

    We   reading   Eagles
  _____   _____   _____

1. Irene and Lee are relaxing under the tree with their pets.

  _____   _____   _____

2. The ten Guyanese teams are extremely talented.

  _____   _____   _____

3. This evening, Esther received a speeding ticket.

  _____   _____   _____

4. The speaker said, "Lean meats have relatively low-fat content."

  _____   _____   _____

5. The students will speak to the dean about the new teachers.

  _____   _____   _____

Classwork

Name: _____ Date: ___/___/_____ Score: _____

Review Lessons 5.2 & 5.3

Reading Short Vowel and Long Vowel Words

Directions: Read the target words in the word box. In the first column, write the words that have the short vowel /ĕ/ sound, as in the word <u>egg</u>. In the second column, write the words that have the long vowel /ē/ sound, as in the word <u>me</u>.

지도: 단어 상자에 있는 대상 단어를 읽으십시오. 첫 번째 칸에는 egg라는 단어처럼 단모음 /ĕ/ 소리가 나는 단어를 씁니다. 두 번째 칸에는 me라는 단어처럼 장모음 /ē/ 소리가 나는 단어를 쓰세요.

Target Word Box				
fled	theme	left	temp	went
these	step	scene	seeing	speed
held	athlete	complete	then	increase
extreme	self	west	free	test

Letter "e" has the /ĕ/ sound as in the word <u>egg</u>

Letter "e" has the /ē/ sound as in the word <u>me</u>

Classwork

 Name: _____ Date: ___/___/_____ Score: _____

Lesson 5.4

Reading Words with Letter "e" Vowel Pairs

✓ Lesson Check Point

 Directions: Read each target word. Circle the word in the column that has the same vowel "ea," "ee," "ei," "eo" or "eu" sound as the target word.
지도: 각 대상 단어를 읽으십시오. 같은 모음 "ea," "ee," "ei," "eo" 또는 "eu"가 대상 단어와 동일한 열의 단어에 동그라미를 치십시오.

| peas | a. easel |
| | b. health |

| veil | a. eight |
| | b. feud |

| seize | a. video |
| | b. people |

| needle | a. been |
| | b. feed |

 Directions: Read each target word. Put a check (✓) under the correct column heading.
지도: 각 대상 단어를 읽으십시오. 올바른 열 제목 아래에 체크(✓)를 하십시오.

Target Words	Words have the long "e" sound as in the word tea	Words do not have the long "e" sound
1. peas		
2. veil		
3. seize		
4. needle		

Classwork

 Name: _____ Date: ___/___/_____ Score: _____

Lesson 5.5

Reading Words with the Final Letter "e"

✓ **Lesson Check Point**

 Directions: Read each target word. Find the letter "e" and put a check (✓) in the column that identifies its position within the syllable.

지도: 각 대상 단어를 읽으십시오. 문자 "e"를 찾아 체크 표시(✓)음 절 내에서 위치를 식별하는 열에서.

Target Words	"e" is at the end of a one syllable word	"e" is at the end of the first syllable	"e" is at the end of a multi-syllable word
1. becoming			
2. he			
3. recording			
4. multiple			
5. we			

 Directions: Read each target word. Put a check (✓) under the correct column heading.

지도: 각 대상 단어를 읽으십시오. 올바른 열 제목 아래에 체크(✓)를 하십시오.

Target Words	"e" has the /ĕ/ sound as in the word <u>egg</u>	"e" has the /ē/ sound as in the word <u>me</u>	"e" has the /ə/ sound as in the word <u>item</u>	"e" is silent as in the word <u>great</u>
6. prefix				
7. made				
8. marvel				
9. season				
10. travel				

Unit E Lesson 5.5

Classwork

 Name: _____ Date:__/___/_____ Score: _____

Lesson 5.6

Reading Letter "e" Words with the Schwa Vowel Sound

✓ **Lesson Check Point**

 Directions: Read each target word. Circle the word in the column that has the same "e" sound as the target word.

지도: 각 대상 단어를 읽으십시오. 목표 단어와 같은 "e" 소리가 나는 열의 단어에 동그라미를 치십시오.

hotter	a. eggs
	b. taken

el<u>e</u>phant	a. camel
	b. meals

father	a. blending
	b. system

poem	a. experiment
	b. chocolate

 Directions: Read each sentence and underline the letter "e" word that has the schwa vowel /ə/ sound. The anchor word for the letter "e" schwa vowel sound is <u>item</u>.

지도: 각 문장을 읽고 슈와 모음 /ə/ 소리가 있는 문자 "e" 단어에 밑줄을 긋습니다. "e" 슈와 모음 소리의 앵커 단어는 <u>item</u>입니다.

1. At dinner, I ate a slice of roast beef.

2. Five movers organized my bedroom set.

3. Every year, we celebrated Andrew's birthday.

4. Three large barrels are located next to cabinets.

5. Our fishermen sailed their ships twenty miles from shore.

6. Large animal populations are scattered throughout Africa.

Classwork

 Name: _____   Date:___/___/_____   Score:_____

Lesson 5.7

Reading Words with the "er" Letter Combination

Dictionary Skills/Vocabulary

✓ **Lesson Check Point**

Directions: Read each target word and its definition. Write the letter of the definition on the line of each target word. Use a dictionary or the Internet to check your answers.

지도: 각 대상 단어와 그 정의를 읽으십시오. 각 대상 단어의 행에 정의의 문자를 씁니다. 사전이나 인터넷을 사용하여 답을 확인하십시오.

Target Words	Definitions
1. __ river	a. something very bad or unacceptable
2. __ sister	b. a body of water that is larger than a creek
3. __ terrible	c. a small fruit that has red or purple drupelets
4. __ raspberry	d. a verbal or written response to a question
5. __ answer	e. a female who has the same parent(s) as another

Directions: Read each sentence and write the target word that correctly completes the sentence.

지도: 각 문장을 읽고 문장을 올바르게 완성하는 목표 단어를 쓰십시오.

6. My younger _____ eats berries and cherries.

7. Jerry did not _____ Sherry's difficult questions.

8. Have you ever eaten a sweet, juicy _____?

9. Sherry's baked herring tasted _____.

10. We are going to take a ferry ride along the _____.

Classwork

 Name: _____ Date:___/___/_____ Score:_____

Lesson 5.8

Reading Words with the "eu" and "ew" Letter Combinations

✓ **Lesson Check Point**

 Directions: Read each sentence and underline the word that has a silent letter "e."
지도: 각 문장을 읽고 묵음 문자"e"가 있는 단어에 밑줄을 긋습니다.

Model
My father said, "The apricot <u>streusel</u> is very tasty."

1. In Germany, I bought many elegant gifts with euros.

2. Jennifer and Cathy painted the ceiling a neutral color.

3. The European bound flight will depart at eleven o'clock.

4. The bridal party was euphoric during the wonderful wedding.

 Directions: Read each sentence and underline the word with an "eu" or "ew" letter combination that has the long vowel /y$\overline{oo}$/ or /$\overline{oo}$/ sound, as in the words <u>feud</u> and <u>flew</u>.
지도: 각 문장을 읽고 단어 feud 그리고 flew에서와 같이 장모음 /y$\overline{oo}$/ 또는 /$\overline{oo}$/ 소리가 있는"eu" 또는"ew" 문자 조합으로 단어에 밑줄을 긋습니다.

5. Mom's apple streusel is delicious.

6. Lieutenant Edwards is a strong leader.

7. The engineering students ate grapes and cashews.

8. Eddie learned a lot of interesting information about Zeus.

9. The Elton family is feuding over Grandmother's possessions.

10. The shower was extremely clean after Jane used mildew remover.

Classwork

Name: _____ Date: ___/___/_____ Score: _____

Lesson 5.9

Reading Words with the "ey" Letter Combination

✓ **Lesson Check Point**

Directions: Read each target word. Put a check (✓) under the correct column heading.

지도: 각 대상 단어를 읽으십시오. 올바른 열 제목 아래에 체크(✓)를 하십시오.

Target Words	"ey" has the long /ē/ sound as in the word <u>honey</u>	"ey" has the long /ā/ sound as in the word <u>hey</u>
1. monkey		
2. survey		
3. convey		
4. kidney		

Directions: Read each sentence and underline the word with the "ey" letter combination. Put a check (✓) under the correct column heading.

지도: 각 문장을 읽고 "ey" 문자 조합으로 단어에 밑줄을 긋습니다. 올바른 열 제목 아래에 체크(✓)를 하십시오.

	"ey" has the long /ē/ sound as in the word <u>honey</u>	"ey" has the long /ā/ sound as in the word <u>hey</u>
5. The survey has ten questions.	_____	_____
6. Lee received a new team jersey.	_____	_____
7. Today, they will have a yard sale.	_____	_____
8. I did not obey my teachers' rules.	_____	_____
9. Ethan enjoys playing volleyball.	_____	_____
10. The jockey's horse is on the track.	_____	_____

Unit E Lesson 5.9

Classwork

 Name: _____ Date: ___/___/_____ Score: _____

Lesson 5.10

Reading Words with a Silent Letter "e"

✓ **Lesson Check Point**

 Directions: Read the target words in the word box. Write the words that have a silent letter "e" in the first column. Write the words that do not have a silent letter "e" in the second column.

지도: 단어 상자에 있는 대상 단어를 읽으십시오. 첫 번째 열에 묵음 문자"e"가 있는 단어를 쓰십시오. 두 번째 열에 묵음 문자"e"가 없는 단어를 쓰십시오.

Target Word Box				
eating	cells	friends	game	vote
seat	base	depend	effect	fresh
tone	size	tube	beds	came
face	zebras	clue	drive	meal

Letter "e" is silent   **Letter "e" has a letter "e" sound**

Learn To Read English With Directions In Korean

Unit E Lesson 5.10

Classwork

✏ Name: _____ Date: ___/___/_____ Score: _____

Unit Review – E/e

Reading Words with Vowel "e" Sounds: /ĕ/, /ē/, /ə/ & Silent

✓ **Lesson Check Point**

Directions: Read each target word. Circle the word in the column that has the same "e" sound as the target word.

지도: 각 대상 단어를 읽으십시오. 목표 단어와 같은 "e" 소리가 나는 열의 단어에 동그라미를 치십시오.

eating	a. coffee
	b. bake

barrel	a. oxygen
	b. these

pollen	a. beat
	b. benefit

check	a. rakes
	b. cells

Directions: Read each target word. Put a check (✓) under the correct column heading.

지도: 각 대상 단어를 읽으십시오. 올바른 열 제목 아래에 체크(✓)를 하십시오.

Target Words	"e" has the /ĕ/ sound as in the word <u>egg</u>	"e" has the /ē/ sound as in the word <u>me</u>	"e" has the /ə/ sound as in the word <u>item</u>	"e" is silent as in the word <u>great</u>
1. eating				
2. barrel				
3. pollen				
4. check				

Classwork

Name: _____ Date: ___/___/_____ Score: _____

The Reading Challenge

Lesson 5.11

Reading Multisyllable Words

✓ **Lesson Check Point**

Directions: Read and divide each target word into syllables. Write each word and place a hyphen (-) between the syllables in the second column. Write the number of syllables in the third column. Use a dictionary or the Internet to check your answers.

지도: 각 대상 단어를 읽고 음절로 나눕니다. 각 단어를 쓰고 두 번째 열의 음절 사이에 하이픈(-)을 넣습니다. 세 번째 열에 음절 수를 쓰십시오. 사전이나 인터넷을 사용하여 답을 확인하십시오.

Target Words	Words Divided into Syllables	Number of Syllables
1. decreasing	_____	_____
2. between	_____	_____
3. peanut	_____	_____
4. shipwreck	_____	_____
5. nutmeg	_____	_____
6. leghorn	_____	_____
7. farewell	_____	_____
8. anthem	_____	_____
9. modem	_____	_____
10. itemize	_____	_____

Learn To Read English With Directions In Korean   Copyrighted Material

Classwork

Name: _____ Date: ___/___/_____ Score: _____

The Reading Challenge

Lesson 5.11

Reading Multisyllable Words

✓ **Lesson Check Point**

Directions: Read each target word. Circle the word in the row that is divided correctly into syllables. Use a dictionary or the Internet to check your answers.

지도: 각 대상 단어를 읽으십시오. 음절로 올바르게 나누어진 행에 있는 단어에 동그라미를 치십시오. 사전이나 인터넷을 사용하여 답을 확인하십시오.

Model

| megabyte | a. me-ga-byte | b. meg-a-byte | c. me-gaby-te |

1. awaken	a. aw-a-ken	b. a-wak-en	c. a-wa-ken
2. legacy	a. le-ga-cy	b. leg-a-cy	c. leg-ac-y
3. forgiven	a. for-giv-en	b. for-gi-ven	c. fo-rgi-ven
4. acknowledge	a. ack-now-ledge	b. ac-know-ledge	c. ac-knowl-edge
5. turtleneck	a. tur-tle-neck	b. turt-len-eck	c. turt-le-neck
6. celebrate	a. cel-eb-rate	b. cel-e-brate	c. ce-le-brate
7. federal	a. fe-de-ral	b. fed-e-ral	c. fed-er-al
8. ascending	a. as-cend-ing	b. asc-end-ing	c. as-cen-ding

Classwork

 Name: _____ Date: ___/___/_____ Score: _____

Lesson 5.12

Reading and Writing

Proper and Common Nouns and Adjectives

✓ **Lesson Check Point**

 Directions: Read the words in the word box. Put an (X) on the line next to each word that is written incorrectly. Remember that all proper nouns and proper adjectives are capitalized. Use a dictionary or the Internet to check your answers.
지도: 단어 상자에 있는 단어를 읽으십시오. 잘못 쓰여진 각 단어 옆의 줄에 (X)를 표시하십시오. 모든 고유 명사와 고유 형용사는 대문자임을 기억하십시오. 사전이나 인터넷을 사용하여 답을 확인하십시오.

Word Box		
__ eiffel Tower	__ Educator	__ east Asia
__ England	__ egyptian	__ el Dorado
__ egocentric	__ Estonia	__ editor
__ Envelope	__ European	__ environment

 Directions: Read each unedited sentence and underline the word that is written incorrectly. Write each sentence correctly on the line.
지도: 편집되지 않은 각 문장을 읽고 잘못 쓰여진 단어에 밑줄을 긋습 니다. 각 문장을 줄에 올바르게 쓰십시오.

Model
All my friends are <u>Excited</u> about the class trip to Europe.
<u>All my friends are excited about the class trip to Europe.</u>

1. I will meet my friend, eileen, at five o'clock EST.
_____

2. evan said, "Many of the citizens of Ethiopia speak English."
_____

3. The address on the envelope indicates that the letter is from egypt.
_____

4. On Earth Day, Mr. eglon's class will discuss environmental issues.
_____

Classwork

Name: _____ Date: ___/___/_____ Score: _____

Lesson 6.1

Reading Words with the Letter F/f

✓ Lesson Check Point

Directions: Read each target word. Find the letter "f" and put a check (✓) in the column that identifies its position: beginning, within or end.
지도: 각 대상 단어를 읽으십시오. 문자 "f"를 찾아 체크 표시(✓)위치를 식별하는 열에서 시작, 내부 또는 끝.

Target Words	Beginning (First Letter)	Within	End (Last Letter)
1. flip			
2. fresh			
3. leaf			
4. defrost			
5. comfort			

Directions: Read each sentence and underline the words that begin with the letter "f." Write all the underlined words in alphabetical order on the lines below.
지도: 각 문장을 읽고 "f"로 시작하는 단어에 밑줄을 긋습니다. 밑줄 친 모든 단어를 아래 줄에 알파벳 순서로 쓰십시오.

6. Ashley and Fred are citizens of France.

7. Brad and Alex are fabulous flute players.

8. The fence in front of the house is dark blue.

9. The flowers in the field are extremely beautiful.

10. The flag of Belgium is flying high over the building.

_____   _____   _____
_____   _____   _____
_____   _____   _____
                          _____

Learn To Read English With Directions In Korean

Classwork

Name: _____ Date: ___/___/_____ Score: _____

Lesson 6.2

Reading Words with the "fr" Letter Combination

Dictionary Skills/ Vocabulary

✓ Lesson Check Point

Directions: Read each target word and its definition. Write the letter of the definition on the line of each target word. Use a dictionary or the Internet to check your answers.
지도: 각 대상 단어와 그 정의를 읽으십시오. 각 대상 단어의 행에 정의의 문자를 씁니다. 사전이나 인터넷을 사용하여 답을 확인하십시오.

Target Words	Definitions
1. __ frog	a. to have broken or cracked something
2. __ framed	b. a branch of a business chain
3. __ franchise	c. to be ahead of someone or something
4. __ fractured	d. a small, smooth, tailless and wet-skinned animal
5. __ front	e. evidence or testimony presented to falsely incriminate

Directions: Read each sentence. Underline the word in the parentheses that correctly completes each sentence. Then, write the underlined word on the line.
지도: 각 문장을 읽으십시오. 각 문장을 올바르게 완성하는 괄호 안에 있는 단어에 밑줄을 긋습니다. 그런 다음 밑줄 친 단어를 줄에 쓰십시오.

6. The _____ is croaking by the water. (frog, framed)

7. On the bus, Freda sat in _____ of Frankie. (front, franchise)

8. At the game, Flo fell and _____ her ankle. (frog, fractured)

9. Frank was _____ for a crime he didn't commit. (front, framed)

10. Flossy purchased a fast food _____. (franchise, framed)

Classwork

Name: _____ Date: ___/___/_____ Score: _____

Lesson 6.3

Reading Words with the "fl" Letter Combination

Dictionary Skills/ Vocabulary

✓ **Lesson Check Point**

Directions: Read each target word and its definition. Write the target word on the line in front of its meaning. Use a dictionary or the Internet to check your answers.
지도: 각 대상 단어와 그 정의를 읽으십시오. 의미 앞 줄에 대상 단어를 쓰십시오. 사전이나 인터넷을 사용하여 답을 확인하십시오.

Target Word Box				
fleet	flash	flower	fluently	fly

1. _____ to travel through the air with wings
2. _____ the colorful part of a plant that contains seeds
3. _____ a number of vehicles owned as a unit
4. _____ a device that provides light to brighten a picture
5. _____ the ability to speak a language correctly

Directions: Read each sentence. Underline the word in the parentheses that correctly completes each sentence. Then, write the underlined word on the line.
지도: 각 문장을 읽으십시오. 각 문장을 올바르게 완성하는 괄호 안에 있는 단어에 밑줄을 긋습니다. 그런 다음 밑줄 친 단어를 줄에 쓰십시오.

6. Fred's camera has a built-in _____. (flash, flower)

7. Flamingos can _____ up to 40 mph in the air. (flash, fly)

8. My friend speaks French and Finnish _____. (fluently, flash)

9. The florist made a beautiful _____ arrangement. (fluently, flower)

10. After the funeral, a _____ of cars drove down the avenue. (fly, fleet)

Classwork

 Name: _____ Date: ___/___/_____ Score: _____

Lesson 6.3

Reading Words with the "fle" Letter Combination

✓ **Lesson Check Point**

 Directions: Read each target word. Find the "fle" letter combination and put a check (✓) in the column that identifies its position: beginning, within or end.
지도: 각 대상 단어를 읽으십시오. "fle" 문자 조합을 찾아해당 위치를식별 하는열에 체크(✓)를 하십시오: 시작, 내부 또는 끝.

Target Words	Beginning (First 3 Letters)	Within	End (Last 3 Letters)
1. waffle			
2. flesh			
3. fleet			
4. reflect			
5. duffle			

 Directions: Read each target word. Put a check (✓) in the "yes" column if the "fle" letter combination has the /f/ + /ə/ + /l/ sounds. Put a check (✓) in the "no" column if the "fle" letter combination does not have the /f/ + /ə/ + /l/ sounds.
지도: 각 대상 단어를 읽으십시오. "fle" 문자 조합에/f/ + /ə/ + /l/ 소리가있으면 "yes" 열에 체크(✓)를 하십시오. "fle" 문자 조합에/f/ + /ə/ + /l/ 소리가"no"아니 오" 열에 체크(✓)를 하십시오.

Target Words	Yes	No
6. waffle		
7. flesh		
8. fleet		
9. reflect		
10. duffle		

Classwork

Name: _____ Date: ___/___/_____ Score: _____

Lesson 6.4

Reading Words with the "ft," "lf" and "ff" Letter Combinations

Dictionary Skills/ Vocabulary

✓ **Lesson Check Point**

Directions: Read each target word and its definition. Write the letter of the definition on the line of each target word. Use a dictionary or the Internet to check your answers.

지도: 각 대상 단어와 그 정의를 읽으십시오. 각 대상 단어의 행에 정의의 문자를 씁니다. 사전이나 인터넷을 사용하여 답을 확인하십시오.

Target Words	Definitions
1. ___ giraffe	a. a piece of writing that is not finalized
2. ___ Gulf	b. to move along by wind or water
3. ___ draft	c. a vehicle that can fly in the air
4. ___ aircraft	d. the tallest land animal with dark spots
5. ___ drift	e. a large body of water partially enclosed by land

Directions: Read each sentence and write the target word that correctly completes the sentence.

지도: 각 문장을 읽고 문장을 올바르게 완성하는 목표 단어를 쓰십시오.

6. I will write the first _____ of the report in class.

7. The _____ flew from New York City to Atlantic City.

8. At sunset, the boats and rafts will _____ along the lake.

9. The hurricane damaged the houses along the _____ Coast.

10. The guide said, "The _____ is the tallest African animal."

Classwork

Name: _____ Date:___/___/_____ Score:_____

Lesson 6.5

Reading Words with a Silent Letter "f"

✓ **Lesson Check Point**

Directions: Read the target words in the word box. Write the words that have a silent letter "f" in the first column. Write the words that do not have a silent letter "f" in the second column.
지도: 단어 상자에 있는 대상 단어를 읽으십시오. 첫 번째 열에 묵음문자 "f"가 있는 단어를 쓰십시오. 두 번째 열에 묵음 문자"f"가 없는 단어를 쓰십시오.

Target Word Box				
muffin	buffalo	infancy	faces	suffocate
wife	after	afresh	afford	flying
defect	effect	cliff	caffeine	officially
fitness	coffee	bullfrog	fast	taffy

Letter "f" is silent	Letter "f" has the /f/ sound
_____	_____
_____	_____
_____	_____
_____	_____
_____	_____
_____	_____
_____	_____
_____	_____
_____	_____
_____	_____

Unit F Lesson 6.5

Learn To Read English With Directions In Korean

Classwork

Name: _____ Date: ___/___/_____ Score: _____

Lesson 6.6

Reading Singular and Plural forms of Words Ending in "-f" & "-fe"

✓ Lesson Check Point

Directions: Read each target word. Put a check (✓) in the second column if the plural form of the target word ends with "-ves." Put a check (✓) in the third column if the plural form of the target word ends with "-s" or "-es."
지도: 각 대상 단어를 읽으십시오. 대상 단어의 복수형이 "-ves"로 끝나는 경우 두 번째 열에 체크(✓)를 하십시오. 대상 단어의 복수형이 "-s" 또는 "-es."로 끝나는 경우 세 번째 열에 체크(✓)를 하십시오.

Target Words	The plural form of the target word ends with "-ves"	The plural form of the target word ends with "-s" or "-es"
1. roof		
2. half		
3. life		
4. thief		
5. chef		

Directions: Read each sentence. Complete each sentence by writing the plural form of the word on the line.
지도: 각 문장을 읽으십시오. 단어의 복수형을 줄에 써서 각 문장을 완성하세요.

6. Doctors save _____ every day. (life)

7. The men gave flowers to their _____. (wife)

8. Frank built five _____ by himself. (shelf)

9. The girls filmed the events by _____. (herself)

10. Many _____ attacked the farmer's chicken. (wolf)

Classwork

Name: _____ Date: ___/___/_____ Score: _____

The Reading Challenge

Lesson 6.7

Reading Multisyllable Words

✓ **Lesson Check Point**

Directions: Read and divide each target word into syllables. Write each word and place a hyphen (-) between the syllables in the second column. Write the number of syllables in the third column. Use a dictionary or the Internet to check your answers.

지도: 각 대상 단어를 읽고 음절로 나눕니다. 각 단어를 쓰고 두 번째 열의 음절 사이에 하이픈(-)을 넣습니다. 세 번째 열에 음절 수를 쓰십시오. 사전이나 인터넷을 사용하여 답을 확인하십시오.

Target Words	Words Divided into Syllables	Number of Syllables
1. fencing	_____	_____
2. fabulous	_____	_____
3. friendship	_____	_____
4. facial	_____	_____
5. flawless	_____	_____
6. franchising	_____	_____
7. falcon	_____	_____
8. finalist	_____	_____
9. florist	_____	_____
10. football	_____	_____

Learn To Read English With Directions In Korean

Classwork

 Name: _____ Date: ___/___/_____ Score: _____

The Reading Challenge

Lesson 6.7

Reading Multisyllable Words

✓ **Lesson Check Point**

 Directions: Read each target word. Circle the word in the row that is divided correctly into syllables. Use a dictionary or the Internet to check your answers.

지도: 각 대상 단어를 읽으십시오. 음절로 올바르게 나누어진 행에 있는 단어에 동그라미를 치십시오. 사전이나 인터넷을 사용하여 답을 확인하십시오.

Model

| factory | a. fac-tor-y | b. fac-to-ry | c. fa-cto-ry |

(b. fac-to-ry is circled)

1. flexible	b. fle-x-ible	b. fle-xi-ble	c. flex-i-ble
2. festival	a. fest-i-val	b. fe-stiv-al	c. fes-ti-val
3. fabricate	a. fab-ri-cate	b. fa-bri-cate	c. fabr-ic-ate
4. finale	a. fin-al-e	b. fi-nal-e	c. fina-le
5. forensic	a. for-e-nsic	b. for-en-sic	c. fo-ren-sic
6. fortify	a. fort-i-fy	b. for-ti-fy	c. for-tif-y
7. familiar	a. fa-mil-iar	b. fam-i-liar	c. fam-il-iar
8. flavoring	a. fla-vor-ing	b. flav-or-ing	c. flav-o-ring

Name: _____ Date: ___/___/_____ Score: _____

Lesson 6.8

Reading and Writing

Proper and Common Nouns and Adjectives

✓ **Lesson Check Point**

Directions: Read the words in the word box. Put an (X) on the line next to each word that is written incorrectly. Remember that all proper nouns and proper adjectives are capitalized. Use a dictionary or the Internet to check your answers.

지도: 단어 상자에 있는 단어를 읽으십시오. 잘못 쓰여진 각 단어 옆의 줄에 (X)를 표시하십시오. 모든 고유 명사와 고유 형용사는 대문자임을 기억하십시오. 사전이나 인터넷을 사용하여 답을 확인하십시오.

Word Box		
__ flower	__ Florida	__ far East
__ franklin	__ flock	__ france
__ french	__ Finalist	__ fashion
__ flamingo	__ frankfort	__ florist

Directions: Read each unedited sentence and underline the word that is written incorrectly. Write each sentence correctly on the line.

지도: 편집되지 않은 각 문장을 읽고 잘못 쓰여진 단어에 밑줄을 긋습 니다. 각 문장을 줄에 올바르게 쓰십시오.

Model
Fiji is my <u>Florist's</u> favorite holiday destination.
<u>Fiji is my florist's favorite holiday destination.</u>

1. Flossy and Frank were born in france.
   _____

2. francis speaks English and French fluently.
   _____

3. Freda works by fort Hamilton Parkway.
   _____

4. Fred's baseball game is at frankfurt Field.
   _____

Classwork

Name: _____ Date:___/___/_____ Score:_____

Lesson 7.1

Reading Words with the Letter G/g

✓ Lesson Check Point

Directions: Read each target word. Find the letter "g" and put a check (✓) in the column that identifies its position: beginning, within or end.
지도: 각 대상 단어를 읽으십시오. 문자"g"를 찾아 체크 표시(✓)위치를 식별하는 열에서 시작, 내부 또는 끝.

Target Words	Beginning (First Letter)	Within	End (Last Letter)
1. glossary			
2. hexagon			
3. landing			
4. oblong			
5. government			

Directions: Read each sentence and underline the words that begin with the letter "g." Write all the underlined words in alphabetical order on the lines below.
지도: 각 문장을 읽고 문자"g"로 시작하는 단어에 밑줄을 긋습니다. 밑줄 친 모든 단어를 아래 줄에 알파벳 순서로 쓰십시오.

6. Billy and Fran ate green grapes.

7. All the boys earned good grades.

8. My guests are going to the airport.

9. The girls forgot to put gas in the car.

10. The golfers play a challenging game.

_____   _____   _____
_____   _____   _____
                   _____

Classwork

Name: _____ Date: ___/ ___/ _____ Score: _____

Lesson 7.1

Reading Words with the Hard Letter "g"

✓ Lesson Check Point

Directions: Read each target word. Put a check (✓) under the correct column heading.

지도: 각 대상 단어를 읽으십시오. 올바른 열 제목 아래에 체크(✓)를 하십시오.

Target Words	Hard "g" has the /g/ sound as in the word gum	Soft "g" has the /j/ sound as in the word gem
1. gills		
2. golden		
3. gentle		
4. geese		
5. gallops		

Directions: Read each sentence and underline the words that have the hard "g" sound. The anchor word for the hard "g" sound is gum. Write all the underlined words in alphabetical order on the lines below.

지도: 각 문장을 읽고 단단한"g" 소리가 나는 단어에 밑줄을 긋습니다. 단단한"g" 소리의 기준어는 gum입니다. 밑줄 친 모든 단어를 아래 줄에 알파벳 순서로 쓰십시오.

6. Gloria and Gina have beautiful blue glasses.

7. Today, Georgette saw a cow, a goat and a gazelle.

8. Jennifer is growing geraniums in her greenhouse.

9. The children in Ms. George's class have good grades.

10. My grandfather has ginger chicken and corn on the grill.

_____   _____   _____
_____   _____   _____
_____   _____
_____

Learn To Read English With Directions In Korean

Classwork

Name: _____ Date: ___/___/_____ Score: _____

Lesson 7.2

Reading Words with the Soft Letter "g"

Directions: Read each target word. Put a check (✓) under the correct column heading.

지도: 각 대상 단어를 읽으십시오. 올바른 열 제목 아래에 체크(✓)를 하십시오.

Target Words	Soft "g" has the /j/ or /zh/ sound as in the words gem & massage	Hard "g" has the /g/ sound as in the word gum	Both soft "g" and hard "g" sounds as in the word gauge
1. garage			
2. gear			
3. intelligent			
4. progress			
5. grammar			

Directions: Read each sentence and underline the words that have the soft "g" sound. The anchor word for the soft "g" sound is gem. Write all the underlined words in alphabetical order on the lines below.

지도: 각 문장을 읽고 부드러운 "g" 소리가 나는 단어에 밑줄을 긋습니다. 부드러운 "g" 소리의 기준어는 gem입니다. 밑줄 친 모든 단어를 아래 줄에 알파벳 순서로 쓰십시오.

6. Gloria's giant gem glistens in the sun.

7. Gianna is chewing gum in the gymnasium.

8. Ginny got a great grade in her biology class.

9. For graduation, I received a gigantic package.

10. The teenagers felt guilty because they did not go to the gym.

_____   _____   _____

_____   _____   _____

_____   _____

_____

Learn To Read English With Directions In Korean

Classwork

Name: _____ Date: ___/___/_____ Score: _____

Review Lessons 7.1 & 7.2

Reading Hard Letter "g" and Soft Letter "g" Words

Directions: Read each target word. Put a check (✓) under the correct column heading.

지도: 각 대상 단어를 읽으십시오. 올바른 열 제목 아래에 체크(✓)를하십시오.

Target Words	Soft "g" has the /j/ or /zh/ sound as in the words gem & massage	Hard "g" has the /g/ sound as in the word gum	Both soft "g" and hard "g" sounds as in the word gauge
1. get			
2. biology			
3. ground			
4. ingested			
5. fragrant			

Directions: Read each sentence and underline the words that have the hard "g" sound. The anchor word for the hard "g" sound is <u>gum</u>. Write all the underlined words in alphabetical order on the lines below.

지도: 각 문장을 읽고 단단한"g" 소리가 나는 단어에 밑줄을 긋습니다. 단단한"g" 소리의 기준어는 gum입니다. 밑줄 친 모든 단어를 아래 줄에 알파벳 순서로 쓰십시오.

6. Georgette has good grades.

7. Greg enjoys going to the gym.

8. Gina's eyeglasses are glamorous.

9. Ben gave me a bronze chain as a gift.

10. My friend, Gio, graduated and traveled to Guyana.

_____ _____ _____
_____ _____ _____
_____ _____
           _____

Learn To Read English With Directions In Korean

Classwork

Name: _____ Date: ___/___/_____ Score: _____

Review Lessons 7.1 & 7.2

Reading Hard Letter "g" and Soft Letter "g" Words

Directions: Read the target words in the word box. In the first column, write the words with the letter "g" that have the /g/ sound, as in the word gum. In the second column, write the words with the letter "g" that have the /j/ sound, as in the word gem.

지도: 단어 상자에 있는 대상 단어를 읽으십시오. 첫 번째 열에는단어 gum에서와 같이 /g/ 소리가 나는 문자"g"가 있는 단어를 씁니다. 두 번째열에 "g"가 포함된 단어를 쓰십시오. /j/ 소리, gem이라는 단어에서와 같이.

Target Word Box				
digital	green	geese	ginger	page
germs	greet	gems	organ	gulf
grandson	glasses	large	sugar	engine
gate	gifts	gym	stage	orange

Hard letter "g" has the /g/ sound as in the word gum

Soft letter "g" has the /j/ sound as in the word gem

Classwork

 Name: _____ Date: ___/___/_____ Score: _____

Lesson 7.3

Reading Words with the "gr" Letter Combination

Dictionary Skills/ Vocabulary

✓ Lesson Check Point

 Directions: Read each target word and its definition. Write the letter of the definition on the line of each target word. Use a dictionary or the Internet to check your answers.
지도: 각 대상 단어와 그 정의를 읽으십시오. 각 대상 단어의 행에 정의의 문자를 씁니다. 사전이나 인터넷을 사용하여 답을 확인하십시오.

Target Words	Definitions
1. __ grabs	a. to make a big, positive impression
2. __ grand	b. to take something quickly with one's hand(s)
3. __ gravel	c. something that contains or is covered with oil
4. __ greasy	d. to hold something firmly with one's hand(s)
5. __ grip	e. a mixture of very small rocks and pebbles

 Directions: Read each sentence. Underline the word in the parentheses that correctly completes each sentence. Then, write the underlined word on the line.
지도: 각 문장을 읽으십시오. 각 문장을 올바르게 완성하는 괄호 안에 있는 단어에 밑줄을 긋습니다. 그런 다음 밑줄 친 단어를 줄에 쓰십시오.

6. Grandpa's driveway is made of _____. (greasy, gravel)

7. I can't eat the burger because it is too _____. (grabs, greasy)

8. The gloves give me a better _____ on the bars. (grip, grabbed)

9. Greg _____ the books with both hands. (grabs, gravel)

10. At the dance, the girls made a _____ entrance. (grand, greasy)

Classwork

Name: _____ Date: ___/___/_____ Score: _____

Lesson 7.4

Reading Words with the "gl" Letter Combination

Dictionary Skills/ Vocabulary

✓ **Lesson Check Point**

Directions: Read each target word and its definition. Write the target word on the line in front of its meaning. Use a dictionary or the Internet to check your answers.
지도: 각 대상 단어와 그 정의를 읽으십시오. 의미 앞 줄에 대상 단어를 쓰십시오. 사전이나 인터넷을 사용하여 답을 확인하십시오.

Target Word Box				
glaze	globe	gloom	glossary	glowing

1. _____ to shine brightly like a light or the sun
2. _____ a state of sadness, hopelessness and/or depression
3. _____ to spread a thin layer of something on a surface
4. _____ a three-dimensional, sphere shaped model of the earth
5. _____ an alphabetical list of text-related words with definitions

Directions: Read each sentence. Underline the word in the parentheses that correctly completes each sentence. Then, write the underlined word on the line.
지도: 각 문장을 읽으십시오. 각 문장을 올바르게 완성하는 괄호 안에 있는 단어에 밑줄을 긋습니다. 그런 다음 밑줄 친 단어를 줄에 쓰십시오.

6. The beautiful, blushing bride is _____. (gloom, glowing)

7. Gerald plans to travel around the _____. (globe, glowing)

8. Gloria _____ the chicken with barbecue sauce. (glazed, globe)

9. The bad report brought deep _____ to the family. (glossary, gloom)

10. The book's _____ helps me define difficult words. (glossary, glowing)

Classwork

 Name: _____ Date: ___/___/_____ Score: _____

Lesson 7.4

Reading Words with the "gle" Letter Combination

✓ Lesson Check Point

 Directions: Read each target word. Find the "gle" letter combination and put a check (✓) in the column that identifies its position: beginning, within or end.
지도: 각 대상 단어를 읽으십시오. "gle" 문자 조합을 찾아 위치를 식별하는 열에 체크(✓)를 하십시오: 시작, 내부 또는 끝.

Target Words	Beginning (First 3 Letters)	Within	End (Last 3 Letters)
1. glee			
2. angle			
3. mangled			
4. gleaming			
5. triangle			

 Directions: Read each target word. Put a check (✓) in the "yes" column if the "gle" letter combination has the /g/ + /ə/ + /l/ sounds. Put a check (✓) in the "no" column if the "gle" letter combination does not have the /g/ + /ə/ + /l/ sounds.
지도: 각 대상 단어를 읽으십시오. "gle" 문자 조합에 /g/ + /ə/ + /l/ 소리가 있으면 "yes" 열에 체크(✓)를 하십시오. "gle" 문자 조합에 /g/ + /ə/ + /l/ 소리가 없으면 "no" 열에 체크(✓)를 하십시오.

Target Words	Yes	No
6. glee		
7. angle		
8. mangled		
9. gleaming		
10. triangle		

Classwork

 Name: _____ Date: ___/ ___/ _____ Score: _____

Lesson 7.5

Reading Words with the "gh" Letter Combination

✓ **Lesson Check Point**

 Directions: Read each target word. Circle the word in the column that has the same "gh" sound as the target word.

지도: 각 대상 단어를 읽으십시오. 대상 단어와 같은 "gh" 소리가 나는 열의 단어에 동그라미를 치십시오.

| enough | a. ghetto |
| | b. cough |

| caught | a. light |
| | b. ghost |

| bright | a. weigh |
| | b. tough |

| Ghana | a. ghee |
| | b. laugh |

 Directions: Read each target word. Put a check (✓) under the correct column heading.

지도: 각 대상 단어를 읽으십시오. 올바른 열 제목 아래에 체크(✓)를 하십시오.

Target Words	"gh" has the /g/ sound as in the word ghetto	"gh" has the /f/ sound as in the word laugh	"gh" is silent as in the word light
1. enough			
2. caught			
3. bright			
4. Ghana			

   Classwork

Name: _____ Date:___/___/_____ Score:_____

Lesson 7.6

Reading Words with the "gn" Letter Combination

✓ **Lesson Check Point**

   Directions: Read each target word. Circle the word in the column that has the same "gn" sound(s) as the target word.
지도: 각 대상 단어를 읽으십시오. 대상 단어와 같은 "gn" 소리가 나는 열의 단어에 동그라미를 치십시오.

ignorance	a. resigned
	b. cognition

designed	a. alignment
	b. magnifying

signature	a. champagne
	b. recognizable

benign	a. foreigner
	b. pregnant

   Directions: Read each target word. Put a check (✓) under the correct column heading.
지도: 각 대상 단어를 읽으십시오. 올바른 열 제목 아래에 체크(✓)를 하십시오.

Target Words	"gn" has the /g/ + /n/ sounds as in the word <u>ignite</u>	"gn" has the silent "g" + /n/ sound as in the word <u>sign</u>
1. ignorance		
2. designed		
3. signature		
4. benign		

Classwork

Name: _____ Date: ___/___/_____ Score: _____

Lesson 7.7

Reading Words with a Silent Letter "g"

✓ **Lesson Check Point**

Directions: Read the target words in the word box. Write the words that have a silent letter "g" in the first column. Write the words that do not have a silent letter "g" in the second column.

지도: 단어 상자에 있는 대상 단어를 읽으십시오. 첫 번째 열에 묵음문자 "g"가 있는 단어를 쓰십시오. 두 번째 열에 묵음 문자"g"가 없는 단어를 쓰십시오.

Target Word Box				
daughter	sleigh	image	hunger	signal
glance	fight	thought	campaign	dough
frog	dignify	sign	magnify	regent
elegant	neighbor	assign	grand	weigh

Letter "g" is silent	Letter "g" has the /g/ or /j/ sound

Classwork

 Name: _____   Date: ___/___/_____   Score: _____

The Reading Challenge

Lesson 7.8

Reading Multisyllable Words

✓ **Lesson Check Point**

 Directions: Read and divide each target word into syllables. Write each word and place a hyphen (-) between the syllables in the second column. Write the number of syllables in the third column. Use a dictionary or the Internet to check your answers.

지도: 각 대상 단어를 읽고 음절로 나눕니다. 각 단어를 쓰고 두 번째 열의 음절 사이에 하이픈(-)을 넣습니다. 세 번째 열에 음절 수를 쓰십시오. 사전이나 인터넷을 사용하여 답을 확인하십시오.

Target Words	Words Divided into Syllables	Number of Syllables
1. grocery	_____	_____
2. Guyana	_____	_____
3. gardening	_____	_____
4. general	_____	_____
5. glamorize	_____	_____
6. grandfather	_____	_____
7. girlfriend	_____	_____
8. generous	_____	_____
9. guardian	_____	_____
10. genetic	_____	_____

Classwork

Name: _____ Date: ___/___/_____ Score: _____

The Reading Challenge

Lesson 7.8

Reading Multisyllable Words

✓ **Lesson Check Point**

Directions: Read each target word. Circle the word in the row that is divided correctly into syllables. Use a dictionary or the Internet to check your answers.

지도: 각 대상 단어를 읽으십시오. 음절로 올바르게 나누어진 행에 있는 단어에 동그라미를 치십시오. 사전이나 인터넷을 사용하여 답을 확인하십시오.

Model

| galaxy | a. ga-lax-y | b. gal-ax-y | c. gal-a-xy |

| 1. glycerol | a. glyc-er-ol | b. gly-cer-ol | c. glyc-e-rol |

| 2. governess | a. go-ver-ness | b. gov-ern-ess | c. gov-er-ness |

| 3. general | a. gen-er-al | b. ge-ner-al | c. gene-r-al |

| 4. graduate | a. gra-du-ate | b. grad-u-ate | c. grad-uat-e |

| 5. granola | a. gra-nol-a | b. gra-no-la | c. gran-ol-a |

| 6. gestation | a. gest-a-tion | b. ge-sta-tion | c. ges-ta-tion |

| 7. germinate | a. ger-mi-nate | b. germ-i-nate | c. ge-rmi-nate |

| 8. gratify | a. grat-i-fy | b. gra-tif-y | c. gr-ati-fy |

Unit G Lesson 7.8

Classwork

Name: _____ Date: ___/___/_____ Score: _____

Lesson 7.9

Reading and Writing

Proper and Common Nouns and Adjectives

✓ **Lesson Check Point**

Directions: Read the words in the word box. Put an (X) on the line next to each word that is written incorrectly. Remember that all proper nouns and proper adjectives are capitalized. Use a dictionary or the Internet to check your answers.

지도: 단어 상자에 있는 단어를 읽으십시오. 잘못 쓰여진 각 단어 옆의 줄에 (X)를 표시하십시오. 모든 고유 명사와 고유 형용사는 대문자임을 기억하십시오. 사전이나 인터넷을 사용하여 답을 확인하십시오.

Word Box		
__ Geology	__ gandhi	__ groom
__ Gym	__ Group	__ grammar
__ Greece	__ globe	__ georgetown
__ Guyana	__ germany	__ Ghana

Directions: Read each unedited sentence and underline the word that is written incorrectly. Write each sentence correctly on the line.

지도: 편집되지 않은 각 문장을 읽고 잘못 쓰여진 단어에 밑줄을긋습 니다. 각 문장을 줄에 올바르게 쓰십시오.

Model
Ginger and <u>gene</u> are going to Georgetown, Guyana.
Ginger and Gene are going to Georgetown, Guyana.

1. The Gambia and ghana are amazing African countries.
_____

2. The bride and the Groom are getting married in Grenada.
_____

3. Everyone says that Mr. Grant will be Georgia's Governor.
_____

4. George and gem said, "Grandma has beautiful new glasses."
_____

Classwork

Name: _____ Date: ___/___/_____ Score: _____

Lesson 8.1

Reading Words with the Letter H/h

✓ Lesson Check Point

Directions: Read each target word. Find the letter "h" and put a check (✓) in the column that identifies its position: beginning, within or end.
지도: 각 대상 단어를 읽으십시오. 문자"h"를 찾아 체크 표시(✓)위치를 식별하는 열에서 시작, 내부 또는 끝.

Target Words	Beginning (First Letter)	Within	End (Last Letter)
1. inch			
2. cheetah			
3. hallway			
4. Fahrenheit			
5. Savannah			

Directions: Read each sentence and underline the words that begin with the letter "h." Write all the underlined words in alphabetical order on the lines below.
지도: 각 문장을 읽고"h"로 시작하는 단어에 밑줄을 긋습니다. 밑줄 친 모든 단어를 아래 줄에 알파벳 순서로 쓰십시오.

6. Barry's home is on top of the hill.

7. Henry lives in the center of Houston.

8. The hummingbirds' eggs are hatching.

9. The cats and hamsters are very hungry.

10. Heather Carrington is an honest person.

_____   _____   _____
_____   _____   _____
_____   _____
              _____

Learn To Read English With Directions In Korean

Classwork

Name: _____ Date: ___/___/_____ Score: _____

Lesson 8.2

Reading Words with the Letter "h" Combinations:
"sh," "wh," "ch," "th," "rh," "ph" and "gh"

✓ Lesson Check Point

Directions: Read the target words in the word box. Identify the words with the following let
er combinations: "sh," "wh," "ch," "th," "rh," "ph" and "gh." Write the word on the line that shows the position of the letter combination: beginning, within or end.

지도: 단어 상자에 있는 대상 단어를 읽으십시오. "sh," "wh," "ch," "th," "rh," "ph" 및 "gh" 문자 조합으로 단어를 식별합니다. 문자 조합의 위치를 나타내는 줄에 단어를 쓰십시오: 시작, 내부 또는 끝.

Target Word Box				
wheel	thanks	rhino	kitchen	sheep
dishes	paragraph	anywhere	phone	laugh
overheard	ghost	myrrh	nephew	brother
chocolate	south	goldfish	reach	caught

	Beginning	Within	End
sh	1. _____	2. _____	3. _____
wh	4. _____	5. _____	
ch	6. _____	7. _____	8. _____
th	9. _____	10. _____	11. _____
rh	12. _____	13. _____	14. _____
ph	15. _____	16. _____	17. _____
gh	18. _____	19. _____	20. _____

Learn To Read English With Directions In Korean   Copyrighted Material

Classwork

Name: _____ Date:___/___/_____ Score:_____

Lesson 8.2

Reading Words with the Letter "h" Combinations:
"sh," "wh," "ch," "th," "rh," "ph," "gh" and "sch"

✓ **Lesson Check Point**

Directions: Read the target words in the word box. Identify the words with the following letter combinations: "sh," "wh," "ch," "th," "rh," "ph," "gh" and "sch." Write the target word that correctly completes each sentence on the line.

지도: 단어 상자에 있는 대상 단어를 읽습니다: "sh," "wh," "ch," "th," "rh," "ph," "gh" 및 "sch"의 문자 조합으로 단어를 식별합니다. 각 문장을 올바르게 완성하는 대상 단어를 줄에 쓰십시오.

Target Word Box		
shower	Ghana	Children
Whales	theater	through
phones		Chemicals
school		rhombus

1. I am learning to read and write in _____.

2. We are not allowed to have cellular _____ in school.

3. The sun was shining brightly _____ the window.

4. Yesterday, Trevor used liquid soap during his _____.

5. Brenda used her ruler to draw the shape of a _____.

6. _____ should obey their parents and teachers.

7. _____ are the largest mammals that live in the ocean.

8. The people from _____ speak many languages.

9. Thelma is hosting her birthday party at the movie _____.

10. _____ found in processed foods may harm your health.

Name: _____ Date: ___/___/_____ Score: _____

Lesson 8.3

Reading Words with a Silent Letter "h"

✓ **Lesson Check Point**

Directions: Read the target words in the word box. Write the words that have a silent letter "h" in the first column. Write the words that do not have a silent letter "h" in the second column.

지도: 단어 상자에 있는 대상 단어를 읽습니다. 첫 번째 열에 묵음문자 "h"가 있는 단어를 쓰십시오. 두 번째 열에 묵음 문자"h"가 없는 단어를 쓰십시오.

Target Word Box				
inherent	beehive	unhappy	myrrh	dehydrate
exhibit	white	fright	hundred	holding
silhouette	behind	exhaust	honor	Fahrenheit
heirloom	house	comprehend	perhaps	whales

Letter "h" is silent

_____
_____
_____
_____
_____
_____
_____
_____

Letter "h" has the /h/ sound

_____
_____
_____
_____
_____
_____
_____
_____

Classwork

Name: _____ Date: ___/___/_____ Score: _____

The Reading Challenge

Lesson 8.4

Reading Multisyllable Words

✓ **Lesson Check Point**

Directions: Read and divide each target word into syllables. Write each word and place a hyphen (-) between the syllables in the second column. Write the number of syllables in the third column. Use a dictionary or the Internet to check your answers.

지도: 각 대상 단어를 읽고 음절로 나눕니다. 각 단어를 쓰고 두 번째 열의 음절 사이에 하이픈(-)을 넣습니다. 세 번째 열에 음절 수를 쓰십시오. 사전이나 인터넷을 사용하여 답을 확인하십시오.

Target Words	Words Divided into Syllables	Number of Syllables
1. hallway	_____	_____
2. heartache	_____	_____
3. honeycomb	_____	_____
4. hyperlink	_____	_____
5. headlights	_____	_____
6. harmonize	_____	_____
7. homonym	_____	_____
8. hardware	_____	_____
9. hesitant	_____	_____
10. hazelnut	_____	_____

Classwork

 Name: _____ Date: ___/___/_____ Score: _____

The Reading Challenge

Lesson 8.4

Reading Multisyllable Words

✓ **Lesson Check Point**

 Directions: Read each target word. Circle the word in the row that is divided correctly into syllables. Use a dictionary or the Internet to check your answers.

지도: 각 대상 단어를 읽으십시오. 음절로 올바르게 나누어진 행에 있는 단어에 동그라미를 치십시오. 사전이나 인터넷을 사용하여 답을 확인하십시오.

Model

| heroic | a. he-roi-c | b. her-o-ic | c. he-ro-ic ⃝ |

1. hatchet	a. hatch-et	b. ha-tch-et	c. hatc-het
2. hazelnut	a. haz-e-lnut	b. haz-el-nut	c. ha-zel-nut
3. hexagon	a. he-xa-gon	b. hex-a-gon	c. hex-ag-on
4. historic	a. hi-stor-ic	b. his-tor-ic	c. hist-or-ic
5. halogen	a. hal-og-en	b. hal-o-gen	c. ha-lo-gen
6. hairdresser	a. hair-dress-er	b. ha-ir-dresser	c. hair-dresse-r
7. harvesting	a. harv-est-ing	b. har-ves-ting	c. har-vest-ing
8. handicap	a. hand-i-cap	b. han-dic-ap	c. hand-ic-ap

Classwork

Name: _____ Date: ___/___/_____ Score: _____

Lesson 8.5

Reading and Writing

Proper and Common Nouns and Adjectives

✓ **Lesson Check Point**

Directions: Read the words in the word box. Put an (X) on the line next to each word that is written incorrectly. Remember that all proper nouns and proper adjectives are capitalized. Use a dictionary or the Internet to check your answers.

지도: 단어 상자에 있는 단어를 읽으십시오. 잘못 쓰여진 각 단어 옆의 줄에 (X)를 표시하십시오. 모든 고유 명사와 고유 형용사는 대문자임을 기억하십시오. 사전이나 인터넷을 사용하여 답을 확인하십시오.

Word Box		
__ Haiti	__ House	__ halifax
__ hebrew	__ Hexagon	__ Hawaii
__ horses	__ Haiku	__ hiccup
__ home	__ Hindu	__ hispanic

Directions: Read each unedited sentence and underline the word that is written incorrectly. Write each sentence correctly on the line.

지도: 편집되지 않은 각 문장을 읽고 잘못 쓰여진 단어에 밑줄을 긋습 니다. 각 문장을 줄에 올바르게 쓰십시오.

Model
Mr. Hitt has a big house on <u>hope</u> Avenue.
<u>Mr. Hitt has a big house on Hope Avenue.</u>

1. Henry is studying haitian history at Hunter College.
_____

2. The local historian lives in hartford's Historic District.
_____

3. The thoroughbred Horses are galloping along Houston Harbor.
_____

4. heather is a hard working housekeeper at the Hilton Garden Hotel.
_____

Classwork

 Name: _____ Date:___/___/_____ Score:_____

Lesson 9.1

Reading Words with the Letter I/i

✓ Lesson Check Point

 Directions: Read each target word. Find the letter "i" and put a check (✓) in the column that identifies its position: beginning, within or end.
지도: 각 대상 단어를 읽으십시오. 문자"i"를 찾아 체크 표시(✓)위치 를 식별하는 열에서 시작, 내부 또는 끝.

Target Words	Beginning (First Letter)	Within	End (Last Letter)
1. incapable			
2. Fuji			
3. alive			
4. broccoli			
5. Ireland			

 Directions: Read each target word. Read the words in the row and circle the word that has a different vowel "i" sound.
지도: 각 대상 단어를 읽으십시오. 행에 있는 단어를 읽고 모음"i" 소리가 다른 단어에 동그라미를 치십시오.

Target Words				
6. blimp	child	this	grim	lid
7. spin	fix	pin	dip	bike
8. trip	hip	nine	fin	pit
9. crib	big	dim	mild	six
10. king	hill	kite	grin	ship

Classwork

 Name: _____ Date: ____/____/_____ Score: _____

Lesson 9.2

Reading Words with the Short Vowel "i" Sound

✓ Lesson Check Point

 Directions: Read the words in the four boxes. Circle two words with the short vowel /ĭ/ sound. The anchor word for the short vowel /ĭ/ sound is <u>insect</u>.

지도: 네 개의 상자에 있는 단어를 읽으십시오. 짧은 모음/ĭ/ 소리로 두 단어에 동그라미를 치십시오. 단모음/ĭ/ 소리의 기준어는 insect입니다.

bin	sip	bike	big	dig	slim
child	mile	hid	fine	bite	pike

line	kite	tint	will	twin	pint
crib	blip	like	nine	taxi	list

 Directions: Read the words in the four boxes. Circle two words that rhyme. Rhyming words have the same ending sound, such as <u>hip</u> and <u>dip</u>.

지도: 네 개의 상자에 있는 단어를 읽으십시오. 운이 맞는 두 단어에동그라미를 치십시오. 운율이 있는 단어는 hip와dip과 같이 끝 소리가같습니다.

pine	bib	clip	wife	fit	sit
hike	rib	rice	slip	life	nice

mile	lime	hide	him	win	pipe
six	mix	dim	mice	tin	side

Classwork

Name: _____ Date: ___/___/_____ Score: _____

Lesson 9.2

Reading & Writing Words with the Short Vowel "i" Sound

✓ **Lesson Check Point**

Directions: Read each sentence and underline three words with the short vowel /ĭ/ sound. Then, write the underlined words on the lines below. The anchor word for the short vowel /ĭ/ sound is <u>insect</u>.

지도: 각 문장을 읽고 세 단어에 짧은 모음 /ĭ/ 소리에 밑줄을 긋습니다. 그런 다음 밑줄 친 단어를 아래 줄에 쓰십시오. 단모음 /ĭ/ 소리의 기준 어는 insect입니다.

Model

<u>Jim</u> placed a <u>big</u> cup of ice on the <u>windowsill</u>.

    Jim   big   windowsill

1. Irene gave Jill a big wig.

   _____   _____   _____

2. The kids did not kick the ball on the field.

   _____   _____   _____

3. Billy said, "Tim licked the ice pop."

   _____   _____   _____

4. Milly sipped the medium-sized drink.

   _____   _____   _____

5. The big dishes used to serve the pizza are by the sink.

   _____   _____   _____

Classwork

 Name: _____ Date: ___/___/_____ Score: _____

Lesson 9.3

Reading Words with the Long Vowel "i" Sound

✓ **Lesson Check Point**

 Directions: Read the words in the four boxes. Circle two words with the long vowel /ī/ sound. The anchor word for the long vowel /ī/ sound is <u>ice</u>.

지도: 네 개의 상자에 있는 단어를 읽으십시오. 장모음/ī/ 소리로두단어에 동그라미를 치십시오. 장모음/ī/ 소리의 기준어는 ice입니다.

brain	wild		bill	bike		hike	taxi
kick	fine		lime	mini		sick	dice

mine	pink		chili	sing		pain	vile
train	tile		mime	tide		miss	side

 Directions: Read the words in the four boxes. Circle two words that rhyme. Rhyming words have the same ending sound, such as <u>rice</u> and <u>nice</u>.

지도: 네 개의 상자에 있는 단어를 읽으십시오. 운이 맞는 두 단어에동그라미를 치십시오. 운율이 있는 단어는 rice와 nice와 같은 끝 소리가같습니다.

lift	dime		nine	link		bite	fill
pick	time		kids	pine		kite	crib

line	skill		like	pike		life	rib
vine	Mali		drill	dim		lick	wife

Classwork

Name: _____ Date: ___/___/_____ Score: _____

Lesson 9.3

Reading & Writing Words with the Long Vowel "i" Sound

✓ **Lesson Check Point**

Directions: Read each sentence and underline three words with the long vowel /ī/ sound. Then, write the underlined words on the lines below. The anchor word for the long vowel /ī/ sound is <u>ice</u>.

지도: 각 문장을 읽고 장모음/ī/ 소리로 세 단어에 밑줄을 긋습니다. 그런 다음 밑줄 친 단어를 아래 줄에 쓰십시오. 장모음/ī/ 소리의 기준어는 ice 입니다.

Model

David and <u>I</u> flew our big, <u>white</u> <u>kite</u> along the riverbank.

     I   white   kite
_____   _____   _____

1. Brian has to fix his mountain bike's tire.

   _____   _____   _____

2. Mike went outside to climb the steep hill.

   _____   _____   _____

3. Jill said, "The bride has a nice, white dress."

   _____   _____   _____

4. Irene's husband retired from working as a firefighter.

   _____   _____   _____

5. The principal invited the entire class to his tiny office.

   _____   _____   _____

Classwork

Name: _____ Date: ___/___/_____ Score: _____

Review Lessons 9.2 & 9.3

Reading Short Vowel and Long Vowel Words

Directions: Read the target words in the word box. In the first column, write the words that have the short vowel /ĭ/ sound, as in the word <u>insect</u>. In the second column, write the words that have the long vowel /ī/ sound, as in the word <u>ice</u>.

지도: 단어 상자에 있는 대상 단어를 읽습니다. 첫 번째 열에는 insect라는 단어와 같이 단모음/ĭ/ 소리가 나는 단어를 씁니다. 두 번째 열에는 ice 라는 단어에서처럼 장모음/ī/ 소리가 나는 단어를 씁니다.

Target Word Box				
child	dinner	trip	bill	gift
tie	hint	I	pink	diner
hi	bike	diet	skim	client
inward	pie	lint	ripe	disk

Letter "i" has the /ĭ/ sound as in the word <u>insect</u>

Letter "i" has the /ī/ sound as in the word <u>ice</u>

Name: _____ Date: ___/___/_____ Score: _____

Lesson 9.4

Reading Words with Letter "i" Vowel Pairs

✓ **Lesson Check Point**

 Directions: Read each target word. Circle the word in the column that has the same vowel "ia," "ie," "io" or "iu" sound(s) as the target word.
지도: 각 대상 단어를 읽으십시오. 대상 단어와 같은 모음 "ia," "ie," "io" 또는 "iu" 소리가 있는 열의 단어에 동그라미를 치십시오.

union	a. allied
	b. civilian

liable	a. radius
	b. diary

vial	a. diet
	b. dialing

believe	a. piece
	b. dried

 Directions: Read each target word. Put a check (✓) under the correct column heading.
지도: 각 대상 단어를 읽으십시오. 올바른 열 제목 아래에 체크(✓)를 하십시오.

Target Words	Words have the long "i" sound as in the word <u>dial</u>	Words do not have the long "i" sound
1. union		
2. liable		
3. vial		
4. believe		

Classwork

 Name: _____ Date: ___/___/_____ Score: _____

Lesson 9.5

Reading Words with the Final Letter "i"

✓ Lesson Check Point

 Directions: Read each target word. Find the letter "i" and put a check (✓) in the column that identifies its position within the syllable.
지도: 각 대상 단어를 읽으십시오. 문자 "i"를 찾아 체크 표시(✓)음절내에서 위치를 식별하는 열에서.

Target Words	"i" is at the end of a one syllable word	"i" is at the end of the first syllable	"i" is at the end of a multi-syllable word
1. hi			
2. final			
3. alib̲i			
4. iron			
5. dinosaur			

 Directions: Read each target word. Put a check (✓) under the correct column heading.
지도: 각 대상 단어를 읽으십시오. 올바른 열 제목 아래에 체크 (✓)를 하십시오.

Target Words	"i" has the /ĭ/ sound as in the word insect	"i" has the /ī/ sound as in the word bike	"i" has the /ə/ sound as in the word pencil	"i" is silent as in the word maid
6. kite				
7. pilgr̲im				
8. himself				
9. business				
10. utensil				

Classwork

 Name: _____ Date: ___/___/_____ Score: _____

Lesson 9.6

Reading Letter "i" Words with the Schwa Vowel Sound

✓ **Lesson Check Point**

 Directions: Read each target word. Circle the word in the column that has the same "i" sound as the target word.
지도: 각 대상 단어를 읽으십시오. 목표 단어와 동일한"i" 소리가 나는 열의 단어에 동그라미를 치십시오.

admiral	a. notified
	b. raisin

incredible	a. instructor
	b. optimize

amplify	a. octopi
	b. festival

estimate	a. stencil
	b. imprints

 Directions: Read each sentence and underline the letter "i" word that has the schwa vowel /ə/ sound. The anchor word for the letter "i" schwa vowel sound is pencil.
지도: 각 문장을 읽고 슈와 모음 /ə/ 소리가 있는 문자"i" 단어에 밑줄을 긋습니다. 문자"i" 슈와 모음 소리의 앵커 단어는 pencil입니다.

1. I will notify the girls about the field trip.
2. The child is experiencing pain in his nostrils.
3. Trinidad's carnival is a major cultural event.
4. The binoculars are inside my white briefcase.
5. I bought vanilla ice cream at the convenience store.
6. The president encouraged every individual to vote.

Classwork

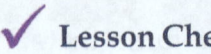 Name: _____ Date: ____/____/_____ Score: _____

Lesson 9.7

Reading Words with the "ir" Letter Combination

Dictionary Skills/ Vocabulary

✓ **Lesson Check Point**

 Directions: Read each target word and its definition. Write the letter of the definition on the line of each target word. Use a dictionary or the Internet to check your answers.
지도: 각 대상 단어와 그 정의를 읽으십시오. 각 대상 단어의 행에 정의의 문자를 씁니다. 사전이나 인터넷을 사용하여 답을 확인하십시오.

Target Words	Definitions
1. __ shirt	a. a bushy-tailed rodent that lives in a tree or a burrow
2. __ birds	b. females
3. __ squirrel	c. clothing worn on the upper part of the body
4. __ twirl	d. to spin or turn something around with one's fingers
5. __ girls	e. egg-laying animals that have wings

 Directions: Read each sentence and write the target word that completes the sentence.
지도: 각 문장을 읽고 문장을 완성하는 목표어를 쓰세요.

6. My white _____ has a clean collar.

7. The cheerleaders _____ their batons.

8. The _____ like to eat ice cream cones.

9. Millions of _____ migrate along the flyway.

10. The _____ climbed up the tree quickly.

Classwork

Name: _____ Date:___/___/_____ Score: _____

Lesson 9.8

Reading Letter "i" Words with the Long Vowel "e" Sound

✓ **Lesson Check Point**

Directions: Read each target word. Circle the word in the column that has the same "i" sound as the target word.
지도: 각 대상 단어를 읽으십시오. 목표 단어와 동일한"i" 소리가나는열의 단어에 동그라미를 치십시오.

chili	a. ivory
	b. Haiti

Miami	a. Hawaii
	b. biology

Hindi	a. kiwi
	b. magi

Pepsi	a. identity
	b. mini

Directions: Read each sentence and underline the letter "i" word that has the long vowel /ē/ sound. Then, write the word on the line. The anchor word, taxi has a letter "i" that represents the long vowel /ē/ sound.
지도: 각 문장을 읽고 장모음 /ē/ 소리가 나는"i" 단어에 밑줄을 긋습니다. 그런 다음 줄에 단어를 쓰십시오. 앵커 단어인 taxi에는 장모음 /ē/ 소리를 나타내는 문자"i"가 있습니다.

1. It is not wise to go skiing at night. _____

2. Jim and Mike enjoy eating pita bread. _____

3. The children admire the police officers. _____

4. My family likes to eat dinner on the patio. _____

5. I will use the sewing machine to sew a pillow. _____

6. Baked ziti is a classic Italian-American dish. _____

Classwork

Name: _____ Date: ___/___/_____ Score: _____

Lesson 9.9

Reading Words with a Silent Letter "i"

✓ **Lesson Check Point**

Directions: Read the target words in the word box. Write the words that have a silent letter "i" in the first column. Write the words that do not have a silent letter "i" in the second column.

지도: 단어 상자에 있는 대상 단어를 읽습니다. 첫 번째 열에 묵음문자 "i"가 있는 단어를 쓰십시오. 두 번째 열에 묵음 문자"i"가 없는 단어를 쓰십시오.

Target Word Box				
aside	camping	Jamaica	sailboat	stained
waist	afraid	giggles	bail	fifteen
bigger	city	hiking	railroad	distinct
attaining	finish	suit	helping	again

Letter "i" is silent

Letter "i" has a letter "i" sound

Learn To Read English With Directions In Korean

Name: _____ Date: ___/___/_____ Score: _____

Unit Review - I/i

Reading Words with Vowel "i" Sounds: /ĭ/, /ī/, /ə/ & Silent

✓ Lesson Check Point

Directions: Read each target word. Circle the word in the column that has the same "i" sound as the target word.
지도: 각 대상 단어를 읽으십시오. 목표 단어와 동일한 "i" 소리가 나는 열의 단어에 동그라미를 치십시오.

fire	a. trip
	b. dine

testify	a. wish
	b. Russia

brick	a. file
	b. fill

milk	a. pinch
	b. time

Directions: Read each target word. Put a check (✓) under the correct column heading.
지도: 각 대상 단어를 읽으십시오. 올바른 열 제목 아래에 체크(✓)를 하십시오.

Target Words	"i" has the /ĭ/ sound as in the word <u>insect</u>	"i" has the /ī/ sound as in the word <u>bike</u>	"i" has the /ə/ sound as in the word <u>pencil</u>	"i" is silent as in the word <u>maid</u>
1. fire				
2. testify				
3. brick				
4. milk				

Classwork

Name: _____ Date: ___/___/_____ Score: _____

The Reading Challenge

Lesson 9.10

Reading Multisyllable Words

✓ Lesson Check Point

Directions: Read and divide each target word into syllables. Write each word and place a hyphen (-) between the syllables in the second column. Write the number of syllables in the third column. Use a dictionary or the Internet to check your answers.

지도: 각 대상 단어를 읽고 음절로 나눕니다. 각 단어를 쓰고 두 번째 열의 음절 사이에 하이픈(-)을 넣습니다. 세 번째 열에 음절 수를 쓰십시오. 사전이나 인터넷을 사용하여 답을 확인하십시오.

Target Words	Words Divided into Syllables	Number of Syllables
1. drinking	_____	_____
2. mentoring	_____	_____
3. spider	_____	_____
4. Haiti	_____	_____
5. kiwi	_____	_____
6. providing	_____	_____
7. diner	_____	_____
8. beside	_____	_____
9. mineral	_____	_____
10. fictional	_____	_____

Classwork

Name: _____ Date: ___/___/_____ Score: _____

The Reading Challenge

Lesson 9.10

Reading Multisyllable Words

✓ Lesson Check Point

Directions: Read each target word. Circle the word in the row that is divided correctly into syllables. Use a dictionary or the Internet to check your answers.

지도: 각 대상 단어를 읽으십시오. 음절로 올바르게 나누어진 행에 있는 단어에 동그라미를 치십시오. 사전이나 인터넷을 사용하여 답을 확인하십시오.

Model

| interesting | a. in-ter-est-ing (circled) | b. int-er-est-ing | c. inte-rest-ing |

1. bifocal	a. bif-o-cal	b. bi-fo-cal	c. bi-foc-al
2. hibernate	a. hi-ber-nate	b. hib-er-nate	c. hi-bern-ate
3. Malawi	a. Ma-la-wi	b. Ma-law-i	c. Mal-a-wi
4. tribunal	a. trib-un-al	b. trib-u-nal	c. tri-bu-nal
5. safari	a. sa-fa-ri	b. saf-a-ri	c. sa-far-i
6. unicorn	a. u-ni-corn	b. un-i-corn	c. u-nic-orn
7. imagine	a. im-a-gine	b. i-ma-gine	c. i-mag-ine
8. dialect	a. di-ale-ct	b. di-a-lect	c. dial-e-ct

Learn To Read English With Directions In Korean   Copyrighted Material

Classwork

Name: _____ Date: ___/___/_____ Score: _____

Lesson 9.11

Reading and Writing

Proper and Common Nouns and Adjectives

✓ **Lesson Check Point**

Directions: Read the words in the word box. Put an (X) on the line next to each word that is written incorrectly. Remember that all proper nouns and proper adjectives are capitalized. Use a dictionary or the Internet to check your answers.

지도: 단어 상자에 있는 단어를 읽으십시오. 잘못 쓰여진 각 단어 옆의 줄에 (X)를 표시하십시오. 모든 고유 명사와 고유 형용사는 대문자임을 기억하십시오. 사전이나 인터넷을 사용하여 답을 확인하십시오.

Word Box		
__ identify	__ illinois	__ Invincible
__ Iroquois	__ Insanity	__ illusion
__ Indo-European	__ itching	__ Ivory Coast
__ italy	__ irish	__ ida Mount

Directions: Read each unedited sentence and underline the word that is written incorrectly. Write each sentence correctly on the line.

지도: 편집되지 않은 각 문장을 읽고 잘못 쓰여진 단어에 밑줄을긋습 니다. 각 문장을 줄에 올바르게 쓰십시오.

Model
New Delhi and Indore are beautiful cities in <u>india</u>.
<u>New Delhi and Indore are beautiful cities in India.</u>

1. My teacher said, "The incas inhabited the Americas."
_____

2. In April, Isabella will attend iowa Community College.
_____

3. Ida looked up information about indonesia on the Internet.
_____

4. On independence Day, Ian ignited a massive display of fireworks.
_____

Classwork

Name: _____ Date: ___/___/_____ Score: _____

Lesson 10.1

Reading Words with the Letter J/j

✓ Lesson Check Point

Directions: Read each target word. Find the letter "j" and put a check (✓) in the column that identifies its position: beginning, within or end.
지도: 각 대상 단어를 읽으십시오. 문자"j"를 찾아 체크 표시(✓)위치를 식별하는 열에서 시작, 내부 또는 끝.

Target Words	Beginning (First Letter)	Within	End (Last Letter)
1. conjunct			
2. jacket			
3. jersey			
4. reject			
5. jumbo			

Directions: Read each sentence and underline the words that begin with the letter "j." Write all the underlined words in alphabetical order on the lines below.
지도: 각 문장을 읽고"j"로 시작하는 단어에 밑줄을 긋습니다. 밑줄 친 모든 단어를 아래 줄에 알파벳 순서로 쓰십시오.

6. Henry has a jug of apple juice.

7. The jockey's horse is named Jupiter.

8. We flew in a jet from New York to Japan.

9. Hadia took a long journey through the jungle.

10. In January, Mrs. Adams is going to Jacksonville, Florida.

_____   _____   _____
_____   _____   _____
_____   _____   _____
               _____

Learn To Read English With Directions In Korean

Classwork

 Name: _____ Date: ___/___/_____ Score: _____

The Reading Challenge

Lesson 10.2

Reading Multisyllable Words

✓ **Lesson Check Point**

 Directions: Read and divide each target word into syllables. Write each word and place a hyphen (-) between the syllables in the second column. Write the number of syllables in the third column. Use a dictionary or the Internet to check your answers.

지도: 각 대상 단어를 읽고 음절로 나눕니다. 각 단어를 쓰고 두 번째 열의 음절 사이에 하이픈(-)을 넣습니다. 세 번째 열에 음절 수를 쓰십시오. 사전이나 인터넷을 사용하여 답을 확인하십시오.

Target Words	Words Divided into Syllables	Number of Syllables
1. jackpot	_____	_____
2. joey	_____	_____
3. jealous	_____	_____
4. judgmental	_____	_____
5. journal	_____	_____
6. judo	_____	_____
7. Japanese	_____	_____
8. joyously	_____	_____
9. justify	_____	_____
10. juicy	_____	_____

Unit J Lesson 10.2

Classwork

 Name: _____   Date: ___/___/_____   Score: _____

The Reading Challenge

Lesson 10.2

Reading Multisyllable Words

✓ **Lesson Check Point**

 Directions: Read each target word. Circle the word in the row that is divided correctly into syllables. Use a dictionary or the Internet to check your answers.

지도: 각 대상 단어를 읽으십시오. 음절로 올바르게 나누어진 행에 있는 단어에 동그라미를 치십시오. 사전이나 인터넷을 사용하여 답을 확인하십시오.

Model

| janitor | a. ja-ni-tor | b. jan-it-or | c. jan-i-tor ⭕ |

1. January	a. Jan-u-ar-y	b. Jan-u-ary	c. Jan-uar-y
2. jeopardize	a. jeop-ard-ize	b. jeop-ar-dize	c. jeo-pard-ize
3. jubilant	a. ju-bila-nt	b. ju-bi-lant	c. ju-bil-ant
4. javelin	a. javel-in	b. jave-lin	c. ja-vel-in
5. judgmental	a. judg-men-tal	b. jud-gmen-tal	c. judg-ment-al
6. jubilance	a. ju-bi-lance	b. ju-bil-ance	c. jub-i-lance
7. justify	a. ju-sti-fy	b. jus-tif-y	c. jus-ti-fy
8. jalopy	a. jal-o-py	b. ja-lop-y	c. jal-op-y

Classwork

Name: _____ Date:___/___/_____ Score:_____

Lesson 10.3

Reading and Writing

Proper and Common Nouns and Adjectives

✓ **Lesson Check Point**

Directions: Read the words in the word box. Put an (X) on the line next to each word that is written incorrectly. Remember that all proper nouns and proper adjectives are capitalized. Use a dictionary or the Internet to check your answers.

지도: 단어 상자에 있는 단어를 읽으십시오. 잘못 쓰여진 각 단어 옆의 줄에 (X)를 표시하십시오. 모든 고유 명사와 고유 형용사는 대문자임을 기억하십시오. 사전이나 인터넷을 사용하여 답을 확인하십시오.

Word Box		
__ Jasmine	__ jupiter	__ jigsaw
__ june	__ jelly	__ january
__ jersey	__ jockey	__ Juice
__ japan	__ Jewelry	__ Jackson

Directions: Read each unedited sentence and underline the word that is written incorrectly. Write each sentence correctly on the line.

지도: 편집되지 않은 각 문장을 읽고 잘못 쓰여진 단어에 밑줄을굿습 니다. 각 문장을 줄에 올바르게 쓰십시오.

Model
Joey and his family live in New <u>jersey</u>.
Joey and his family live in New Jersey.

1. In january, Jack will wear a warm jacket.
_____

2. In june, Jordan had five jars of jalapenos.
_____

3. The kids are playing with a Jigsaw puzzle and a jet.
_____

4. jillian has a new job at Johnson and Johnson Incorporated.
_____

Classwork

Name: _____ Date:___/___/_____ Score:_____

Lesson 11.1

Reading Words with the Letter K/k

✓ Lesson Check Point

Directions: Read each target word. Find the letter "k" and put a check (✓) in the column that identifies its position: beginning, within or end.
지도: 각 대상 단어를 읽으십시오. 문자"k"를 찾아 체크 표시(✓)위치를 식별하는 열에서 시작, 내부 또는 끝.

Target Words	Beginning (First Letter)	Within	End (Last Letter)
1. shock			
2. king			
3. choke			
4. homework			
5. keycard			

Directions: Read each sentence and underline the words that begin with the letter "k." Write all the underlined words in alphabetical order on the lines below.
지도: 각 문장을 읽고 문자"k"로 시작하는 단어에 밑줄을 긋습니다. 밑줄 친 모든 단어를 아래 줄에 알파벳 순서로 쓰십시오.

6. Kangaroos and koalas live in Australia.

7. Alex is learning to kick in his karate class.

8. King George III had a very powerful kingdom.

9. My friend, Karen, was born in Kingston, Jamaica.

10. Some keys on the computer keyboard are not working.

_____   _____   _____
_____   _____   _____
_____   _____   _____
            _____

Learn To Read English With Directions In Korean

Classwork

 Name: _____ Date: ___/___/_____ Score: _____

Lesson 11.2

Reading Words with the Letter "k" and "ck" Letter Combination

✓ **Lesson Check Point**

 Directions: Read each target word. Put a check (✓) in the second column if the target word has one vowel. Put a check (✓) in the third column if the target word has two vowels.

지도: 각 대상 단어를 읽으십시오. 대상 단어에 모음이 하나 있는 경우 두 번째 열에 체크(✓)를 합니다. 대상 단어에 두 개의 모음이 있는경우제삼 열에 체크(✓)를 합니다.

Target Words	Words with 1 Vowel	Words with 2 Vowels
1. pike		
2. smack		
3. sneak		
4. lock		
5. broke		

 Directions: Read each target word in the first column and write the number of vowels within the word in the second column. Read each target word in the third column and write the number of vowels within the word in the fourth column.

지도: 첫 번째 열의 각 대상 단어를 읽고 두 번째 열의 단어 내 모음 수를 쓰십시오. 세 번째 열의 각 대상 단어를 읽고 네 번째 열의 단어에 포함된 모음의 수를 쓰십시오.

Target Words	Number of Vowels	Target Words	Number of Vowels
6. stoke		stock	
7. smock		smoke	
8. Blake		black	
9. tack		take	
10. pick		pike	

Classwork

 Name: _____ Date: ___/___/_____ Score: _____

Lesson 11.3

Reading Words with the "kle" Letter Combination

✓ Lesson Check Point

 Directions: Read each target word. Find the "kle" letter combination and put a check (✓) in the column that identifies its position: beginning, within or end.

지도: 각 대상 단어를 읽으십시오. "kle" 문자 조합을 찾아 해당 위치를 식별하는 열에 체크(✓)를 하십시오: 시작, 내부 또는 끝.

Target Words	Beginning (First 3 Letters)	Within	End (Last 3 Letters)
1. knuckle			
2. Kleenex			
3. anklets			
4. sparkles			
5. wrinkle			

 Directions: Read each target word. Put a check (✓) in the "yes" column if the "kle" letter combination has the /k/ + /ə/ + /l/ sounds. Put a check (✓) in the "no" column if the "kle" letter combination does not have the /k/ + /ə/ + /l/ sounds.

지도: 각 대상 단어를 읽으십시오. "kle" 문자 조합에 /k/ + /ə/ + /l/ 소리가있으 면 "yes" 열에 체크(✓)를 하십시오. "kle" 문자 조합에 /k/ + /ə/ + /l/ 소리가없으 면 "no" 열에 체크(✓)를 하십시오.

Target Words	Yes	No
6. knuckle		
7. Kleenex		
8. anklets		
9. sparkles		
10. wrinkle		

Classwork

Name: _____ Date: ___/___/_____ Score: _____

Lesson 11.4

Reading Words with a Silent Letter "k"

✓ **Lesson Check Point**

Directions: Read the target words in the word box. Write the words that have a silent letter "k" in the first column. Write the words that do not have a silent letter "k" in the second column.

지도: 단어 상자에 있는 대상 단어를 읽으십시오. 첫 번째 열에 묵음문자 "k"가 있는 단어를 쓰십시오. 두 번째 열에 묵음 문자"k"가 없는 단어를 쓰십시오.

Target Word Box				
knee	known	doorknob	seeking	knead
shaking	parking	knocking	keyboard	knew
keeping	karate	kennel	knap	sharks
knish	knives	knuckle	milky	kneed

Letter "k" is silent   **Letter "k" has the /k/ sound**

_____ _____
_____ _____
_____ _____
_____ _____
_____ _____
_____ _____
_____ _____
_____ _____
_____ _____
_____ _____

Classwork

Name: _____ Date: ___/___/_____ Score: _____

The Reading Challenge

Lesson 11.5

Reading Multisyllable Words

✓ **Lesson Check Point**

Directions: Read and divide each target word into syllables. Write each word and place a hyphen (-) between the syllables in the second column. Write the number of syllables in the third column. Use a dictionary or the Internet to check your answers.

지도: 각 대상 단어를 읽고 음절로 나눕니다. 각 단어를 쓰고 두 번째 열의 음절 사이에 하이픈(-)을 넣습니다. 세 번째 열에 음절 수를 쓰십시오. 사전이나 인터넷을 사용하여 답을 확인하십시오.

Target Words	Words Divided into Syllables	Number of Syllables
1. kayak		
2. Kenya		
3. Korean		
4. kindly		
5. ketchup		
6. keyboard		
7. Kuwaiti		
8. kidnap		
9. knowledge		
10. kudos		

Unit K
Lesson 11.5

Classwork

Name: _____ Date: ___/___/_____ Score: _____

The Reading Challenge

Lesson 11.5

Reading Multisyllable Words

✓ **Lesson Check Point**

Directions: Read each target word. Circle the word in the row that is divided correctly into syllables. Use a dictionary or the Internet to check your answers.

지도: 각 대상 단어를 읽으십시오. 음절로 올바르게 나누어진 행에 있는 단어에 동그라미를 치십시오. 사전이나 인터넷을 사용하여 답을 확인하십시오.

Model

| kangaroo | a. kang-a-roo | b. kan-ga-roo | c. kan-gar-oo |

1. karate	a. ka-ra-te	b. ka-rate	c. kar-ate
2. kilobyte	a. ki-lo-byte	b. kil-o-byte	c. kil-ob-yte
3. Kentucky	a. Ken-tuc-ky	b. Kent-uck-y	c. Ken-tuck-y
4. kilowatt	a. ki-lo-watt	b. kil-o-watt	c. ki-low-att
5. keratin	a. ke-ra-tin	b. ker-at-in	c. ker-a-tin
6. Korea	a. Ko-r-ea	b. Ko-re-a	c. Kor-e-a
7. koala	a. ko-a-la	b. koa-la	c. ko-ala
8. kilogram	a. ki-log-ram	b. ki-lo-gram	c. kil-o-gram

Classwork

Name: _____ Date: ___/___/_____ Score: _____

Lesson 11.6

Reading and Writing

Proper and Common Nouns and Adjectives

✓ **Lesson Check Point**

Directions: Read the words in the word box. Put an (X) on the line next to each word that is written incorrectly. Remember that all proper nouns and proper adjectives are capitalized. Use a dictionary or the Internet to check your answers.

지도: 단어 상자에 있는 단어를 읽으십시오. 잘못 쓰여진 각 단어 옆의 줄에 (X)를 표시하십시오. 모든 고유 명사와 고유 형용사는 대문자임을 기억하십시오. 사전이나 인터넷을 사용하여 답을 확인하십시오.

Word Box		
__ Kenya	__ key Largo	__ Korea
__ Kept	__ Kensington	__ Know
__ Kid	__ knock	__ knight
__ kansas	__ kentucky	__ kind

Directions: Read each unedited sentence and underline the word that is written incorrectly. Write each sentence correctly on the line.

지도: 편집되지 않은 각 문장을 읽고 잘못 쓰여진 단어에 밑줄을 긋습 니다. 각 문장을 줄에 올바르게 쓰십시오.

Model
Helen <u>keller</u> was a kind person.
<u>Helen Keller was a kind person.</u>

1. karen and Kim speak Korean fluently.
_____

2. Kimberly is going to kingston, Jamaica.
_____

3. My best friend, Kara, is from kuwait.
_____

4. Kennedy and I are reading about king George III.
_____

Classwork

Name: _____ Date: ___/ ___/ _____ Score: _____

Lesson 12.1

Reading Words with the Letter L/l

✓ **Lesson Check Point**

Directions: Read each target word. Find the letter "l" and put a check (✓) in the column that identifies its position: beginning, within or end.
지도: 각 대상 단어를 읽으십시오. 문자"l"을 찾아 체크 표시(✓)위치를 식별하는 열에서 시작, 내부 또는 끝.

Target Words	Beginning (First Letter)	Within	End (Last Letter)
1. kneel			
2. imply			
3. leave			
4. juvenile			
5. lasting			

Directions: Read each sentence and underline the words that begin with the letter "l." Write all the underlined words in alphabetical order on the lines below.
지도: 각 문장을 읽고 문자"l"로 시작하는 단어에 밑줄을 긋습니다. 밑줄 친 모든 단어를 아래 줄에 알파벳 순서로 쓰십시오.

6. The little light bulb is very bright.

7. We are learning about Lewis and Clark.

8. Abraham Lincoln was a brilliant lawyer.

9. My friend, Tim, enjoys licking cherry lollipops.

10. Everyone in my Latin class speaks another language.

_____   _____   _____
_____   _____   _____
_____   _____   _____
                  _____

Classwork

 Name: _____ Date:___/___/_____ Score:_____

Lesson 12.2

Reading Words with the Letter "l" Combinations:
"cl," "fl," "pl" & "sl"

Dictionary Skills/ Vocabulary

✓ Lesson Check Point

 Directions: Read each target word and its definition. Write the target word on the line in front of its meaning. Use a dictionary or the Internet to check your answers.
지도: 각 대상 단어와 그 정의를 읽으십시오. 의미 앞 줄에대상단어를 쓰십시오. 사전이나 인터넷을 사용하여 답을 확인하십시오.

Target Word Box				
class	flowers	placed	play	sleet

1. _____ the act of doing something fun
2. _____ small icy pieces that fall from the sky
3. _____ the colorful part of a plant that contains seeds
4. _____ to put something in a particular position or location
5. _____ group of students who is taught by the same teacher

 Directions: Read each sentence. Underline the word in the parentheses that correctly completes each sentence. Then, write the underlined word on the line.
지도: 각 문장을 읽으십시오. 각 문장을 올바르게 완성하는 괄호 안에 있는 단어에 밑줄을 긋습니다. 그런 다음 밑줄 친 단어를 줄에 쓰십시오.

6. I _____ two plants in large pots. (class, placed)

7. The kids like to _____ at the playground. (placed, play)

8. The _____ caused the skiers to stop skiing. (sleet, flowers)

9. The garden in your backyard has beautiful _____. (flowers, play)

10. Ms. Brown's _____ is going on an exciting trip. (class, sleet)

Classwork

Name: _____ Date: ___/___/_____ Score: _____

Lesson 12.3

Reading Words with a Silent Letter "l"

✓ **Lesson Check Point**

Directions: Read the target words in the word box. Write the words that have a silent letter "l" in the first column. Write the words that do not have a silent letter "l" in the second column.

지도: 단어 상자에 있는 대상 단어를 읽으십시오. 첫 번째 열에 묵음문자 "l"이 있는 단어를 쓰십시오. 두 번째 열에 묵음 문자"l"이 없는 단어를 쓰십 시오.

Target Word Box				
could	build	soul	cool	likes
yolk	halves	salmon	slam	behalf
calf	loves	talking	helpful	pencil
leaf	slime	chalk	should	almond

Letter "l" is silent

Letter "l" has the /l/ sound

Classwork

 Name: _____ Date: ___/___/_____ Score: _____

The Reading Challenge

Lesson 12.4

Reading Multisyllable Words

✓ **Lesson Check Point**

 Directions: Read and divide each target word into syllables. Write each word and place a hyphen (-) between the syllables in the second column. Write the number of syllables in the third column. Use a dictionary or the Internet to check your answers.

지도: 각 대상 단어를 읽고 음절로 나눕니다. 각 단어를 쓰고 두 번째 열의 음절 사이에 하이픈(-)을 넣습니다. 세 번째 열에 음절 수를 쓰십시오. 사전이나 인터넷을 사용하여 답을 확인하십시오.

Target Words	Words Divided into Syllables	Number of Syllables
1. limber		
2. lumber		
3. leveling		
4. licensing		
5. liberty		
6. loyalty		
7. landlord		
8. liable		
9. lioness		
10. leotard		

Classwork

Name: _____ Date: ___/___/_____ Score: _____

The Reading Challenge

Lesson 12.4

Reading Multisyllable Words

✓ Lesson Check Point

Directions: Read each target word. Circle the word in the row that is divided correctly into syllables. Use a dictionary or the Internet to check your answers.

지도: 각 대상 단어를 읽으십시오. 음절로 올바르게 나누어진 행에 있는 단어에 동그라미를 치십시오. 사전이나 인터넷을 사용하여 답을 확인하십시오.

Model

| liberty | a. li-ber-ty | b. lib-er-ty (circled) | c. lib-ert-y |

| 1. luxury | a. lux-u-ry | b. lu-xu-ry | c. lux-ur-y |

| 2. lasagna | a. las-a-gna | b. la-sa-gna | c. la-sag-na |

| 3. lemonade | a. lem-o-nade | b. lem-on-ade | c. le-mo-nade |

| 4. limited | a. lim-it-ed | b. li-mit-ed | c. lim-i-ted |

| 5. levitate | a. le-vi-tate | b. lev-i-tate | c. lev-it-ate |

| 6. lavender | a. lav-en-der | b. lave-n-der | c. la-ven-der |

| 7. legislate | a. leg-i-slate | b. le-gis-late | c. leg-is-late |

| 8. levity | a. le-vit-y | b. le-vi-ty | c. lev-i-ty |

Classwork

Name: _____ Date: ___/___/_____ Score: _____

Lesson 12.5

Reading and Writing

Proper and Common Nouns and Adjectives

✓ **Lesson Check Point**

Directions: Read the words in the word box. Put an (X) on the line next to each word that is written incorrectly. Remember that all proper nouns and proper adjectives are capitalized. Use a dictionary or the Internet to check your answers.

지도: 단어 상자에 있는 단어를 읽으십시오. 잘못 쓰여진 각 단어 옆의 줄에 (X)를 표시하십시오. 모든 고유 명사와 고유 형용사는 대문자임을 기억하십시오. 사전이나 인터넷을 사용하여 답을 확인하십시오.

Word Box		
__ ladder	__ leopard	__ Ladybug
__ lincoln	__ lebanon	__ language
__ Laos	__ Lobster	__ London
__ latin	__ Labrador	__ Lawyer

Directions: Read each unedited sentence and underline the word that is written incorrectly. Write each sentence correctly on the line.

지도: 편집되지 않은 각 문장을 읽고 잘못 쓰여진 단어에 밑줄을긋습 니다. 각 문장을 줄에 올바르게 쓰십시오.

Model
I am studying <u>latin</u> at Lutheran Life Academy.
<u>I am studying Latin at Lutheran Life Academy.</u>

1. My family and I had a Lovely time in Liberia.
_____

2. Abraham lincoln was a loyal American president.
_____

3. Lucy said, "The labrador Current is a cold ocean current."
_____

4. Larry learned that the capital of Arkansas is little Rock.
_____

Classwork

Name: _____ Date: ___/___/_____ Score: _____

Lesson 13.1

Reading Words with the Letter M/m

Directions: Read each target word. Find the letter "m" and put a check (✓) in the column that identifies its position: beginning, within or end.
지도: 각 대상 단어를 읽으십시오. 문자"m"을 찾아 체크 표시(✓)위치 를 식별하는 열에서 시작, 내부 또는 끝.

Target Words	Beginning (First Letter)	Within	End (Last Letter)
1. money			
2. common			
3. multiple			
4. eardrum			
5. dilemma			

Directions: Read each sentence and underline the words that begin with the letter "m." Write all the underlined words in alphabetical order on the lines below.
지도: 각 문장을 읽고 문자"m"으로 시작하는 단어에 밑줄을 긋습니다. 밑줄 친 모든 단어를 아래 줄에 알파벳 순서로 쓰십시오.

6. Danny has more mittens than gloves.

7. Our aunt, Mary, is baking macaroons.

8. Dan and Madison are from Morocco.

9. Did Miller eat the mozzarella cheese?

10. His mom baked mini pies for our snack.

_____   _____   _____
_____   _____   _____
_____   _____

Classwork

Name: _____ Date: ___/___/_____ Score: _____

Lesson 13.2

Reading Words with a Silent Letter "m"

✓ Lesson Check Point

Directions: Read each target word. Find the letter "m" and put a check (✓) in the column that identifies its position: beginning, within or end.
지도: 각 대상 단어를 읽으십시오. 문자"m"을 찾아 체크 표시(✓)위치 를 식별하는 열에서 시작, 내부 또는 끝.

Target Words	Beginning (First Letter)	Within	End (Last Letter)
1. program			
2. immediate			
3. basement			
4. submarine			
5. moving			

Directions: Read each target word. Put a check (✓) in the "yes" column if the target word has a silent letter "m" Put a check (✓) in the "no" column if the target word does not have a silent letter "m."
지도: 각 대상 단어를 읽으십시오. 대상 단어에 묵음"m"이 있는 경우"yes" 열에 체크(✓) 표시 대상 단어에 묵음"m"이 없는 경우"no" 열에체크 (✓) 표시.

Target Words	Yes	No
6. mnemonic		
7. immense		
8. commit		
9. compromise		
10. momentum		

Learn To Read English With Directions In Korean

Classwork

Name: _____ Date: ___/___/_____ Score: _____

The Reading Challenge

Lesson 13.3

Reading Multisyllable Words

✓ **Lesson Check Point**

Directions: Read and divide each target word into syllables. Write each word and place a hyphen (-) between the syllables in the second column. Write the number of syllables in the third column. Use a dictionary or the Internet to check your answers.

지도: 각 대상 단어를 읽고 음절로 나눕니다. 각 단어를 쓰고 두 번째 열의 음절 사이에 하이픈(-)을 넣습니다. 세 번째 열에 음절 수를 쓰십시오. 사전이나 인터넷을 사용하여 답을 확인하십시오.

Target Words	Words Divided into Syllables	Number of Syllables
1. menu		
2. minuteman		
3. monsoon		
4. meaningful		
5. migrant		
6. monkey		
7. macaroni		
8. meadow		
9. morsel		
10. Mexico		

Learn To Read English With Directions In Korean

Classwork

 Name: _____ Date:___/___/_____ Score:_____

The Reading Challenge

Lesson 13.3

Reading Multisyllable Words

✓ **Lesson Check Point**

 Directions: Read each target word. Circle the word in the row that is divided correctly into syllables. Use a dictionary or the Internet to check your answers.

지도: 각 대상 단어를 읽으십시오. 음절로 올바르게 나누어진 행에 있는 단어에 동그라미를 치십시오. 사전이나 인터넷을 사용하여 답을 확인하십시오.

Model

| magazine | a. mag-a-zine (circled) | b. ma-ga-zine | c. mag-az-ine |

1. mineral	a. mi-ner-al	b. min-er-al	c. min-e-ral
2. magnify	a. mag-ni-fy	b. mag-nif-y	c. ma-gni-fy
3. malpractice	a. mal-prac-tice	b. mal-pract-ice	c. ma-lprac-tice
4. mechanics	a. mech-an-ics	b. me-cha-nics	c. me-chan-ics
5. monopoly	a. mon-op-o-ly	b. mo-no-po-ly	c. mo-nop-o-ly
6. metaphor	a. me-ta-phor	b. met-aph-or	c. met-a-phor
7. monument	a. mon-um-ent	b. mon-u-ment	c. mo-nu-ment
8. memorize	a. mem-o-rize	b. mem-or-ize	c. me-mor-ize

Learn To Read English With Directions In Korean

Classwork

Name: _____ Date: ___/___/_____ Score: _____

Lesson 13.4

Reading and Writing

Proper and Common Nouns and Adjectives

✓ **Lesson Check Point**

Directions: Read the words in the word box. Put an (X) on the line next to each word that is written incorrectly. Remember that all proper nouns and proper adjectives are capitalized. Use a dictionary or the Internet to check your answers.

지도: 단어 상자에 있는 단어를 읽으십시오. 잘못 쓰여진 각 단어 옆의 줄에 (X)를 표시하십시오. 모든 고유 명사와 고유 형용사는 대문자임을 기억하십시오. 사전이나 인터넷을 사용하여 답을 확인하십시오.

Word Box		
__ Manager	__ Monkey	__ menu
__ Manchester	__ market	__ mentor
__ manhattan	__ Margaret	__ Mailbox
__ malawi	__ malta	__ Mother

Directions: Read each unedited sentence and underline the word that is written incorrectly. Write each sentence correctly on the line.

지도: 편집되지 않은 각 문장을 읽고 잘못 쓰여진 단어에 밑줄을긋습 니다. 각 문장을 줄에 올바르게 쓰십시오.

Model
My son, Mark, is going to attend MIT in <u>massachusetts</u>.
<u>My son, Mark, is going to attend MIT in Massachusetts.</u>

1. My Mom is cooking macaroni and cheese for dinner.
   _____

2. Mary and max read a book about the planet Mars.
   _____

3. Beth and Mom will meet in Midtown manhattan.
   _____

4. I received my master's degree from mombasa College.
   _____

Classwork

Name: _____ Date: ___/___/_____ Score: _____

Lesson 14.1

Reading Words with the Letter N/n

✓ Lesson Check Point

Directions: Read each target word. Find the letter "n" and put a check (✓) in the column that identifies its position: beginning, within or end.
지도: 각 대상 단어를 읽으십시오. 문자"n"을 찾아 체크 표시(✓)위치를 식별하는 열에서 시작, 내부 또는 끝.

Target Words	Beginning (First Letter)	Within	End (Last Letter)
1. university			
2. glutton			
3. twin			
4. nurse			
5. newspaper			

Directions: Read each sentence and underline the words that begin with the letter "n." Write all the underlined words in alphabetical order on the lines below.
지도: 각 문장을 읽고"n"으로 시작하는 단어에 밑줄을 긋습니다. 밑줄 친 모든 단어를 아래 줄에 알파벳 순서로 쓰십시오.

6. Mommy never tasted chicken noodle soup.

7. Napoleon read ten books about the Nile River.

8. My neighbors enjoy celebrating New Year's Eve.

9. Nick wants to move from Kansas to North Dakota.

10. Everyone knows that many nice people live in Norway.

_____ _____ _____
_____ _____ _____
_____ _____ _____
           _____

Unit N
Lesson 14.1

Learn To Read English With Directions In Korean

Classwork

Name: _____ Date: ___/___/_____ Score: _____

Lesson 14.2

Reading Words with the "ng" Letter Combination

✓ Lesson Check Point

Directions: Read each target word. Circle the word in the column that has the same "ng" sound(s) as the target word.
지도: 각 대상 단어를 읽으십시오. 대상 단어와 같은 "ng" 소리가 나는 열의 단어에 동그라미를 치십시오.

anger	a. exchange
	b. language

congratulate	a. congruence
	b. engineer

congeniality	a. jingle
	b. danger

singer	a. boxing
	b. triangle

Directions: Read each target word. Put a check (✓) under the correct column heading.
지도: 각 대상 단어를 읽으십시오. 올바른 열 제목 아래에 체크(✓)를 하십시오.

Target Words	"ng" has the /n/ + /g/ sounds as in the word <u>ingrain</u>	"ng" has the /n/ + /j/ sounds as in the word <u>ginger</u>	"ng" has the /ng/ sound as in the word <u>bang</u>	"ng" has the /ng/ + /g/ sounds as in the word <u>congress</u>
1. anger				
2. congratulate				
3. congeniality				
4. singer				

Name: _____ Date: ___/___/_____ Score: _____

Lesson 14.3

Reading Words with a Silent Letter "n"

✓ **Lesson Check Point**

Directions: Read the target words in the word box. Write the words that have a silent letter "n" in the first column. Write the words that do not have a silent letter "n" in the second column.

지도: 단어 상자에 있는 대상 단어를 읽으십시오. 첫 번째 열에 묵음문자 "n"이 있는 단어를 쓰십시오. 두 번째 열에 묵음 문자"n"이 없는 단어를 쓰십시오.

Target Word Box				
animals	hymn	encounter	botanical	annex
comments	behind	hunter	nouns	penny
autumn	annual	cinnamon	monsieur	condemn
chimneys	tennis	handy	nominate	columns

Letter "n" is silent

_____
_____
_____
_____
_____
_____
_____
_____

Letter "n" has the /n/ sound

_____
_____
_____
_____
_____
_____
_____
_____

Classwork

Name: _____ Date: ___/___/_____ Score: _____

The Reading Challenge

Lesson 14.4

Reading Multisyllable Words

✓ Lesson Check Point

Directions: Read and divide each target word into syllables. Write each word and place a hyphen (-) between the syllables in the second column. Write the number of syllables in the third column. Use a dictionary or the Internet to check your answers.

지도: 각 대상 단어를 읽고 음절로 나눕니다. 각 단어를 쓰고 두 번째 열의 음절 사이에 하이픈(-)을 넣습니다. 세 번째 열에 음절 수를 쓰십시오. 사전이나 인터넷을 사용하여 답을 확인하십시오.

Target Words	Words Divided into Syllables	Number of Syllables
1. nighttime	_____	_____
2. nationwide	_____	_____
3. nuance	_____	_____
4. needlessly	_____	_____
5. normalize	_____	_____
6. ninety	_____	_____
7. nimbleness	_____	_____
8. noble	_____	_____
9. nectarine	_____	_____
10. notion	_____	_____

Classwork

Name: _____ Date: ___/___/_____ Score: _____

The Reading Challenge

Lesson 14.4

Reading Multisyllable Words

✓ **Lesson Check Point**

Directions: Read each target word. Circle the word in the row that is divided correctly into syllables. Use a dictionary or the Internet to check your answers.

지도: 각 대상 단어를 읽으십시오. 음절로 올바르게 나누어진 행에 있는 단어에 동그라미를 치십시오. 사전이나 인터넷을 사용하여 답을 확인하십시오.

Model

| napkin | a. na-pkin | b. napk-in | c. nap-kin (circled) |

1. neighbor	a. neighb-or	b. neigh-bor	c. nei-gh-bor
2. notify	a. no-ti-fy	b. no-tif-y	c. not-i-fy
3. natural	a. nat-u-ral	b. na-tu-ral	c. na-tur-al
4. nevermore	a. ne-ver-more	b. nev-erm-ore	c. nev-er-more
5. nobody	a. no-bod-y	b. no-body	c. no-bo-dy
6. newcomer	a. ne-wcom-er	b. new-co-mer	c. new-com-er
7. nutrition	a. nu-tri-tion	b. nut-ri-tion	c. nu-trit-ion
8. nausea	a. na-us-ea	b. n-au-sea	c. nau-se-a

Unit N
Lesson 14.4

Learn To Read English With Directions In Korean

Classwork

Name: _____ Date:___/___/_____ Score:_____

Lesson 14.5

Reading and Writing

Proper and Common Nouns and Adjectives

✓ Lesson Check Point

Directions: Read the words in the word box. Put an (X) on the line next to each word that is written incorrectly. Remember that all proper nouns and proper adjectives are capitalized. Use a dictionary or the Internet to check your answers.

지도: 단어 상자에 있는 단어를 읽으십시오. 잘못 쓰여진 각 단어 옆의 줄에 (X)를 표시하십시오. 모든 고유 명사와 고유 형용사는 대문자임을 기억하십시오. 사전이나 인터넷을 사용하여 답을 확인하십시오.

Word Box		
__ Nugget	__ north Africa	__ nigeria
__ Nepal	__ nile	__ napkin
__ Napoleon	__ news	__ Noodle
__ New Delhi	__ Number	__ Nicaragua

Directions: Read each unedited sentence and underline the word that is written incorrectly. Write each sentence correctly on the line.

지도: 편집되지 않은 각 문장을 읽고 잘못 쓰여진 단어에 밑줄을긋습 니다. 각 문장을 줄에 올바르게 쓰십시오.

Model
Nick and Nancy live in the <u>netherlands</u>.
<u>Nick and Nancy live in the Netherlands.</u>

1. I received a Needle from Nurse Nutley.
_____

2. The Newscasters collaborate about national news stories.
_____

3. Mrs. Newton taught a lesson about the Nervous system.
_____

4. The nile River derives its name from the Greek word, Nelios.
_____

Classwork

 Name: _____ Date:___/___/_____ Score:_____

Lesson 15.1

Reading Words with the Letter O/o

✓ **Lesson Check Point**

 Directions: Read each target word. Find the letter "o" and put a check (✓) in the column that identifies its position: beginning, within or end.
지도: 각 대상 단어를 읽으십시오. 문자"o"를 찾아 체크 표시(✓)위치 를 식별하는 열에서 시작, 내부 또는 끝.

Target Words	Beginning (First Letter)	Within	End (Last Letter)
1. combine			
2. older			
3. outreach			
4. cargo			
5. embargo			

 Directions: Read each target word. Read the words in the row and circle the word that has a different vowel "o" sound.
지도: 각 대상 단어를 읽으십시오. 행에 있는 단어를 읽고 모음"o" 소리가 다른 단어에 동그라미를 치십시오.

Target Words				
6. almost	go	code	song	dole
7. drop	host	prom	stop	clog
8. solo	lock	joke	tone	coat
9. gold	soap	toss	aloe	so
10. shopping	rock	clock	frost	poll

Classwork

 Name: _____ Date: ___/___/_____ Score: _____

Lesson 15.2

Reading Words with the Short Vowel "o" Sound

✓ **Lesson Check Point**

 Directions: Read the words in the four boxes. Circle two words with the short vowel /ŏ/ or /ô/ sound. The anchor word for the short vowel /ŏ/ and /ô/ sounds is <u>frog</u>.

지도: 네 개의 상자에 있는 단어를 읽으십시오. 짧은 모음/ŏ/ 또는 /ô/ 소리로 두 단어에 동그라미를 치십시오. 단모음/ŏ/ 및 /ô/ 소리의 앵커 단어는 frog입니다.

stop	poll
old	plot

colt	flog
host	drop

post	both
slot	chop

fond	prom
told	go

blot	mole
knot	don't

rock	clop
hold	roll

 Directions: Read the words in the four boxes. Circle two words that rhyme. Rhyming words have the same ending sound, such as <u>hot</u> and <u>not</u>.

지도: 네 개의 상자에 있는 단어를 읽으십시오. 운이 맞는 두 단어에동그라미를 치십시오. 운율이 있는 단어는 hot 및 not과 같이 끝 소리가같습니다.

shot	spot
no	chosen

shop	roll
solo	crop

hydro	phone
bond	pond

ago	lock
gold	dock

boss	toss
ocean	hotel

long	joke
song	sold

Classwork

L Name: _____ Date: ___/___/_____ Score: _____

Lesson 15.2

Reading & Writing Words with the Short Vowel "o" Sound

✓ **Lesson Check Point**

Directions: Read each sentence and underline three words with the short vowel /ŏ/ or /ô/ sound. Then, write the underlined words on the lines below. The anchor word for the short vowel /ŏ/ and /ô/ sounds is frog.
지도: 각 문장을 읽고 짧은 모음 /ŏ/ 또는 /ô/ 소리로 세 단어에 밑줄을 긋습니다. 그런 다음 밑줄 친 단어를 아래 줄에 쓰십시오. 단모음 /ŏ/ 및 /ô/ 소리의 앵커 단어는 frog입니다.

Model
Everyone saw the frog hop close to the rock.

    frog   hop   rock
 _____   _____   _____

1. The ropes on the mop are very soft.

 _____   _____   _____

2. The policeman stopped the robber in the office.

 _____   _____   _____

3. Tom walked around the block in his socks.

 _____   _____   _____

4. Joan's job assignment is to mop the spotty tiles.

 _____   _____   _____

5. Moss develops from spores and grows in damp logs.

 _____   _____   _____

Classwork

 Name: _____   Date: ___/___/_____   Score: _____

Lesson 15.3

Reading Words with the Long Vowel "o" Sound

✓ **Lesson Check Point**

 Directions: Read the words in the four boxes. Circle two words with the long vowel /ō/ sound. The anchor word for the long vowel /ō/ sound is <u>open</u>.

지도: 네 개의 상자에 있는 단어를 읽으십시오. 장모음 /ō/ 소리로 두 단어에 동그라미를 치십시오. 장모음 /ō/ 소리의 기준어는 open입니다.

cross	yo-yo		boss	joke		rock	took
roll	lock		lost	so		pony	sold

both	pond		drop	shop		prompt	soap
boat	sock		poke	toad		floss	poll

 Directions: Read the words in the four boxes. Circle two words that rhyme. Rhyming words have the same ending sound, such as <u>hope</u> and <u>soap</u>.

지도: 네 개의 상자에 있는 단어를 읽으십시오. 운이 맞는 두 단어에 동그라미를 치십시오. 운율이 있는 단어는 hope 및 soap과 같이 끝 소리가 같습니다.

go	folk		boat	coat		toss	home
yolk	clock		rose	song		post	most

frost	pole		so	cold		poet	roast
told	role		strong	sold		toast	spot

Classwork

Name: _____ Date: ___/___/_____ Score: _____

Lesson 15.3

Reading & Writing Words with the Long Vowel "o" Sound

✓ **Lesson Check Point**

Directions: Read each sentence and underline three words with the long vowel /ō/ sound. Then, write the underlined words on the lines below. The anchor word for the long vowel /ō/ sound is <u>open</u>.

지도: 각 문장을 읽고 장모음 /ō/소리로 세 단어에 밑줄을 긋습니다. 그런 다음 밑줄 친 단어를 아래 줄에 쓰십시오. 장모음 /ō/ 소리의 앵커 단어는 open입니다.

Model

We will <u>go</u> to the <u>rodeo</u> and <u>limbo</u> competitions for fun.

    go   rodeo   limbo
_____   _____   _____

1. Owen said hello to the ponies in the zoo.

     _____   _____   _____

2. The hotel's frozen donuts do not taste good.

     _____   _____   _____

3. The coeducational golf team is going to enroll in the competition.

     _____   _____   _____

4. Tom, the yodeler, will change his tempo in a moment.

     _____   _____   _____

5. My son said, "Both hippos and dodo birds are interesting animals."

     _____   _____   _____

Classwork

Name: _____   Date: ___/___/_____   Score: _____

Review Lessons 15.2 & 15.3

Reading Short Vowel and Long Vowel Words

Directions: Read the target words in the word box. In the first column, write the words that have the short vowel /ŏ/ or /ô/ sound, as in the word <u>frog</u>. In the second column, write the words that have the long vowel /ō/ sound, as in the word <u>open</u>.

지도: 단어 상자에 있는 대상 단어를 읽으십시오. 첫 번째 열에는 frog라는 단어에서와 같이 단모음 /ŏ/ 또는 /ô/ 소리가 나는 단어를 씁니다. 두번째 열에는 open이라는 단어에서와 같이 장모음 /ō/ 소리가 나는 단어를 씁니다.

Target Word Box				
scaffold	cross	billfold	prompt	shopping
disposal	postal	bonding	going	rocking
stock	revolt	lost	enroll	grocery
plot	clock	mostly	strong	hippos

Letter "o" has the /ŏ/ or /ô/ sound as in the word <u>frog</u>

Letter "o" has the /ō/ sound as in the word <u>open</u>

Classwork

Name: _____ Date:___/___/_____ Score: _____

Lesson 15.4

Reading Words with Letter "o" Vowel Pairs

✓ Lesson Check Point

Directions: Read each target word. Circle the word in the column that has the same vowel "oa," "oe," "oo" or "ou" sound(s) as the target word.
지도: 각 대상 단어를 읽으십시오. 대상 단어와 동일한 모음"oa," "oe," "oo" 또는"ou" 소리가 있는 열의 단어에 동그라미를 치십시오.

| carousel | a. detour |
| | b. camouflage |

| gloat | a. mangoes |
| | b. aboard |

| banjoes | a. maroon |
| | b. toast |

| coast | a. oboe |
| | b. moody |

Directions: Read each target word. Put a check (✓) under the correct column heading.
지도: 각 대상 단어를 읽으십시오. 올바른 열 제목 아래에 체크(✓)를하십시오.

Target Words	Words have the long "o" sound as in the word <u>coat</u>	Words do not have the long "o" sound
1. carousel		
2. gloat		
3. banjoes		
4. coast		

Classwork

 Name: _____ Date: ___/___/_____ Score: _____

Lesson 15.5

Reading Words with the Final Letter "o"

✓ Lesson Check Point

 Directions: Read each target word. Find the letter "o" and put a check (✓) in the column that identifies its position within the syllable.

지도: 각 대상 단어를 읽으십시오. 문자"o"를 찾아 체크 표시(✓)음절 내에서 위치를 식별하는 열에서.

Target Words	"o" is at the end of a one syllable word	"o" is at the end of the first syllable	"o" is at the end of a multi-syllable word
1. motor			
2. piano			
3. chosen			
4. go			
5. ago			

 Directions: Read each target word. Put a check (✓) under the correct column heading.

지도: 각 대상 단어를 읽으십시오. 올바른 열 제목 아래에 체크(✓)를 하십시오.

Target Words	"o" has the /ŏ/ sound as in the word frog	"o" has the /ō/ sound as in the word go	"o" has the /ə/ sound as in the word carrot	"o" is silent as in the word people
6. roaches				
7. turbo				
8. contain				
9. mopping				
10. vaporize				

Classwork

 Name: _____ Date: ___/___/_____ Score: _____

Lesson 15.6

Reading Letter "o" Words with the Schwa Vowel Sound

✓ Lesson Check Point

 Directions: Read each target word. Circle the word in the column that has the same "o" sound as the target word.
지도: 각 대상 단어를 읽으십시오. 대상 단어와 동일한"o" 소리가 나는 열의 단어에 동그라미를 치십시오.

other	a. opening
	b. sons

collector	a. socks
	b. inspector

factor	a. occur
	b. toads

parrot	a. lemons
	b. boxer

 Directions: Read each sentence and underline the letter "o" word that has the schwa vowel /ə/ sound or short vowel /ŭ/ sound. The anchor word for the letter "o" schwa vowel /ə/ sound is carrot and the letter "o" short vowel /ŭ/ sound is dove.
지도: 각 문장을 읽고 슈와 모음/ə/ 소리 또는 단모음/ŭ/ 소리가 있는 문자"o" 단어에 밑줄을 긋습니다. 문자"o" 슈와 모음/ə/ 소리의 앵커 단어는 carrot이고 문자"o" 단모음/ŭ/ 소리는 dove입니다.

1. The orange sponge is in the old pot.

2. The boys won the bowling tournament.

3. Mommy enjoys eating onion noodle soup.

4. This year, our school will start at eight o'clock.

5. On Monday, I closed the window before the storm.

6. In October, my doctor gave me an intensive examination.

Classwork

 Name: _____ Date: ___/___/_____ Score: _____

Lesson 15.7

Reading Words with Vowel "o" Sounds: /ŏ/, /ō/ & /o͞o/

✓ Lesson Check Point

 Directions: Read each target word. Put a check (✓) under the correct column heading.
지도: 각 대상 단어를 읽으십시오. 올바른 열 제목 아래에 체크(✓)를 하십시오.

Target Words	"o" has the /ŏ/ sound as in the word <u>frog</u>	"o" has the /ō/ sound as in the word <u>go</u>	"o" has the /o͞o/ sound as in the word <u>to</u>
1. mopping			
2. who			
3. moving			
4. October			
5. soul			

 Directions: Read each sentence and underline the word that has a letter "o" that has the vowel /o͞o/ sound, as in the word <u>two</u>.
지도: 각 문장을 읽고 two라는 단어에서처럼 모음/o͞o/소리가 있는 문자 "o"가 있는 단어에 밑줄을 긋습니다.

6. Do we have a box of colorful rocks?

7. On Monday, Ron and Tom will move out.

8. We may lose our money in the stock market.

9. Who read the book about the fox in the woods?

10. The outspoken lawyer proved that his client is not guilty.

Classwork

 Name: _____ Date: ___/___/_____ Score: _____

Lesson 15.8

Reading Words with the "or" Letter Combination

✓ **Lesson Check Point**

 Directions: Read each target word. Circle the word in the column that has the same "o" + "r" sounds as the target word.
지도: 각 대상 단어를 읽으십시오. 가 있는 열에 있는 단어에 동그라미를 치십시오. 동일한"o" + "r"이 대상 단어로 들립니다.

| forensic | a. forth |
| | b. correct |

| boring | a. core |
| | b. horizon |

| portion | a. morning |
| | b. corral |

| original | a. memory |
| | b. fork |

 Directions: Read each target word. Put a check (✓) under the correct column heading.
지도: 각 대상 단어를 읽으십시오. 올바른 열 제목 아래에 체크(✓)를 하십시오.

Target Words	"or" has the /ô/ + /r/ sounds as in the word door	"or" has the /ə/ + /r/ sounds as in the word doctor
1. forensic		
2. boring		
3. portion		
4. original		

Classwork

Name: _____ Date:___/___/_____ Score: _____

Lesson 15.8

Reading Words with the "or" Letter Combination

Dictionary Skills/ Vocabulary

✓ **Lesson Check Point**

Directions: Read each target word and its definition. Write the target word on the line in front of its meaning. Use a dictionary or the Internet to check your answers.

지도: 각 대상 단어와 그 정의를 읽으십시오. 의미 앞 줄에대상단어를 쓰십시오. 사전이나 인터넷을 사용하여 답을 확인하십시오.

Target Word Box				
worn	orbits	important	story	forgot

1. _____ inability to remember

2. _____ something or someone of great value

3. _____ fabric that has become thinner or damaged

4. _____ the act of moving around another object

5. _____ a spoken or written description of characters and events

Directions: Read each sentence and write the target word that correctly completes the sentence.

지도: 각 문장을 읽고 문장을 올바르게 완성하는 목표 단어를 쓰십시오.

6. My old blue jeans are _____ out.

7. The science teacher said, "The Earth _____ the Sun."

8. It is _____ to attend school every day.

9. Molly told the teacher she _____ to do her homework.

10. The _____ "The Fox and the Wise Owl" has a great plot.

Unit O
Lesson 15.8

Classwork

 Name: _____ Date: ___/___/_____ Score: _____

Lesson 15.9

Reading Words with a Silent Letter "o"

✓ Lesson Check Point

 Directions: Read the target words in the word box. Write the words that have a silent letter "o" in the first column. Write the words that do not have a silent letter "o" in the second column.

지도: 단어 상자에 있는 대상 단어를 읽으십시오. 첫 번째 열에 묵음 문자 "o"가 있는 단어를 쓰십시오. 두 번째 열에 묵음 문자 "o"가 없는 단어를 쓰십시오.

Target Word Box

combat	leopards	horse	Phoenician	subpoena
body	jeopardy	subpoenas	know	hold
Leonard	assort	open	leopard	collect
expose	phoenix	people	octopus	jeopardize

Letter "o" is silent	Letter "o" has a letter "o" sound
_____	_____
_____	_____
_____	_____
_____	_____
_____	_____
_____	_____
_____	_____
_____	_____
_____	_____
_____	_____

Classwork

Name: _____ Date: ___/___/_____ Score: _____

Unit Review - O/o

Reading Words with Vowel "o" Sounds: /ŏ/, /ō/, /ə/ & Silent

✓ **Lesson Check Point**

Directions: Read each target word. Circle the word in the column that has the same "o" sound as the target word.

지도: 각 대상 단어를 읽으십시오. 대상 단어와 동일한 "o" 소리가 나는 열의 단어에 동그라미를 치십시오.

forget	a. corral
	b. avoid

toaster	a. spotted
	b. goals

jeopardy	a. ponder
	b. people

robbing	a. hopping
	b. hoping

Directions: Read each target word. Put a check (✓) under the correct column heading.

지도: 각 대상 단어를 읽으십시오. 올바른 열 제목 아래에 체크(✓)를 하십시오.

Target Words	"o" has the /ŏ/ sound as in the word <u>frog</u>	"o" has the /ō/ sound as in the word <u>go</u>	"o" has the /ə/ sound as in the word <u>carrot</u>	"o" is silent as in the word <u>people</u>
1. forget				
2. toaster				
3. jeopardy				
4. robbing				

Classwork

Name: _____ Date: ___/___/_____ Score: _____

The Reading Challenge

Lesson 15.10

Reading Multisyllable Words

✓ **Lesson Check Point**

Directions: Read and divide each target word into syllables. Write each word and place a hyphen (-) between the syllables in the second column. Write the number of syllables in the third column. Use a dictionary or the Internet to check your answers.

지도: 각 대상 단어를 읽고 음절로 나눕니다. 각 단어를 쓰고 두 번째 열의 음절 사이에 하이픈(-)을 넣습니다. 세 번째 열에 음절 수를 쓰십시오. 사전이나 인터넷을 사용하여 답을 확인하십시오.

Target Words	Words Divided into Syllables	Number of Syllables
1. solar	_____	_____
2. motel	_____	_____
3. token	_____	_____
4. composer	_____	_____
5. Romania	_____	_____
6. lotion	_____	_____
7. orderly	_____	_____
8. rodent	_____	_____
9. provoking	_____	_____
10. Bohemian	_____	_____

Unit O
Lesson 15.10

Classwork

 Name: _____ Date: ___/___/_____ Score: _____

The Reading Challenge

Lesson 15.10

Reading Multisyllable Words

✓ **Lesson Check Point**

 Directions: Read each target word. Circle the word in the row that is divided correctly into syllables. Use a dictionary or the Internet to check your answers.

지도: 각 대상 단어를 읽으십시오. 음절로 올바르게 나누어진 행에 있는 단어에 동그라미를 치십시오. 사전이나 인터넷을 사용하여 답을 확인하십시오.

Model

| proposal | a. prop-o-sal | b. pro-po-sal | c. pro-pos-al |

1. portable	a. por-table	b. por-ta-ble	c. port-a-ble
2. asteroid	a. as-te-roid	b. ast-e-roid	c. as-ter-oid
3. corporate	a. cor-po-rate	b. corpo-ra-te	c. corp-o-rate
4. potato	a. pot-at-o	b. po-ta-to	c. pot-a-to
5. repertoire	a. rep-er-toire	b. re-pert-oire	c. re-per-toire
6. investor	a. in-ves-tor	b. in-vest-or	c. i-nvest-or
7. cockatoo	a. cock-at-oo	b. co-cka-too	c. cock-a-too
8. October	a. Oct-o-ber	b. Oc-to-ber	c. Oct-ob-er

Unit O
Lesson 15.10

Learn To Read English With Directions In Korean

Classwork

 Name: _____   Date: ___/___/_____   Score: _____

Lesson 15.11

Reading and Writing

Proper and Common Nouns and Adjectives

✓ Lesson Check Point

 Directions: Read the words in the word box. Put an (X) on the line next to each word that is written incorrectly. Remember that all proper nouns and proper adjectives are capitalized. Use a dictionary or the Internet to check your answers.

지도: 단어 상자에 있는 단어를 읽으십시오. 잘못 쓰여진 각 단어 옆의 줄에 (X)를 표시하십시오. 모든 고유 명사와 고유 형용사는 대문자임을 기억하십시오. 사전이나 인터넷을 사용하여 답을 확인하십시오.

Word Box		
__ Oxbridge	__ octopus	__ orlando
__ ontario	__ Onega Bay	__ organizer
__ Old English	__ october	__ Atlantic ocean
__ Occasion	__ objective	__ Original

 Directions: Read each unedited sentence and underline the word that is written incorrectly. Write each sentence correctly on the line.

지도: 편집되지 않은 각 문장을 읽고 잘못 쓰여진 단어에 밑줄을 긋습 니다. 각 문장을 줄에 올바르게 쓰십시오.

Model
At <u>One</u> o'clock, the Owens family went to Onega Bay.
<u>At one o'clock, the Owens family went to Onega Bay.</u>

1. Mr. o'Connor is planning an outstanding trip to the Orient.
   _____

2. Marie, Octavia and I are Overjoyed about our trip to Oktoberfest.
   _____

3. Mr. O'Keeffe gave the class a fact sheet about the oregon Trail.
   _____

4. In October, the official olympic Games tryouts will begin.
   _____

Classwork

Name: _____ Date: ___/___/_____ Score: _____

Lesson 16.1

Reading Words with the Letter P/p

✓ **Lesson Check Point**

Directions: Read each target word. Find the letter "p" and put a check (✓) in the column that identifies its position: beginning, within or end.
지도: 각 대상 단어를 읽으십시오. 문자"p"를 찾아 체크 표시(✓)위치를 식별하는 열에서 시작, 내부 또는 끝.

Target Words	Beginning (First Letter)	Within	End (Last Letter)
1. price			
2. pest			
3. plans			
4. asleep			
5. concept			

Directions: Read each sentence and underline the words that begin with the letter "p." Write all the underlined words in alphabetical order on the lines below.
지도: 각 문장을 읽고"p"로 시작하는 단어에 밑줄을 긋습니다. 아래 줄에 밑줄 친 단어를 알파벳 순서로 모두 쓰십시오.

6. The pitcher threw powerful fastballs.

7. Lydia is sending a package to Panama.

8. Gabby's pageant gown is white and purple.

9. The police officer is patrolling our college campus.

10. People in the courtroom said the plaintiff has a strong case.

_____ _____ _____
_____ _____ _____
_____ _____ _____
              _____

Classwork

 Name: _____ Date:___/___/_____ Score: _____

Lesson 16.2

Reading Words with the "ph" Letter Combination

✓ Lesson Check Point

 Directions: Read each target word. Circle the word in the column that has the same "ph" sound(s) as the target word.
지도: 각 대상 단어를 읽으십시오. 대상 단어와 동일한 "ph" 소리를 가진 열의 단어에 동그라미를 치십시오.

orphan	a. pamphlet
	b. haphazard

upheaval	a. haphazard
	b. photograph

alphabet	a. uphold
	b. biography

amphibian	a. esophagus
	b. shepherd

 Directions: Read each target word. Put a check (✓) under the correct column heading.
지도: 각 대상 단어를 읽으십시오. 올바른 열 제목 아래에 체크(✓)를 하십시오.

Target Words	"ph" has the /f/ sound as in the word phone	"ph" has the /p/ + /h/ sounds as in the word uphill
1. orphan		
2. upheaval		
3. alphabet		
4. amphibian		

Classwork

Name: _____ Date: ___/___/_____ Score: _____

Lesson 16.3

Reading Words with the "pr" Letter Combination

Dictionary Skills/ Vocabulary

✓ **Lesson Check Point**

Directions: Read each target word and its definition. Write the letter of the definition on the line of each target word. Use a dictionary or the Internet to check your answers.

지도: 각 대상 단어와 그 정의를 읽으십시오. 각 대상 단어의 행에 정의의 문자를 씁니다. 사전이나 인터넷을 사용하여 답을 확인하십시오.

Target Words	Definitions
1. __ praised	a. an educator/instructor at a university or college
2. __ predators	b. to have expressed words of admiration or approval
3. __ president	c. animals that kill and eat other animals for survival
4. __ professor	d. an elected or appointed leader of a country
5. __ program	e. an organized business that provides activities

Directions: Read each sentence and write the target word that correctly completes the sentence.

지도: 각 문장을 읽고 문장을 올바르게 완성하는 목표 단어를 쓰십시오.

6. The great white whales and lions are alpha _____.

7. Dr. Pringle is a _____ at Pratt University.

8. The _____ was elected for a four-year term.

9. The teacher _____ her hardworking students.

10. My sister and I attend an after-school _____.

Classwork

 Name: _____ Date: ___/___/_____ Score: _____

Lesson 16.4

Reading Words with the "pl" Letter Combination

Dictionary Skills/ Vocabulary

✓ **Lesson Check Point**

 Directions: Read each target word and its definition. Write the target word on the line in front of its meaning. Use a dictionary or the Internet to check your answers.
지도: 각 대상 단어와 그 정의를 읽으십시오. 의미 앞 줄에 대상단어를 쓰십시오. 사전이나 인터넷을 사용하여 답을 확인하십시오.

Target Word Box				
plaintiff	pleasure	plowing	plum	plush

1. _____ the act of breaking up the land for farming
2. _____ a luxury item that is nice and expensive
3. _____ a person or group of people who file a lawsuit
4. _____ an experience that is enjoyable or satisfying
5. _____ purple, smooth-skinned fruit that is very sweet

 Directions: Read each sentence. Underline the word in the parentheses that correctly completes each sentence. Then, write the underlined word on the line.
지도: 각 문장을 읽으십시오. 각 문장을 올바르게 완성하는 괄호 안에 있는 단어에 밑줄을 긋습니다. 그런 다음 밑줄 친 단어를 줄에 쓰십시오.

6. The _____ filed a case at the courthouse. (pleasure, plaintiff)

7. The farmer is _____ the center of his field. (plowing, plush)

8. I spent a lot of money for my _____ condo. (plum, plush)

9. I bought peaches and _____ from the fruit store. (plums, pleasure)

10. I agree that it is a _____ to work with children. (pleasure, plaintiff)

Classwork

 Name: _____ Date: ___/___/_____ Score: _____

Lesson 16.4

Reading Words with the "ple" Letter Combination

✓ **Lesson Check Point**

 Directions: Read each target word. Find the "ple" letter combination and put a check (✓) in the column that identifies its position: beginning, within or end.

지도: 각 대상 단어를 읽으십시오. "ple"문자 조합을 찾고 위치를 식별하는 열에 체크(✓)를 하십시오: 시작, 내 또는 끝.

Target Words	Beginning (First 3 Letters)	Within	End (Last 3 Letters)
1. participle			
2. multiple			
3. displeased			
4. simple			
5. plentiful			

 Directions: Read each target word. Put a check (✓) in the "yes" column if the "ple" letter combination has the /p/ + /ə/ + /l/ sounds. Put a check (✓) in the "no" column if the "ple" letter combination does not have the /p/ + /ə/ + /l/ sounds.

지도: 각 대상 단어를 읽으십시오. "ple" 문자 조합에 /p/ + /ə/ + /l/ 소리가 있는 경우 "yes" 열에 체크(✓)를 하십시오. "ple" 문자 조합에 /p/ + /ə/ + /l/ 소리가 없으면 "no" 열에 체크(✓)를 하십시오.

Target Words	Yes	No
6. participle		
7. multiple		
8. displeased		
9. simple		
10. plentiful		

Classwork

Name: _____ Date: ___/___/_____ Score: _____

Lesson 16.5

Reading Words with a Silent Letter "p"

✓ **Lesson Check Point**

Directions: Read the target words in the word box. Write the words that have a silent letter "p" in the first column. Write the words that do not have a silent letter "p" in the second column.

지도: 단어 상자에 있는 대상 단어를 읽으십시오. 첫 번째 열에 묵음 문자"p"가 있는 단어를 쓰십시오. 두 번째 열에 묵음 문자"p"가 없는 단어를 쓰십시오.

Target Word Box				
apple	receipt	sleep	compose	slippery
suppose	point	puppy	hopping	raspberry
tips	sample	corps	predict	play
plot	psychic	cupboard	stamps	surprise

Letter "p" is silent	Letter "p" has the /p/ sound

Unit P
Lesson 16.5

Learn To Read English With Directions In Korean   165   Copyrighted Material

Classwork

Name: _____ Date: ___/___/_____ Score: _____

The Reading Challenge

Lesson 16.6

Reading Multisyllable Words

✓ **Lesson Check Point**

Directions: Read and divide each target word into syllables. Write each word and place a hyphen (-) between the syllables in the second column. Write the number of syllables in the third column. Use a dictionary or the Internet to check your answers.

지도: 각 대상 단어를 읽고 음절로 나눕니다. 각 단어를 쓰고 두 번째 열의 음절 사이에 하이픈(-)을 넣습니다. 세 번째 열에 음절 수를 쓰십시오. 사전이나 인터넷을 사용하여 답을 확인하십시오.

Target Words	Words Divided into Syllables	Number of Syllables
1. people	_____	_____
2. plural	_____	_____
3. powder	_____	_____
4. privatized	_____	_____
5. platform	_____	_____
6. politeness	_____	_____
7. plastic	_____	_____
8. persistence	_____	_____
9. parsley	_____	_____
10. peanut	_____	_____

Classwork

Name: _____ Date:___/___/_____ Score: _____

The Reading Challenge

Lesson 16.6

Reading Multisyllable Words

✓ **Lesson Check Point**

Directions: Read each target word. Circle the word in the row that is divided correctly into syllables. Use a dictionary or the Internet to check your answers.

지도: 각 대상 단어를 읽으십시오. 음절로 올바르게 나누어진 행에 있는 단어에 동그라미를 치십시오. 사전이나 인터넷을 사용하여 답을 확인하십시오.

Model

paragraph	(a. par-a-graph)	b. pa-ra-graph	c. par-ag-raph

1. period	a. per-i-od	b. pe-ri-od	c. pe-r-iod

2. pyramid	a. pyr-a-mid	b. py-ra-mid	c. pyr-am-id

3. personal	a. per-son-al	b. pers-on-al	c. per-so-nal

4. parakeet	a. pa-ra-keet	b. par-a-keet	c. pa-rak-eet

5. punctual	a. pun-ctu-al	b. punc-t-ual	c. punc-tu-al

6. Panama	a. Pan-am-a	b. Pan-a-ma	c. Pa-na-ma

7. perigee	a. pe-rig-ee	b. per-i-gee	c. per-ig-ee

8. peculiar	a. pec-u-liar	b. pe-cul-iar	c. pe-cu-liar

Learn To Read English With Directions In Korean

Classwork

Name: _____ Date: ___/___/_____ Score: _____

Lesson 16.7

Reading and Writing

Proper and Common Nouns and Adjectives

✓ Lesson Check Point

Directions: Read the words in the word box. Put an (X) on the line next to each word that is written incorrectly. Remember that all proper nouns and proper adjectives are capitalized. Use a dictionary or the Internet to check your answers.

지도: 단어 상자에 있는 단어를 읽으십시오. 잘못 쓰여진 각 단어 옆의 줄에 (X)를 표시하십시오. 모든 고유 명사와 고유 형용사는 대문자임을 기억하십시오. 사전이나 인터넷을 사용하여 답을 확인하십시오.

Word Box		
___ Poland	___ philippine	___ place
___ passport	___ Peruvian	___ panama
___ Penguin	___ people	___ Passenger
___ pharmacist	___ pennsylvania	___ Poodle

Directions: Read each unedited sentence and underline the word that is written incorrectly. Write each sentence correctly on the line.

지도: 편집되지 않은 각 문장을 읽고 잘못 쓰여진 단어에 밑줄을 긋습 니다. 각 문장을 줄에 올바르게 쓰십시오.

Model
The poem, "<u>puddles</u>," was written by Patrick Parker.
The poem, "Puddles," was written by Patrick Parker.

1. The panama Canal is a powerful structure.
_____

2. The City of philadelphia is located in Pennsylvania.
_____

3. The peruvian coast bordering the Pacific Ocean is a desert strip.
_____

4. perry the Platypus is the star of the hit show "Phineas and Ferb."
_____

Classwork

Name: _____ Date: ___/___/_____ Score: _____

Lesson 17.1

Reading Words with the Letter Q/q

✓ Lesson Check Point

Directions: Read each target word. Find the letter "q" and put a check (✓) in the column that identifies its position: beginning, within or end.
지도: 각 대상 단어를 읽으십시오. 문자"q"를 찾아 체크 표시(✓)위치를 식별하는 열에서 시작, 내부 또는 끝.

Target Words	Beginning (First Letter)	Within	End (Last Letter)
1. question			
2. squabbled			
3. quotation			
4. Iraq			
5. consequent			

Directions: Read each sentence and underline the words that begin with the letter "q." Write all the underlined words in alphabetical order on the lines below.
지도: 각 문장을 읽고"q"로 시작하는 단어에 밑줄을 긋습니다. 아래 줄에 밑줄 친 단어를 알파벳 순서로 모두 쓰십시오.

6. Quincy and his family are from Quebec, Canada.

7. The new quilts are made with high quality fabrics.

8. My sister, Queenisha, sleeps on a queen-sized bed.

9. All the children in the Quinn family have four quarters.

10. All the candidates are highly qualified for the job at Quick Inc.

_____ _____ _____
_____ _____ _____
_____ _____ _____
_____

Learn To Read English With Directions In Korean

Classwork

 Name: _____ Date:___/___/_____ Score:_____

Lesson 17.2

Reading Words with the Letter "q" and "qu" Letter Combination

✓ Lesson Check Point

 Directions: Read each target word. Circle the word in the column that has the same "q" or "qu" sound(s) as the target word.
지도: 각 대상 단어를 읽으십시오. 대상 단어와 동일한 "q" 또는 "qu" 소리가 있는 열의 단어에 동그라미를 치십시오.

equip	a. antique
	b. quickly

conquer	a. liquid
	b. Qatar

equal	a. queen
	b. quetzal

conquest	a. opaque
	b. quench

 Directions: Read each target word. Put a check (✓) under the correct column heading.
지도: 각 대상 단어를 읽으십시오. 올바른 열 제목 아래에 체크(✓)를 하십시오.

Target Words	"qu" has the /k/ sound as in the word <u>plaque</u>	"qu" has the /k/ + /w/ sounds as in the word <u>queen</u>
1. equip		
2. conquer		
3. equal		
4. conquest		

Classwork

 Name: _____ Date: ___/ ___/ _____ Score: _____

Lesson 17.2

Reading Words with the "qu" Letter Combination

✓ Lesson Check Point

 Directions: Read each target word. Circle the word in the column that has the same "qu" sound(s) as the target word.
지도: 각 대상 단어를 읽으십시오. 대상 단어와 동일한 "qu" 소리가 있는 열의 단어에 동그라미를 치십시오.

| inquire | a. queen |
| | b. boutique |

| lacquer | a. quilt |
| | b. racquet |

| technique | a. antique |
| | b. conquest |

| questions | a. quarterly |
| | b. techniques |

 Directions: Read each target word. Put a check (✓) under the correct column heading.
지도: 각 대상 단어를 읽으십시오. 올바른 열 제목 아래에 체크(✓)를 하십시오.

Target Words	"qu" has the /k/ + /w/ sounds as in the word <u>queen</u>	"qu" has the /k/ sound as in the word <u>plaque</u>	"qu" is silent as in the word <u>racquet</u>
1. inquire			
2. lacquer			
3. technique			
4. questions			

Classwork

 Name: _____ Date:___/___/_____ Score:_____

The Reading Challenge

Lesson 17.3

Reading Multisyllable Words

✓ **Lesson Check Point**

 Directions: Read and divide each target word into syllables. Write each word and place a hyphen (-) between the syllables in the second column. Write the number of syllables in the third column. Use a dictionary or the Internet to check your answers.

지도: 각 대상 단어를 읽고 음절로 나눕니다. 각 단어를 쓰고 두 번째 열의 음절 사이에 하이픈(-)을 넣습니다. 세 번째 열에 음절 수를 쓰십시오. 사전이나 인터넷을 사용하여 답을 확인하십시오.

Target Words	Words Divided into Syllables	Number of Syllables
1. quarantine	_____	_____
2. quintet	_____	_____
3. quiver	_____	_____
4. quota	_____	_____
5. query	_____	_____
6. quartet	_____	_____
7. quantities	_____	_____
8. qualified	_____	_____
9. quadruple	_____	_____
10. quietness	_____	_____

Classwork

Name: _____ Date: ___/___/_____ Score: _____

The Reading Challenge

Lesson 17.3

Reading Multisyllable Words

✓ **Lesson Check Point**

Directions: Read each target word. Circle the word in the row that is divided correctly into syllables. Use a dictionary or the Internet to check your answers.

지도: 각 대상 단어를 읽으십시오. 음절로 올바르게 나누어진 행에 있는 단어에 동그라미를 치십시오. 사전이나 인터넷을 사용하여 답을 확인하십시오.

Model

| quarter | a. quart-er | b. quar-ter (circled) | c. qu-arter |

1. quantum	a. quan-tum	b. quant-um	c. qua-ntum
2. qualify	a. qual-i-fy	b. qua-li-fy	c. qua-lif-y
3. quiver	a. qui-ver	b. quiv-er	c. qu-iver
4. question	a. ques-tion	b. quest-ion	c. que-stion
5. quotient	a. quot-ient	b. qu-otient	c. quo-tient
6. quota	a. qu-ota	b. quo-ta	c. quot-a
7. Quebec	a. Qu-ebec	b. Que-bec	c. Queb-ec
8. quietude	a. qui-e-tude	b. quiet-ude	c. quie-tu-de

Learn To Read English With Directions In Korean 173 Copyrighted Material

Classwork

👤 Name: _____ Date: ___/___/_____ Score: _____

Lesson 17.4

Reading and Writing

Proper and Common Nouns and Adjectives

✓ **Lesson Check Point**

Directions: Read the words in the word box. Put an (X) on the line next to each word that is written incorrectly. Remember that all proper nouns and proper adjectives are capitalized. Use a dictionary or the Internet to check your answers.

지도: 단어 상자에 있는 단어를 읽으십시오. 잘못 쓰여진 각 단어 옆의 줄에 (X)를 표시하십시오. 모든 고유 명사와 고유 형용사는 대문자임을 기억하십시오. 사전이나 인터넷을 사용하여 답을 확인하십시오.

Word Box		
__ quarrel	__ quebec	__ Quakers
__ Quotient	__ Qatar	__ questionable
__ Quotes	__ quickly	__ queen Anne
__ Quiver	__ Quiche	__ Quincy

Directions: Read each unedited sentence and underline the word that is written incorrectly. Write each sentence correctly on the line.

지도: 편집되지 않은 각 문장을 읽고 잘못 쓰여진 단어에 밑줄을 긋습 니다. 각 문장을 줄에 올바르게 쓰십시오.

Model
The <u>queen</u> of England is very quiet.
<u>The Queen of England is very quiet.</u>

1. According to my Quartz watch, it is a Quarter after two.
_____

2. My good friends, Mr. and Mrs. Quinn, are quakers.
_____

3. The queen is going to visit quezon City in the Philippines.
_____

4. After reading the article, I asked a Question about Queen Elizabeth.
_____

Classwork

Name: _____ Date: ___/___/_____ Score: _____

Lesson 18.1

Reading Words with the Letter R/r

✓ Lesson Check Point

Directions: Read each target word. Find the letter "r" and put a check (✓) in the column that identifies its position: beginning, within or end.
지도: 각 대상 단어를 읽으십시오. 문자"r"을 찾아 체크 표시(✓)위치를 식별하는 열에서 시작, 내부 또는 끝.

Target Words	Beginning (First Letter)	Within	End (Last Letter)
1. cashier			
2. recent			
3. folder			
4. grape			
5. runaway			

Directions: Read each sentence and underline the words that begin with the letter "r." Write all the underlined words in alphabetical order on the lines below.
지도: 각 문장을 읽고 문자"r"로 시작하는 단어에 밑줄을 긋습니다. 아래 줄에 밑줄 친 단어를 알파벳 순서로 모두 쓰십시오.

6. At recess, Brianna and I ran quickly on the track.

7. The green rowboat is floating along the Nile River.

8. Brian rode his bike along the base of the Rocky Mountains.

9. The residents have the new Long Island Railroad schedule.

10. We can preserve our planet by recycling and reusing items.

_____ _____ _____
_____ _____ _____
_____ _____ _____
                _____

Classwork

Name: _____ Date: ___/ ___/ _____ Score: _____

Lesson 18.2

Reading Words with the Letter "r" Combinations:
"br," "cr," "dr," "fr," "gr," "pr" and "tr"

✓ **Lesson Check Point**

Directions: Read the target words in the word box. Identify the words with the following letter combinations: "br," "cr," "dr," "fr," "gr," "pr" and "tr." Write the target word on the line that correctly completes each sentence.

지도: 단어 상자에 있는 대상 단어를 읽으십시오. "br," "cr," "dr," "fr," "gr," "pr" 및 "tr" 문자 조합으로 단어를 식별합니다. 각 문장을 올바르게 완성하는 행에 목표 단어를 쓰십시오.

Target Word Box				
friends	traveling		bread	groom
principal	cruise			drifting
brochure	program			trucks

1. The _____ brochure is on the brass table.

2. Francis and Brad are best _____.

3. The new _____ is our school's leader.

4. Yesterday, I saw logs _____ along the riverbank.

5. The two loaves of _____ are fresh out of the oven.

6. The train is _____ from New York to Chicago.

7. The college admission _____ is very informative.

8. My social service _____ distributes food to needy families.

9. Testa's electric _____ travel up to 100 miles without recharging.

10. The bride and _____ received lots of expensive wedding presents.

Classwork

 Name: _____ Date: ___/___/_____ Score: _____

The Reading Challenge

Lesson 18.3

Reading Multisyllable Words

✓ Lesson Check Point

 Directions: Read and divide each target word into syllables. Write each word and place a hyphen (-) between the syllables in the second column. Write the number of syllables in the third column. Use a dictionary or the Internet to check your answers.

지도: 각 대상 단어를 읽고 음절로 나눕니다. 각 단어를 쓰고 두 번째 열의 음절 사이에 하이픈(-)을 넣습니다. 세 번째 열에 음절 수를 쓰십시오. 사전이나 인터넷을 사용하여 답을 확인하십시오.

Target Words	Words Divided into Syllables	Number of Syllables
1. reviewing	_____	_____
2. rigorously	_____	_____
3. rapidly	_____	_____
4. ready	_____	_____
5. rocky	_____	_____
6. rather	_____	_____
7. reading	_____	_____
8. rapture	_____	_____
9. reflection	_____	_____
10. reporting	_____	_____

Learn To Read English With Directions In Korean   Copyrighted Material

Classwork

Name: _____ Date: ___/___/_____ Score: _____

The Reading Challenge

Lesson 18.3

Reading Multisyllable Words

✓ **Lesson Check Point**

Directions: Read each target word. Circle the word in the row that is divided correctly into syllables. Use a dictionary or the Internet to check your answers.

지도: 각 대상 단어를 읽으십시오. 음절로 올바르게 나누어진 행에 있는 단어에 동그라미를 치십시오. 사전이나 인터넷을 사용하여 답을 확인하십시오.

Model

| runaway | a. ru-na-way | b. run-a-way (circled) | c. run-aw-ay |

| 1. robotics | a. ro-bot-ics | b. rob-ot-ics | c. ro-bo-tics |

| 2. radius | a. ra-di-us | b. rad-i-us | c. ra-diu-s |

| 3. radical | a. rad-i-cal | b. ra-dic-al | c. ra-di-cal |

| 4. reception | a. re-cept-ion | b. rec-ep-tion | c. re-cep-tion |

| 5. royalist | a. ro-yal-ist | b. roy-a-list | c. roy-al-ist |

| 6. reconcile | a. re-con-cile | b. rec-on-cile | c. rec-onc-ile |

| 7. recliner | a. rec-lin-er | b. re-cli-ner | c. re-clin-er |

| 8. refresher | a. re-fresh-er | b. ref-res-her | c. ref-resh-er |

Learn To Read English With Directions In Korean

Classwork

Name: _____ Date: ___/___/_____ Score: _____

Lesson 18.4

Reading and Writing

Proper and Common Nouns and Adjectives

✓ **Lesson Check Point**

Directions: Read the words in the word box. Put an (X) on the line next to each word that is written incorrectly. Remember that all proper nouns and proper adjectives are capitalized. Use a dictionary or the Internet to check your answers.

지도: 단어 상자에 있는 단어를 읽으십시오. 잘못 쓰여진 각 단어 옆의 줄에 (X)를 표시하십시오. 모든 고유 명사와 고유 형용사는 대문자임을 기억하십시오. 사전이나 인터넷을 사용하여 답을 확인하십시오.

Word Box		
__ runner	__ Amazon river	__ Red CRoss
__ Richard	__ Ryan	__ rainforest
__ romanian	__ Richmond, VA	__ Railroad
__ The rockies	__ roaches	__ rome

Directions: Read each unedited sentence and underline the word that is written incorrectly. Write each sentence correctly on the line.

지도: 편집되지 않은 각 문장을 읽고 잘못 쓰여진 단어에 밑줄을긋습 니다. 각 문장을 줄에 올바르게 쓰십시오.

Model
We saw two <u>Retired</u> racehorses at Richardson Ranch.
<u>We saw two retired racehorses at Richardson Ranch.</u>

1. Raphael said, "russia is the world's largest country."
   _____

2. My friends, Rachel and Ricky, went to the Amazon rainforest.
   _____

3. Mr. Richards received the rockefeller Merit Award for Excellence.
   _____

4. Do you know that Rose Robin restaurant serves the best ribs?
   _____

Classwork

Name: _____ Date: ___/___/_____ Score: _____

Lesson 19.1

Reading Words with the Letter S/s

✓ **Lesson Check Point**

Directions: Read each target word. Find the letter "s" and put a check (✓) in the column that identifies its position: beginning, within or end.
지도: 각 대상 단어를 읽으십시오. 문자"s"를 찾아 체크 표시(✓)위치를 식별하는 열에서 시작, 내부 또는 끝.

Target Words	Beginning (First Letter)	Within	End (Last Letter)
1. safety			
2. matches			
3. runners			
4. shower			
5. construct			

Directions: Read each sentence and underline the words that begin with the letter "s." Write all the underlined words in alphabetical order on the lines below.
지도: 각 문장을 읽고"s"로 시작하는 단어에 밑줄을 긋습니다. 아래 줄에 밑줄 친 단어를 알파벳 순서로 모두 쓰십시오.

6. Dexter ate a tasty salami sandwich for lunch.

7. My brother received two scholarships for school.

8. Melanie said, "My grandmother is a great singer."

9. Melissa is using scissors to cut ten sheets of paper.

10. Both Josiah and Simone are seventy-six years old.

_____ _____ _____

_____ _____ _____

_____

Classwork

 Name: _____   Date: ___/___/_____   Score: _____

Lesson 19.1

Reading Words with the Letter S/s

✓ **Lesson Check Point**

 Directions: Read each target word. Circle the word in the column that has the same "s" sound as the target word.
지도: 각 대상 단어를 읽으십시오. 대상 단어와 동일한 "s" 소리가 나는 열의 단어에 동그라미를 치십시오.

aspect	a. summer
	b. diversion

instant	a. insurance
	b. cross

cheese	a. music
	b. swim

issue	a. assurance
	b. jets

 Directions: Read each target word. Put a check (✓) under the correct column heading.
지도: 각 대상 단어를 읽으십시오. 올바른 열 제목 아래에 체크(✓)를 하십시오.

Target Words	"s" has the /s/ sound as in the word <u>sun</u>	"s" has the /sh/ sound as in the word <u>sugar</u>	"s" has the /z/ sound as in the word <u>his</u>	"s" has the /zh/ sound as in the word <u>vision</u>
1. aspect				
2. instant				
3. cheese				
4. issue				

Classwork

Name: _____ Date: ___/___/_____ Score: _____

Lesson 19.2

Reading Words with the "sion," "sial" & "scious" Suffixes

✓ **Lesson Check Point**

Directions: Read each target word. Circle the word in the column that has the same "sion," "sial" or "scious" sound as the target word.

지도: 각 대상 단어를 읽으십시오. 대상 단어와 동일한 "sion," "sial" 또는 "scious" 소리가 나는 열의 단어에 동그라미를 치십시오.

| commission | a. controversial |
| | b. passion |

| conversion | a. fusion |
| | b. percussion |

| compulsion | a. inclusion |
| | b. ambrosial |

| unconscious | a. vision |
| | b. conscious |

Directions: Read each target word. Put a check (✓) under the correct column heading.

지도: 각 대상 단어를 읽으십시오. 올바른 열 제목 아래에 체크(✓)를 하십시오.

Target Words	"sion" has the /sh/ +/ə/+/n/ sounds as in the word <u>passion</u>	"sion" has the /zh/ +/ə/+/n/ sounds as in the word <u>vision</u>	"scious" has the /sh/ +/ə/+/s/ sounds as in the word <u>conscious</u>
1. commission			
2. conversion			
3. compulsion			
4. unconscious			

Classwork

 Name: _____ Date:___/___/_____ Score:_____

Lesson 19.3

Reading Words with the "sch" Letter Combination

✓ Lesson Check Point

 Directions: Read each target word. Circle the word in the column that has the same "sch" sound(s) as the target word.
지도: 각 대상 단어를 읽으십시오. 대상 단어와 같은 "sch" 소리가 나는 열의 단어에 동그라미를 치십시오.

schmear	a. schilling
	b. school

schedule	a. schizoid
	b. schlep

schema	a. schmooze
	b. scholars

scholarly	a. schism
	b. scheme

 Directions: Read each target word. Put a check (✓) under the correct column heading.
지도: 각 대상 단어를 읽으십시오. 올바른 열 제목 아래에 체크(✓)를 하십시오.

Target Words	"sch" has the /s/ + /k/ sounds as in the word school	"sch" has the /sh/ sound as in the word schilling
1. schmear		
2. schedule		
3. schema		
4. scholarly		

Classwork

Name: _____ Date: ___/___/_____ Score: _____

Lesson 19.4

Reading Words with the "scr," "shr," "spr" & "str" Letter Combinations

Dictionary Skills/ Vocabulary

✓ **Lesson Check Point**

Directions: Read each target word and its definition. Write the letter of the definition on the line of each target word. Use a dictionary or the Internet to check your answers.
지도: 각 대상 단어와 그 정의를 읽으십시오. 각 대상 단어의 행에 정의의 문자를 씁니다. 사전이나 인터넷을 사용하여 답을 확인하십시오.

Target Words	Definitions
1. __ scrub	a. a device used to sprinkle water on a lawn
2. __ strawberries	b. sweet, red berries with a green leaf on top
3. __ shredder	c. to clean something by brushing
4. __ street	d. a paved road in a town or city
5. __ sprinkler	e. a machine that cuts paper into small pieces

Directions: Read each sentence. Underline the word in the parentheses that correctly completes each sentence. Then, write the underlined word on the line.
지도: 각 문장을 읽으십시오. 각 문장을 올바르게 완성하는 괄호 안에 있는 단어에 밑줄을 긋습니다. 그런 다음 밑줄 친 단어를 줄에 쓰십시오.

6. I will water my grass with a _____ system. (street, sprinkler)

7. She will _____ the dirty floor with a firm brush. (street, scrub)

8. Stan shreds documents with a _____. (shredder, sprinkler)

9. The driver drove down the _____ at a high speed. (street, scrub)

10. I enjoy _____ with my breakfast cereal. (shredder, strawberries)

Classwork

Name: _____ Date: ___/___/_____ Score: _____

Lesson 19.5

Reading Words with the "sl" & "sle" Letter Combinations

Dictionary Skills/ Vocabulary

✓ **Lesson Check Point**

Directions: Read each target word and its definition. Write the target word on the line in front of its meaning. Use a dictionary or the Internet to check your answers.
지도: 각 대상 단어와 그 정의를 읽으십시오. 의미 앞 줄에 대상단어를 쓰십시오. 사전이나 인터넷을 사용하여 답을 확인하십시오.

Target Word Box				
sleeves	slippery	slope	sloth	sly

1. _____ causing to slip and/or slide
2. _____ a characteristic of a tricky person
3. _____ a furry mammal that moves very slowly
4. _____ a falling or rising land surface
5. _____ the parts of a garment that cover a person's arms

Directions: Read each sentence. Underline the word in the parentheses that correctly completes each sentence. Then, write the underlined word on the line.
지도: 각 문장을 읽으십시오. 각 문장을 올바르게 완성하는 괄호 안에 있는 단어에 밑줄을 긋습니다. 그런 다음 밑줄 친 단어를 줄에 쓰십시오.

6. In the woods, the tricky fox has a _____ smile. (sloth, sly)

7. I could not hold the _____ starfish. (slippery, slopes)

8. The _____ is hanging on the tropical tree. (sloth, slippery)

9. Sam is wearing a shirt with short _____. (sly, sleeves)

10. The ski _____ are covered with snow and ice. (slopes, sleeves)

Learn To Read English With Directions In Korean

Classwork

 Name: _____ Date: ___/___/_____ Score: _____

Lesson 19.5

Reading Words with the "sle" Letter Combination

✓ **Lesson Check Point**

 Directions: Read each target word. Find the "sle" letter combination and put a check (✓) in the column that identifies its position: beginning, within or end.

지도: 각 대상 단어를 읽으십시오. "sle" 문자 조합을 찾고위치를 식별하는 열에 체크(✓)를 하십시오: 시작, 내또는 끝.

Target Words	Beginning (First 3 Letters)	Within	End (Last 3 Letters)
1. sleet			
2. sleeves			
3. sleigh			
4. tussle			
5. measles			

 Directions: Read each target word. Put a check (✓) in the "yes" column if the "sle" letter combination has the /s/ + /ə/ + /l/ or /z/ + /ə/ + /l/ sounds. Put a check (✓) in the "no" column if the "sle" letter combination does not have the /s/ + /ə/ + /l/ or /z/ + /ə/ + /l/ sounds.

지도: 각 대상 단어를 읽으십시오. "sle" 문자 조합에/s/ + /ə/ + /l/ 또는/z/ + /ə/ + /l/소리 가 있으면"yes" 열에 체크(✓)를 하십시오. "sle" 문자 조합에/s/ + /ə/ + /l/ 또는/z/ + /ə/ + /소리가 없으면"no" 열에 체크(✓)를 하십시오.

Target Words	Yes	No
6. sleet		
7. sleeves		
8. sleigh		
9. tussle		
10. measles		

Classwork

 Name: _____ Date: ___/___/_____ Score: _____

Lesson 19.6

Reading Words with the "sm" Letter Combination

✓ Lesson Check Point

 Directions: Read each target word. Circle the word in the column that has the same "sm" sounds as the target word.
지도: 각 대상 단어를 읽으십시오. 대상 단어와 동일한 "sm" 소리가 나는 열의 단어에 동그라미를 치십시오.

dismay	a. dualism	smile	a. charisma
	b. smoke		b. mismatch

newsman	a. smooth	racism	a. realism
	b. cosmetic		b. plasma

 Directions: Read each target word. Put a check (✓) under the correct column heading.
지도: 각 대상 단어를 읽으십시오. 올바른 열 제목 아래에 체크(✓)를 하십시오.

Target Words	"sm" has the /s/ + /m/ sounds as in the word smell	"sm" has the /z/ + /m/ sounds as in the word cosmic	"sm" has the /z/ + /ə/ + /m/ sounds as in the word autism
1. dismay			
2. smile			
3. newsman			
4. racism			

Classwork

Name: _____ Date: ___/___/_____ Score: _____

Lesson 19.7

Reading Words with the "ss" Letter Combination

✓ **Lesson Check Point**

Directions: Read each target word. Circle the word in the column that has the same "ss" sound(s) as the target word.

지도: 각 대상 단어를 읽으십시오. 대상 단어와 동일한 "ss" 소리가 나는 열의 단어에 동그라미를 치십시오.

| misshaped | a. dissolve |
| | b. dissatisfy |

| Missouri | a. compassion |
| | b. dissolve |

| expression | a. misstated |
| | b. concussion |

| mission | a. misspell |
| | b. aggression |

Directions: Read each target word. Put a check (✓) under the correct column heading.

지도: 각 대상 단어를 읽으십시오. 올바른 열 제목 아래에 체크(✓)를 하십시오.

Target Words	"ss" has the /sh/ sound as in the word <u>tissue</u>	"ss" has the /s/ + /s/ sounds as in the word <u>misspell</u>	"ss" has the /z/ sound as in the word <u>dissolve</u>
1. misshaped			
2. Missouri			
3. expression			
4. mission			

Name: _____ Date: ___/___/_____ Score: _____

Lesson 19.8

Reading Words with a Silent Letter "s"

✓ **Lesson Check Point**

 Directions: Read the target words in the word box. Write the words that have a silent letter "s" in the first column. Write the words that do not have a silent letter "s" in the second column.

지도: 단어 상자에 있는 대상 단어를 읽으십시오. 첫 번째 열에 묵음문자 "s"가 있는 단어를 씁니다. 두 번째 열에 묵음 문자"s"가 없는 단어를쓰십시오.

Target Word Box				
class	horses	handsome	island	debris
aisle	passage	estate	assess	becomes
request	hotels	Arkansas	consider	aside
optimist	address	discover	embassy	isle

Letter "s" is silent | Letter "s" has the /s/, /z/ or /sh/ sound

Classwork

Name: _____ Date: ___/___/_____ Score: _____

The Reading Challenge

Lesson 19.9

Reading Multisyllable Words

✓ **Lesson Check Point**

Directions: Read and divide each target word into syllables. Write each word and place a hyphen (-) between the syllables in the second column. Write the number of syllables in the third column. Use a dictionary or the Internet to check your answers.

지도: 각 대상 단어를 읽고 음절로 나눕니다. 각 단어를 쓰고 두 번째 열의 음절 사이에 하이픈(-)을 넣습니다. 세 번째 열에 음절 수를 쓰십시오. 사전이나 인터넷을 사용하여 답을 확인하십시오.

Target Words	Words Divided into Syllables	Number of Syllables
1. safety		
2. senior		
3. sampling		
4. shampoo		
5. seaport		
6. soldiers		
7. satisfaction		
8. sequential		
9. shadowing		
10. sisterhood		

Classwork

 Name: _____ Date:___/___/_____ Score:_____

The Reading Challenge

Lesson 19.9

Reading Multisyllable Words

✓ Lesson Check Point

 Directions: Read each target word. Circle the word in the row that is divided correctly into syllables. Use a dictionary or the Internet to check your answers.
지도: 각 대상 단어를 읽으십시오. 음절로 올바르게 나누어진 행에 있는 단어에 동그라미를 치십시오. 사전이나 인터넷을 사용하여 답을 확인하십시오.

Model

| Saturday | a. Sa-tur-day | b. Sat-ur-day | c. Sa-turd-ay |

| 1. seminar | a. sem-i-nar | b. se-mi-nar | c. se-min-ar |

| 2. satisfy | a. sa-tis-fy | b. sa-tisf-y | c. sat-is-fy |

| 3. seasonal | a. seas-on-al | b. sea-so-nal | c. sea-son-al |

| 4. several | a. se-ver-al | b. sev-er-al | c. sev-e-ral |

| 5. singular | a. sing-u-lar | b. sin-gu-lar | c. sin-gul-ar |

| 6. semester | a. se-mest-er | b. sem-est-er | c. se-mes-ter |

| 7. skeleton | a. skel-e-ton | b. ske-le-ton | c. ske-let-on |

| 8. salary | a. sa-lar-y | b. sal-ar-y | c. sal-a-ry |

Learn To Read English With Directions In Korean

Classwork

Name: _____ Date: ___/___/_____ Score: _____

Lesson 19.10

Reading and Writing

Proper and Common Nouns and Adjectives

✓ Lesson Check Point

Directions: Read the words in the word box. Put an (X) on the line next to each word that is written incorrectly. Remember that all proper nouns and proper adjectives are capitalized. Use a dictionary or the Internet to check your answers.

지도: 단어 상자에 있는 단어를 읽으십시오. 잘못 쓰여진 각 단어 옆의 줄에 (X)를 표시하십시오. 모든 고유 명사와 고유 형용사는 대문자임을 기억하십시오. 사전이나 인터넷을 사용하여 답을 확인하십시오.

Word Box		
__ Sandbox	__ siberia	__ Samoa
__ Salon	__ shrimp	__ Dr. samuel
__ San Juan	__ sample	__ Sailor
__ seagull	__ senator Sam	__ seahorse

Directions: Read each unedited sentence and underline the word that is written incorrectly. Write each sentence correctly on the line.

지도: 편집되지 않은 각 문장을 읽고 잘못 쓰여진 단어에 밑줄을긋습 니다. 각 문장을 줄에 올바르게 쓰십시오.

Model
<u>sandy</u> is going to Salt Lake City on Sunday.
<u>Sandy is going to Salt Lake City on Sunday.</u>

1. On saturday, we are going sailing around South Bay.
_____

2. My Siblings received scholarships to Sidney School.
_____

3. On Sunday, I am going to have lunch with sergeant Smith.
_____

4. My grandparents, Samuel and Samantha, are Senior citizens.
_____

Classwork

Name: _____ Date: ___/___/_____ Score: _____

Lesson 20.1

Reading Words with the Letter T/t

Directions: Read each target word. Find the letter "t" and put a check (✓) in the column that identifies its position: beginning, within or end.
지도: 각 대상 단어를 읽으십시오. 문자"t"를 찾아 체크 표시(✓)위치를 식별하는 열에서 시작, 내부 또는 끝.

Target Words	Beginning (First Letter)	Within	End (Last Letter)
1. reporter			
2. teenager			
3. merchant			
4. Tuesday			
5. section			

Directions: Read each sentence and underline the words that begin with the letter "t." Write all the underlined words in alphabetical order on the lines below.
지도: 각 문장을 읽고 문자"t"로 시작하는 단어에 밑줄을 긋습니다. 아래 줄에 밑줄 친 단어를 알파벳 순서로 모두 쓰십시오.

6. My teacher, Ms. Peters, does not like tarantulas.

7. My sister tossed her interactive toys everywhere.

8. At Thanksgiving dinner, Danny ate rice and turkey.

9. Terrence likes putting tartar sauce on his fish sandwiches.

10. An intense thunderstorm caused damage throughout our county.

_____   _____   _____
_____   _____   _____
_____   _____   _____
              _____

Classwork

 Name: _____ Date: ___/___/_____ Score: _____

Lesson 20.2

Reading Words with the "thm" Letter Combination

✓ **Lesson Check Point**

 Directions: Read each target word. Circle the word in the column that has the same "thm" sound(s) as the target word.
지도: 각 대상 단어를 읽으십시오. 대상 단어와 동일한"thm" 소리가 있는 열의 단어에 동그라미를 치십시오.

logarithm	a. biorhythm
	b. bathmat

isthmus	a. rhythm
	b. asthma

algorithm	a. isthmian
	b. logarithm

birthmark	a. bathmat
	b. biorhythm

 Directions: Read each target word. Put a check (✓) under the correct column heading.
지도: 각 대상 단어를 읽으십시오. 올바른 열 제목 아래에 체크(✓)를 하십시오.

Target Words	"thm" has the /th/ + /ə/ + /m/ sounds as in the word <u>rhythm</u>	"thm" has the /th/ + /m/ sounds as in the word <u>bathmat</u>	"thm" silent "th" + /m/ sound as in the word <u>asthma</u>
1. logarithm			
2. isthmus			
3. algorithm			
4. birthmark			

Classwork

 Name: _____ Date: ___/___/_____ Score: _____

Lesson 20.3

Reading Words with the "tion," "tial" & "tious" Suffixes

✓ **Lesson Check Point**

 Directions: Read each target word. Circle the word in the column that has the same "tion," "tial" or "tious" sound as the target word.
지도: 각 대상 단어를 읽으십시오. 대상 단어와 같은 "tion," "tial" 또는 "tious" 소리가 나는 열의 단어에 동그라미를 치십시오.

distinction	a. assumption
	b. substantially

substantial	a. confidential
	b. celebration

infectious	a. cautiously
	b. animation

conditional	a. admiration
	b. bumptious

 Directions: Read each target word. Put a check (✓) under the correct column heading.
지도: 각 대상 단어를 읽으십시오. 올바른 열 제목 아래에 체크(✓)를 하십시오.

Target Words	"tion" has the /sh/ +/ə/+/n/ sounds as in the word <u>education</u>	"tial" has the /sh/ +/ə/+/l/ sounds as in the word <u>partial</u>	"tious" has the /sh/ +/ə/+/s/ sounds as in the word <u>ambitious</u>
1. distinction			
2. substantial			
3. infectious			
4. conditional			

Classwork

Name: _____ Date: ___/___/_____ Score: _____

Lesson 20.4

Reading Words with the "tr" Letter Combination

Dictionary Skills/ Vocabulary

✓ **Lesson Check Point**

Directions: Read each target word and its definition. Write the letter of the definition on the line of each target word. Use a dictionary or the Internet to check your answers.

지도: 각 대상 단어와 그 정의를 읽으십시오. 각 대상 단어의 행에 정의의 문자를 씁니다. 사전이나 인터넷을 사용하여 답을 확인하십시오.

Target Words	Definitions
1. __ tragic	a. a problematic situation, a conflict
2. __ trampled	b. to write words from one language to another
3. __ transfer	c. to move from one place to another
4. __ translate	d. a disastrous occurrence or event
5. __ trouble	e. the act of beating a surface down with one's feet

Directions: Read each sentence. Underline the word in the parentheses that correctly completes each sentence. Then, write the underlined word on the line.

지도: 각 문장을 읽으십시오. 각 문장을 올바르게 완성하는 괄호 안에 있는 단어에 밑줄을 긋습니다. 그런 다음 밑줄 친 단어를 줄에 쓰십시오.

6. I _____ the report from English to Arabic. (translated, tragic)

7. He got in _____ for breaking the class rules. (trouble, transfer)

8. Tress cried when she read the story's _____ ending. (tragic, trample)

9. Terrance will _____ to his connecting flight. (transfer, translate)

10. The horse _____ the crops in the field. (trouble, trampled)

Classwork

 Name: _____ Date: ___/___/_____ Score: _____

Lesson 20.5

Reading Words with the "tle" Letter Combination

✓ **Lesson Check Point**

 Directions: Read each target word. Find the "tle" letter combination and put a check in the column that identifies its position: beginning, within or end.

지도: 각 대상 단어를 읽으십시오. "tle" 문자 조합을 찾고 위치를 식별하는 열에 체크(✓)를 하십시오: 시작, 내 또는 끝.

Target Words	Beginning (First 3 Letters)	Within	End (Last 3 Letters)
1. hurtle			
2. cutlet			
3. outlet			
4. settle			
5. countless			

 Directions: Read each target word. Put a check (✓) in the "yes" column if the "tle" letter combination has the /t/ + /ə/ + /l/ sounds. Put a check (✓) in the "no" column if the "tle" letter combination does not have the /t/ + /ə/ + /l/ sounds.

지도: 각 대상 단어를 읽으십시오. "tle" 문자 조합에 /t/ + /ə/ + /l/ 소리가 있으면 "yes" 열에 체크(✓)를 하십시오. "tle" 문자 조합에 /t/ + /ə/ + /l/ 소리가 없으면 "no" 열에 체크(✓)를 하십시오.

Target Words	Yes	No
6. hurtle		
7. cutlet		
8. outlet		
9. settle		
10. countless		

Classwork

Name: _____ Date: ___/___/_____ Score: _____

Lesson 20.6

Reading Words with the Letter "t" Sounds

✓ **Lesson Check Point**

Directions: Read each target word. Circle the word in the column that has the same "t" sound as the target word.

지도: 각 대상 단어를 읽으십시오. 대상 단어와 "t" 소리가 같은 열의 단어에 동그라미를 치십시오.

mention	a. ambition
	b. righteous

culture	a. picture
	b. contact

electric	a. connect
	b. action

actual	a. denture
	b. expect

Directions: Read each target word. Put a check (✓) under the correct column heading.

지도: 각 대상 단어를 읽으십시오. 올바른 열 제목 아래에 체크(✓)를 하십시오.

Target Words	"t" has the /t/ sound as in the word <u>multiply</u>	"t" has the /ch/ sound as in the word <u>picture</u>	"t" has the /sh/ sound as in the word <u>position</u>
1. mention			
2. culture			
3. electric			
4. actual			

Classwork

 Name: _____ Date:___/___/_____ Score:_____

Lesson 20.7

Reading Words with a Silent Letter "t"

✓ **Lesson Check Point**

 Directions: Read the target words in the word box. Write the words that have a silent letter "t" in the first column. Write the words that do not have a silent letter "t" in the second column.

지도: 단어 상자에 있는 대상 단어를 읽으십시오. 첫 번째 열에 묵음문자 "t"가 있는 단어를 쓰십시오. 두 번째 열에 묵음 문자"t"가 없는 단어를 쓰십시오.

Target Word Box				
continue	itch	crochet	entrance	totally
pottery	curtain	kitchen	heart	factory
clothes	defeat	denote	listening	dieting
castle	postman	sitting	mortgage	snitch

Letter "t" is silent

_____
_____
_____
_____
_____
_____
_____
_____

Letter "t" has the /t/ sound

_____
_____
_____
_____
_____
_____
_____
_____

Learn To Read English With Directions In Korean

Classwork

Name: _____ Date: ___/___/_____ Score: _____

The Reading Challenge

Lesson 20.8

Reading Multisyllable Words

✓ **Lesson Check Point**

Directions: Read and divide each target word into syllables. Write each word and place a hyphen (-) between the syllables in the second column. Write the number of syllables in the third column. Use a dictionary or the Internet to check your answers.

지도: 각 대상 단어를 읽고 음절로 나눕니다. 각 단어를 쓰고 두 번째 열의 음절 사이에 하이픈(-)을 넣습니다. 세 번째 열에 음절 수를 쓰십시오. 사전이나 인터넷을 사용하여 답을 확인하십시오.

Target Words	Words Divided into Syllables	Number of Syllables
1. traveling	_____	_____
2. tiny	_____	_____
3. treasure	_____	_____
4. textbooks	_____	_____
5. tonight	_____	_____
6. timbering	_____	_____
7. tweezers	_____	_____
8. turquoise	_____	_____
9. transplanting	_____	_____
10. title	_____	_____

Classwork

 Name: _____ Date:___/___/_____ Score:_____

The Reading Challenge

Lesson 20.8

Reading Multisyllable Words

✓ **Lesson Check Point**

 Directions: Read each target word. Circle the word in the row that is divided correctly into syllables. Use a dictionary or the Internet to check your answers.

지도: 각 대상 단어를 읽으십시오. 음절로 올바르게 나누어진 행에 있는 단어에 동그라미를 치십시오. 사전이나 인터넷을 사용하여 답을 확인하십시오.

Model

| telephone | a. te-lep-hone | b. tel-e-phone (circled) | c. te-le-phone |

1. teenager	a. teen-ag-er	b. teen-a-ger	c. teena-g-er
2. taxicab	a. ta-xic-ab	b. tax-ic-ab	c. tax-i-cab
3. technical	a. te-chnic-al	b. tech-nic-al	c. tech-ni-cal
4. triangle	a. tri-ang-le	b. tri-an-gle	c. tria-n-gle
5. testify	a. tes-ti-fy	b. te-stif-y	c. tes-tif-y
6. temperate	a. temp-er-ate	b. tem-pe-rate	c. tem-per-ate
7. typical	a. ty-pi-cal	b. ty-pic-al	c. typ-i-cal
8. translated	a. trans-lat-ed	b. transl-a-ted	c. tran-slat-ed

Classwork

Name: _____ Date: ___/___/_____ Score: _____

Lesson 20.9

Reading and Writing

Proper and Common Nouns and Adjectives

✓ **Lesson Check Point**

Directions: Read the words in the word box. Put an (X) on the line next to each word that is written incorrectly. Remember that all proper nouns and proper adjectives are capitalized. Use a dictionary or the Internet to check your answers.

지도: 단어 상자에 있는 단어를 읽으십시오. 잘못 쓰여진 각 단어 옆의 줄에 (X)를 표시하십시오. 모든 고유 명사와 고유 형용사는 대문자임을 기억하십시오. 사전이나 인터넷을 사용하여 답을 확인하십시오.

Word Box		
__ taiwan	__ thursday	__ thousand
__ Togo	__ Today	__ Tonga
__ thunder	__ Tokyo	__ tunisia
__ Twins	__ target	__ Tomato

Directions: Read each unedited sentence and underline the word that is written incorrectly. Write each sentence correctly on the line.

지도: 편집되지 않은 각 문장을 읽고 잘못 쓰여진 단어에 밑줄을 긋습 니다. 각 문장을 줄에 올바르게 쓰십시오.

Model
On <u>thursday</u>, a tornado destroyed my hometown.
<u>On Thursday, a tornado destroyed my hometown.</u>

1. I ate tasty thai food at Lemongrass Thailand Restaurant.
_____

2. My dentist, Dr. Tracks, Takes good care of my teeth.
_____

3. In tanzania, the townspeople have tremendous hearts.
_____

4. I will travel to the beautiful twin islands of Trinidad and tobago.
_____

Unit T Lesson 20.9

Learn To Read English With Directions In Korean   Copyrighted Material

Classwork

 Name: _____ Date:___/___/_____ Score:_____

Lesson 21.1

Reading Words with the Letter U/u

✓ Lesson Check Point

 Directions: Read each target word. Find the letter "u" and put a check (✓) in the column that identifies its position: beginning, within or end.
지도: 각 대상 단어를 읽으십시오. 문자"u"를 찾아 체크 표시(✓)위치를 식별하는 열에서 시작, 내부 또는 끝.

Target Words	Beginning (First Letter)	Within	End (Last Letter)
1. under			
2. menu			
3. success			
4. you			
5. university			

 Directions: Read each target word. Read the words in the row and circle the word that has a different vowel "u" sound.
지도: 각 대상 단어를 읽으십시오. 줄에 있는 단어를 읽고 모음"u" 소리가 다른 단어에 동그라미를 치세요.다른 단어에 동그라미를 치세요.

Target Words				
6. swum	mud	June	tug	sub
7. chum	thru	bum	cut	hum
8. snub	nut	bud	tube	bun
9. thug	pun	cub	nun	juke
10. funny	burst	makeup	snuff	tux

Classwork

 Name: _____ Date: ___/___/_____ Score: _____

Lesson 21.2

Reading Words with the Short Vowel "u" Sound

✓ **Lesson Check Point**

 **Directions:** Read the words in the four boxes. Circle two words with the short vowel /ŭ/ sound. The anchor word for the short vowel /ŭ/ sound is up.

지도: 네 개의 상자에 있는 단어를 읽으십시오. 짧은 모음 /ŭ/ 소리로 두 단어에 동그라미를 치십시오. 단모음 /ŭ/ 소리의 기준어는 up입니다.

fume	buck	bump	rust	suck	null
June	dull	crude	brute	rule	truce

chute	lush	drunk	mute	dune	flute
used	punch	fuse	plush	duck	buff

 Directions: Read the words in the four boxes. Circle two words that rhyme. Rhyming words have the same ending sound, such as just and must.

지도: 네 개의 상자에 있는 단어를 읽으십시오. 해당하는 두 단어에 동그라미 표시운. 운율이 있는 단어는 just 및 must와 같이 끝 소리가 같습니다.

tuba	dump	luck	gush	grub	rush
lump	drug	tuck	flu	hush	use

stub	rust	cute	slug	super	much
tune	dust	brush	crush	smug	such

Classwork

L Name: _____ Date:___/___/_____ Score:_____

Lesson 21.2

Reading & Writing Words with the Short Vowel "u" Sound

✓ **Lesson Check Point**

Directions: Read each sentence and underline three words with the short vowel /ŭ/ sound. Then, write the underlined words on the lines below. The anchor word for the short vowel /ŭ/ sound is up.
지도: 각 문장을 읽고 세 단어에 짧은 모음 /ŭ/ 소리에 밑줄을 긋습니다. 그런 다음 밑줄 친 단어를 아래 줄에 쓰십시오. 단모음 /ŭ/ 소리의기준 어는 up입니다.

Model
Ulysses, the <u>drummer</u>, <u>jumps</u> when he plays the <u>drums</u>.

  drummer   jumps   drums
  _____   _____   _____

1. As Luke trudged in, he got mud on the rug.

  _____   _____   _____

2. The oatmeal in the cup is usually not lumpy and mushy.

  _____   _____   _____

3. The groomer brushed the puppy's fur with a soft brush.

  _____   _____   _____

4. In June, I was lucky to see the ducks and cubs at the zoo.

  _____   _____   _____

5. The club's members sat on the rug and ate blueberry muffins.

  _____   _____   _____

L Learn To Read English With Directions In Korean Copyrighted Material

Classwork

 Name: _____ Date: ___/___/_____ Score: _____

Lesson 21.3

Reading Words with the Long Vowel "u" Sound

✓ Lesson Check Point

 Directions: Read the words in the four boxes. Circle two words with the long vowel /yoo/ or /oo/ sound. The anchor word for the long vowel /yoo/ and /oo/ sounds is tube.
지도: 네 개의 상자에 있는 단어를 읽으십시오. 장모음 /yoo/ 또는 /oo/ 소리 로 두 단어에 동그라미를 치십시오. 장모음의 앵커 단어 /yoo/ 및 /oo/ 소리는 tube입니다.

guard	June		brute	junk		yucky	dilute
biscuit	use		bunch	volume		guest	reduce

stump	gulp		must	prune		sunken	salute
nude	accuse		confuse	quiet		lungs	include

 Directions: Read the words in the four boxes. Circle two words that rhyme. Rhyming words have the same ending sound, such as rule and mule.
지도: 네 개의 상자에 있는 단어를 읽으십시오. 해당하는 두 단어에 동그라미 표시운. 운율이 있는 단어는 rule 및 mule과 같이 끝 소리가 같습니다.

dump	cruel		dusk	lumpy		June	duckling
Just	fuel		glue	blue		lucky	tune

mute	Dutch		sung	rude		munch	rushing
flute	pumps		crude	bumper		excuse	refuse

Classwork

Name: _____ **Date:** ___/ ___/ _____ **Score:** _____

Lesson 21.3

Reading & Writing Words with the Long Vowel "u" Sound

✓ **Lesson Check Point**

Directions: Read each sentence and underline three words with the long vowel /yōō/ or /ōō/ sound. Then, write the underlined words on the lines below. The anchor word for the long vowel /yōō/ and /ōō/ sounds is <u>tube</u>.

지도: 각 문장을 읽고 긴 단어로 세 단어에 밑줄을 긋습니다. 모음/yōō/ 또는 /ōō/ 소리. 그런 다음 밑줄 친 단어를 아래 줄에 쓰십시오. 장모음/yōō/ 및 /ōō/ 소리의 앵커 워드는 tube입니다.

Model

<u>Bruce</u> is going to play the <u>tuba</u> and drums in <u>Uganda</u>.

    Bruce   tuba   Uganda
   _____   _____   _____

1. At lunch, Lucy enjoys eating juicy fruits.

   _____   _____   _____

2. The students' blue uniforms are dull and unattractive.

   _____   _____   _____

3. My aunt used flowers to produce a fragrant perfume.

   _____   _____   _____

4. In June, the club's rules gradually changed for the better.

   _____   _____   _____

5. Mr. Gus Underhill refused to accept the students' excuses.

   _____   _____   _____

Classwork

Name: _____ Date: ___/___/_____ Score: _____

Review Lessons 21.2 & 21.3

Reading Short Vowel and Long Vowel Words

Directions: Read the target words in the word box. In the first column, write the words that have the short vowel /ŭ/ sound, as in the word <u>up</u>. In the second column, write the words that have the long vowel /yoō/ or /oō/ sound, as in the word <u>tube</u>.

지도: 단어 상자에 있는 대상 단어를 읽으십시오. 첫 번째 열에는 up 단어와 같이 단모음 /ŭ/ 소리가 나는 단어를 씁니다. 두 번째 칸에는 장모음 /yoō/ 또는 /oō/ 소리, 단어 tube에서와 같이.

Target Word Box				
lucky	bunch	consume	hunter	rung
using	dull	bumpers	accuse	truce
computer	tofu	lungs	commute	jumping
rushing	debut	music	dusty	uniform

Letter "u" has the /ŭ/ sound as in the word <u>up</u>

Letter "u" has the /yoō/ or /oō/ sound as in the word <u>tube</u>

Classwork

Name: _____ Date: ___/___/_____ Score: _____

Lesson 21.4

Reading Words with Letter "u" Vowel Pairs

✓ Lesson Check Point

Directions: Read each target word. Circle the word in the column that has the same vowel "ua," "ue" or "ui" sound(s) as the target word.
지도: 각 대상 단어를 읽으십시오. 대상 단어와 동일한 모음 "ua," "ue" 또는 "ui" 소리를 갖는 열의 단어에 동그라미를 치십시오.

| fruits | a. clue |
| | b. dual |

| avenue | a. suite |
| | b. juicy |

| perpetual | a. gradual |
| | b. recruit |

| built | a. ritual |
| | b. building |

Directions: Read each target word. Put a check (✓) under the correct column heading.
지도: 각 대상 단어를 읽으십시오. 올바른 열 제목 아래에 체크(✓)를 하십시오.

Target Words	Words have the long "u" sound as in the word blue	Words do not have the long "u" sound
1. builds		
2. affluent		
3. factual		
4. suites		

Classwork

 Name: _____ Date: ___/___/_____ Score: _____

Lesson 21.5

Reading Words with the Final Letter "u"

✓ **Lesson Check Point**

 Directions: Read each target word. Find the letter "u" and put a check (✓) in the column that identifies its position within the syllable.
지도: 각 대상 단어를 읽으십시오. 문자"u"를 찾아 체크 표시(✓)음절 내에서 위치를 식별하는 열에서.

Target Words	"u" is at the end of a one syllable word	"u" is at the end of the first syllable	"u" is at the end of a multi-syllable word
1. July			
2. you			
3. impromptu			
4. Utah			
5. uniform			

 Directions: Read each target word. Put a check (✓) under the correct column heading.
지도: 각 대상 단어를 읽으십시오. 올바른 열 제목 아래에체크(✓)를 하십 시오.

Target Words	"u" has the /ŭ/ sound as in the word <u>tub</u>	"u" has the /yōō/ sound as in the word <u>tube</u>	"u" has the /ə/ sound as in the word <u>circus</u>	"u" is silent as in the word <u>build</u>
6. vague				
7. radius				
8. clue				
9. drums				
10. survive				

Classwork

 Name: _____ Date: ___/___/_____ Score: _____

Lesson 21.6

Reading Letter "u" Words with the Schwa Vowel Sound

✓ **Lesson Check Point**

 Directions: Read each target word. Circle the word in the column that has the same "u" sound as the target word.
지도: 각 대상 단어를 읽으십시오. 대상 단어와 "u" 소리가 같은 열의 단어에 동그라미를 치십시오.

faculty	a. plateau
	b. upon

lettuce	a. umbrella
	b. hopeful

suggested	a. campus
	b. used

adjust	a. supply
	b. upside

 Directions: Read each sentence and underline the letter "u" word that has the schwa vowel /ə/ sound. The anchor word for the letter "u" schwa vowel sound is <u>campus</u>.
지도: 각 문장을 읽고 슈와 모음 /ə/ 소리가 있는 문자 "u" 단어에 밑줄을 긋습니다. 문자 "u" 슈와 모음 소리의 앵커 단어는 campus입니다.

1. The umpire is not very popular.

2. Some of my students are very playful.

3. Hugo has nice pictures and gifts from Guyana.

4. In January, Eugene will visit Portugal and Uganda.

5. The Museum of Urban Studies is close to Pace University.

6. During class, I tend to focus on the bilingual presentations.

Classwork

 Name: _____ Date:____/____/_____ Score: _____

Lesson 21.7

Reading Words with the "ur" Letter Combination

Dictionary Skills/ Vocabulary

✓ **Lesson Check Point**

 Directions: Read each target word and its definition. Write the letter of the definition on the line of each target word. Use a dictionary or the Internet to check your answers.
지도: 각 대상 단어와 그 정의를 읽으십시오. 각 대상 단어의 행에 정의의 문자를 씁니다. 사전이나 인터넷을 사용하여 답을 확인하십시오.

Target Words	Definitions
1. __ purse	a. the possessive form of the word, you
2. __ journey	b. a small bag used to carry money and items
3. __ Your	c. a trip; to go from one place to another
4. __ Failure	d. to have felt extreme sadness or sorrow
5. __ mourned	e. act of not succeeding

 Directions: Read each sentence and write the target word on the line that correctly completes the sentence.
지도: 각 문장을 읽고 문장을 올바르게 완성하는 목표 단어를 쓰십시오.

6. My teacher shouted, "_____ in school is unacceptable."

7. Jimmy _____ the loss of his pet goldfish.

8. Grandma carries keys and money in her _____.

9. _____ brother is going to join the basketball team.

10. The characters are on a dangerous _____ in the woods.

Classwork

Name: _____ Date:___/___/_____ Score:_____

Lesson 21.8

Reading Words with a Silent Letter "u"

✓ **Lesson Check Point**

Directions: Read the target words in the word box. Write the words that have a silent letter "u" in the first column. Write the words that do not have a silent letter "u" in the second column.

지도: 단어 상자에 있는 대상 단어를 읽으십시오. 첫 번째 열에 묵음문자 "u"가 있는 단어를 쓰십시오. 두 번째 열에 묵음 문자"u"가 없는 단어를 쓰십시오.

Target Word Box				
fatigue	continuum	circuit	laughing	Guinea
guiding	avenue	Tuesday	rulers	attitude
unison	under	annual	guessing	visual
impromptu	building	tongues	biscuit	shoulder

Letter "u" is silent

_____
_____
_____
_____
_____
_____
_____
_____

Letter "u" has a letter "u" sound

_____
_____
_____
_____
_____
_____
_____
_____

Classwork

Name: _____ Date: ___/___/_____ Score: _____

Unit Review - U/u

Reading Words with Vowel "u" Sounds: /ŭ/, /o͞o/, /ə/ & Silent

✓ **Lesson Check Point**

Directions: Read each target word. Circle the word in the column that has the same "u" sound as the target word.
지도: 각 대상 단어를 읽으십시오. 대상 단어와 "u" 소리가 같은 열의단어에 동그라미를 치십시오.

suggest	a. unicorn
	b. subtract

duckling	a. hutch
	b. music

student	a. super
	b. dumping

tongue	a. menu
	b. guests

Directions: Read each target word. Put a check (✓) under the correct column heading.
지도: 각 대상 단어를 읽으십시오. 올바른 열 제목 아래에 체크(✓)를하십시오.

Target Words	"u" has the /ŭ/ sound as in the word **tub**	"u" has the /o͞o/ sound as in the word **tube**	"u" has the /ə/ sound as in the word **circus**	"u" is silent as in the word **build**
1. suggest				
2. duckling				
3. student				
4. tongue				

Learn To Read English With Directions In Korean   214   Copyrighted Material

Classwork

Name: _____ Date: ___/___/_____ Score: _____

The Reading Challenge

Lesson 21.9

Reading Multisyllable Words

✓ **Lesson Check Point**

Directions: Read and divide each target word into syllables. Write each word and place a hyphen (-) between the syllables in the second column. Write the number of syllables in the third column. Use a dictionary or the Internet to check your answers.

지도: 각 대상 단어를 읽고 음절로 나눕니다. 각 단어를 쓰고 두 번째 열의 음절 사이에 하이픈(-)을 넣습니다. 세 번째 열에 음절 수를 쓰십시오. 사전이나 인터넷을 사용하여 답을 확인하십시오.

Target Words	Words Divided into Syllables	Number of Syllables
1. luncheon	_____	_____
2. bunches	_____	_____
3. duckling	_____	_____
4. crushing	_____	_____
5. sugary	_____	_____
6. pulpit	_____	_____
7. bumper	_____	_____
8. intruding	_____	_____
9. denouncing	_____	_____
10. capsulate	_____	_____

Learn To Read English With Directions In Korean

Classwork

Name: _____ Date: ___/___/_____ Score: _____

The Reading Challenge

Lesson 21.9

Reading Multisyllable Words

✓ Lesson Check Point

Directions: Read each target word. Circle the word in the row that is divided correctly into syllables. Use a dictionary or the Internet to check your answers.

지도: 각 대상 단어를 읽으십시오. 음절로 올바르게 나누어진 행에 있는 단어에 동그라미를 치십시오. 사전이나 인터넷을 사용하여 답을 확인하십시오.

Model

| visualize | a. vis-ua-lize | b. vi-su-al-ize | c. vis-u-a-lize |

| 1. habitual | a. ha-bit-u-al | b. ha-bit-ual | c. hab-it-ual |

| 2. avenue | a. av-e-nue | b. ave-nu-e | c. a-ve-nue |

| 3. diluting | a. dil-u-ting | b. di-lut-ing | c. di-lu-ting |

| 4. amusing | a. a-mu-sing | b. a-mus-ing | c. am-u-sing |

| 5. confusion | a. con-fu-sion | b. con-fus-ion | c. conf-u-sion |

| 6. saluting | a. sa-lut-ing | b. sal-u-ting | c. sa-lu-ting |

| 7. fortunate | a. fort-u-nate | b. for-tun-ate | c. for-tu-nate |

| 8. truancy | a. tru-anc-y | b. tru-a-ncy | c. tru-an-cy |

Unit U Lesson 21.9

Learn To Read English With Directions In Korean

Classwork

Name: _____ Date: ___/___/_____ Score: _____

Lesson 21.10

Reading and Writing

Proper and Common Nouns and Adjectives

✓ Lesson Check Point

Directions: Read the words in the word box. Put an (X) on the line next to each word that is written incorrectly. Remember that all proper nouns and proper adjectives are capitalized. Use a dictionary or the Internet to check your answers.

지도: 단어 상자에 있는 단어를 읽으십시오. 잘못 쓰여진 각 단어 옆의 줄에 (X)를 표시하십시오. 모든 고유 명사와 고유 형용사는 대문자임을 기억하십시오. 사전이나 인터넷을 사용하여 답을 확인하십시오.

Word Box		
__ University	__ ukraine	__ URL
__ USSR	__ ubangi	__ upbeat
__ Universal	__ umbrella	__ Uncle
__ Ultra	__ Uruguay	__ Uncovered

Directions: Read each unedited sentence and underline the word that is written incorrectly. Write each sentence correctly on the line.

지도: 편집되지 않은 각 문장을 읽고 잘못 쓰여진 단어에 밑줄을긋습 니다. 각 문장을 줄에 올바르게 쓰십시오.

Model
Mrs. Ubangi usually has union meetings at a local <u>University</u>.
<u>Mrs. Ubangi usually has union meetings at a local university.</u>

1. We are studying the planet Uranus in Mrs. ubet's class.
_____

2. Professor Utrecht said, "The united Nations is very influential."
_____

3. In 1971, uzbekistan became independent from the U.S.S.R.
_____

4. I found information about two universities in upper Canada.
_____

Learn To Read English With Directions In Korean

Classwork

Name: _____ Date: ___/___/_____ Score: _____

Lesson 22.1

Reading Words with the Letter V/v

✓ Lesson Check Point

Directions: Read each target word. Find the letter "v" and put a check (✓) in the column that identifies its position: beginning, within or end.
지도: 각 대상 단어를 읽으십시오. 문자"v"를 찾아 체크 표시(✓)위치를 식별하는 열에서 시작, 내부 또는 끝.

Target Words	Beginning (First Letter)	Within	End (Last Letter)
1. visitor			
2. travel			
3. veterans			
4. silver			
5. Yugoslav			

Directions: Read each sentence and underline the words that begin with the letter "v." Write all the underlined words in alphabetical order on the lines below.
지도: 각 문장을 읽고"v"로 시작하는 단어에 밑줄을 긋습니다. 아래 줄에 밑줄 친 단어를 알파벳 순서로 모두 쓰십시오.

6. My guitar case has a valuable velvet lining.

7. Samantha's vintage dress is violet and white.

8. Our vice president has a vibrant personality.

9. The character in the video game vanished into thin air.

10. Joshua plays volleyball for his school's team, The Vikings.

_____ _____ _____
_____ _____ _____
_____ _____
            _____

Classwork

 Name: _____ Date: ___/___/_____ Score: _____

The Reading Challenge

Lesson 22.2

Reading Multisyllable Words

✓ Lesson Check Point

 Directions: Read and divide each target word into syllables. Write each word and place a hyphen (-) between the syllables in the second column. Write the number of syllables in the third column. Use a dictionary or the Internet to check your answers.

지도: 각 대상 단어를 읽고 음절로 나눕니다. 각 단어를 쓰고 두 번째 열의 음절 사이에 하이픈(-)을 넣습니다. 세 번째 열에 음절 수를 쓰십시오. 사전이나 인터넷을 사용하여 답을 확인하십시오.

Target Words	Words Divided into Syllables	Number of Syllables
1. visionary	_____	_____
2. vocalized	_____	_____
3. vantage	_____	_____
4. visiting	_____	_____
5. volume	_____	_____
6. verdict	_____	_____
7. vanishing	_____	_____
8. victorious	_____	_____
9. vineyard	_____	_____
10. various	_____	_____

Unit V
Lesson 22.2

Learn To Read English With Directions In Korean   219   Copyrighted Material

Classwork

Name: _____ Date: ___/___/_____ Score: _____

The Reading Challenge

Lesson 22.2

Reading Multisyllable Words

✓ **Lesson Check Point**

Directions: Read each target word. Circle the word in the row that is divided correctly into syllables. Use a dictionary or the Internet to check your answers.

지도: 각 대상 단어를 읽으십시오. 음절로 올바르게 나누어진 행에 있는 단어에 동그라미를 치십시오. 사전이나 인터넷을 사용하여 답을 확인하십시오.

Model

| volcano | a. vo-lcan-o | b. vol-can-o | c. (vol-ca-no) |

| 1. victory | a. vic-tor-y | b. vic-to-ry | c. vi-ctor-y |

| 2. varsity | a. var-sit-y | b. va-rsi-ty | c. var-si-ty |

| 3. visual | a. vis-u-al | b. vi-su-al | c. visu-a-l |

| 4. vacation | a. va-cat-ion | b. vac-a-tion | c. va-ca-tion |

| 5. volunteer | a. vol-un-teer | b. vo-lun-teer | c. vol-u-nteer |

| 6. vitamin | a. vit-a-min | b. vi-tam-in | c. vi-ta-min |

| 7. vehement | a. ve-hem-ent | b. veh-e-ment | c. ve-he-ment |

| 8. vehicle | a. ve-hi-cle | b. veh-i-cle | c. ve-hicl-e |

Classwork

Name: _____ Date: ___/___/_____ Score: _____

Lesson 22.3

Reading and Writing

Proper and Common Nouns and Adjectives

✓ **Lesson Check Point**

Directions: Read the words in the word box. Put an (X) on the line next to each word that is written incorrectly. Remember that all proper nouns and proper adjectives are capitalized. Use a dictionary or the Internet to check your answers.

지도: 단어 상자에 있는 단어를 읽으십시오. 잘못 쓰여진 각 단어 옆의 줄에 (X)를 표시하십시오. 모든 고유 명사와 고유 형용사는 대문자임을 기억하십시오. 사전이나 인터넷을 사용하여 답을 확인하십시오.

Word Box		
__ vision	__ vienna	__ vikings
__ Las vegas	__ Vietnam	__ velvet
__ Village	__ vehicle	__ Virginia
__ Volume	__ VIP	__ Vice president

Directions: Read each unedited sentence and underline the word that is written incorrectly. Write each sentence correctly on the line.

지도: 편집되지 않은 각 문장을 읽고 잘못 쓰여진 단어에 밑줄을 긋습 니다. 각 문장을 줄에 올바르게 쓰십시오.

Model
In the fall, the leaves in <u>vermont</u> have vibrant colors.
<u>In the fall, the leaves in Vermont have vibrant colors.</u>

1. valerie is attending Valor Vocational School.
_____

2. Vince voted to go to the British virgin Islands.
_____

3. Washington's troops were victorious at valley Forge.
_____

4. This summer, I am going on Vacation to Victoria Falls.
_____

Unit V Lesson 22.3

Classwork

Name: _____ Date: ___/___/_____ Score: _____

Lesson 23.1

Reading Words with the Letter W/w

✓ Lesson Check Point

Directions: Read each target word. Find the letter "w" and put a check (✓) in the column that identifies its position: beginning, within or end.
지도: 각 대상 단어를 읽으십시오. 문자"w"를 찾아 체크 표시(✓)위치를 식별하는 열에서 시작, 내부 또는 끝.

Target Words	Beginning (First Letter)	Within	End (Last Letter)
1. bowling			
2. arrow			
3. western			
4. bookworm			
5. shadow			

Directions: Read each sentence and underline the words that begin with the letter "w." Write all the underlined words in alphabetical order on the lines below.
지도: 각 문장을 읽고"w"로 시작하는 단어에 밑줄을 긋습니다. 아래 줄에 밑줄 친 단어를 알파벳 순서로 모두 쓰십시오.

6. The wildcats have very long whiskers.

7. The tourists are walking along the waterfront.

8. The wilderness is home to wolves and eagles.

9. There are beautiful waterfalls in the West Indies.

10. My wife placed the clothes in the new washing machine.

_____   _____   _____

_____   _____   _____

_____   _____
              _____

Unit W Lesson 23.1

Learn To Read English With Directions In Korean

Classwork

 Name: _____ Date: ___/___/_____ Score: _____

Lesson 23.2

Reading Words with a Vowel before the Letter "w"

✓ Lesson Check Point

 Directions: Read each target word. Circle the word in the column that has the same "aw," "ew" or "ow" sound as the target word.
지도: 각 대상 단어를 읽으십시오. 대상 단어와 같은 "aw," "ew" 또는 "ow" 소리가 나는 열의 단어에 동그라미를 치십시오.

window	a. vowel
	b. yellow

renew	a. sew
	b. threw

drawing	a. awaiting
	b. awful

township	a. glow
	b. crown

 Directions: Read each target word. Put a check (✓) under the correct column heading.
지도: 각 대상 단어를 읽으십시오. 올바른 열 제목 아래에 체크(✓)를 하십시오.

Target Words	Underlined letters have /ōō/ sound as in the word <u>few</u>	Underlined letters have /ȯ/ sound as in the word <u>law</u>	Underlined letters have /ō/ sound as in the word <u>sew</u>	Underlined letters have /ou/ sound as in the word <u>cow</u>
1. wind<u>ow</u>				
2. ren<u>ew</u>				
3. dr<u>aw</u>ing				
4. t<u>ow</u>nship				

Learn To Read English With Directions In Korean

Classwork

Name: _____ Date: ___/___/_____ Score: _____

Lesson 23.3

Reading Words with a Silent "w" and "wr" Letter Combination

Dictionary Skills/ Vocabulary

✓ **Lesson Check Point**

Directions: Read each target word and its definition. Write the letter of the definition on the line of each target word. Use a dictionary or the Internet to check your answers.
지도: 각 대상 단어와 그 정의를 읽으십시오. 각 대상 단어의 행에 정의의 문자를 씁니다. 사전이나 인터넷을 사용하여 답을 확인하십시오.

Target Words	Definitions
1. __ wrap	a. to have destroyed something with intense force
2. __ wrestling	b. a circular decoration made with flowers or evergreens
3. __ wreath	c. the act of arguing or debating a topic
4. __ wrecked	d. to fold in a fitted covering
5. __ wrangling	e. a physical sport

Directions: Read each sentence. Underline the word in the parentheses that correctly completes each sentence. Then, write the underlined word on the line.
지도: 각 문장을 읽으십시오. 각 문장을 올바르게 완성하는 괄호 안에 있는 단어에 밑줄을 긋습니다. 그런 다음 밑줄 친 단어를 줄에 쓰십시오.

6. Wendy placed a beautiful _____ on the door. (wrestling, wreath)

7. His house was _____ by the tornado. (wrangling, wrecked)

8. The wrestler has a _____ match tonight. (wrestling, wrap)

9. The mothers will _____ their babies in warm blankets. (wrap, wreath)

10. He was _____ with his teacher over an unfair grade. (wrangling, wrap)

Classwork

Name: _____ Date: ___/___/_____ Score: _____

Lesson 23.3

Reading Words with a Silent Letter "w"

✓ **Lesson Check Point**

Directions: Read the target words in the word box. Write the words that have a silent letter "w" in the first column. Write the words that do not have a silent letter "w" in the second column.

지도: 단어 상자에 있는 대상 단어를 읽으십시오. 첫 번째 열에 묵음 문자 "w"가 있는 단어를 쓰십시오. 두 번째 열에 묵음 문자 "w"가 없는 단어를 쓰십시오.

Target Word Box				
sword	tomorrow	below	dwell	disown
winner	bandwidth	eastward	two	freewill
afterward	answer	farewell	firewall	writing
wrap	doorway	wreck	wrongly	went

Letter "w" is silent

_____
_____
_____
_____
_____
_____
_____
_____

Letter "w" has the /w/ sound

_____
_____
_____
_____
_____
_____
_____
_____

Classwork

Name: _____ Date:___/___/_____ Score:_____

The Reading Challenge

Lesson 23.4

Reading Multisyllable Words

✓ **Lesson Check Point**

Directions: Read and divide each target word into syllables. Write each word and place a hyphen (-) between the syllables in the second column. Write the number of syllables in the third column. Use a dictionary or the Internet to check your answers.

지도: 각 대상 단어를 읽고 음절로 나눕니다. 각 단어를 쓰고 두 번째 열의 음절 사이에 하이픈(-)을 넣습니다. 세 번째 열에 음절 수를 쓰십시오. 사전이나 인터넷을 사용하여 답을 확인하십시오.

Target Words	Words Divided into Syllables	Number of Syllables
1. waistband	_____	_____
2. woman	_____	_____
3. whistle	_____	_____
4. western	_____	_____
5. wondering	_____	_____
6. washing	_____	_____
7. writer	_____	_____
8. worthless	_____	_____
9. willful	_____	_____
10. waterfall	_____	_____

Classwork

 Name: _____ Date: ___/___/_____ Score: _____

The Reading Challenge

Lesson 23.4

Reading Multisyllable Words

✓ **Lesson Check Point**

 Directions: Read each target word. Circle the word in the row that is divided correctly into syllables. Use a dictionary or the Internet to check your answers.
지도: 각 대상 단어를 읽으십시오. 음절로 올바르게 나누어진 행에 있는 단어에 동그라미를 치십시오. 사전이나 인터넷을 사용하여 답을 확인하십시오.

Model

wonderful	a. wo-nder-ful	(b. won-der-ful)	c. won-derf-ul

1. waterbed	a. wa-ter-bed	b. wa-terb-ed	c. wat-er-bed

2. wandering	a. wand-er-ing	b. wand-e-ring	c. wan-der-ing

3. Wyoming	a. Wy-o-ming	b. Wy-om-ing	c. Wyo-mi-ng

4. whenever	a. whe-nev-er	b. when-ev-er	c. wh-ene-ver

5. withdrawal	a. withdr-aw-al	b. with-draw-al	c. with-dra-wal

6. watermark	a. wat-er-mark	b. wa-term-ark	c. wa-ter-mark

7. workable	a. wor-ka-ble	b. wor-kab-le	c. work-a-ble

8. weekender	a. wee-kend-er	b. week-end-er	c. week-en-der

Classwork

Name: _____ Date: ___/___/_____ Score: _____

Lesson 23.5

Reading and Writing

Proper and Common Nouns and Adjectives

✓ **Lesson Check Point**

Directions: Read the words in the word box. Put an (X) on the line next to each word that is written incorrectly. Remember that all proper nouns and proper adjectives are capitalized. Use a dictionary or the Internet to check your answers.

지도: 단어 상자에 있는 단어를 읽으십시오. 잘못 쓰여진 각 단어 옆의 줄에 (X)를 표시하십시오. 모든 고유 명사와 고유 형용사는 대문자임을 기억하십시오. 사전이나 인터넷을 사용하여 답을 확인하십시오.

Word Box		
__ wakefield, NY	__ wrappers	__ whiplash
__ Wealth	__ wisconsin	__ West Virginia
__ Washington	__ Wheelchair	__ white House
__ waterfall	__ Wake Island	__ Workforce

Directions: Read each unedited sentence and underline the word that is written incorrectly. Write each sentence correctly on the line.

지도: 편집되지 않은 각 문장을 읽고 잘못 쓰여진 단어에 밑줄을 긋습 니다. 각 문장을 줄에 올바르게 쓰십시오.

Model

We walked along the winding path that led to the <u>Waterfalls</u>.
<u>We walked along the winding path that led to the waterfalls.</u>

1. The Warden works for the Wisconsin Prison System.
_____

2. The waterfalls in the west Indies are breathtaking.
_____

3. The new Waitress is from Washington, D.C.
_____

4. The woodpeckers made their homes in wilmington.
_____

Classwork

☺ Name: _____   Date:___/___/_____   Score: _____

Lesson 24.1

Reading Words with the Letter X/x

✓ **Lesson Check Point**

Directions: Read each target word. Find the letter "x" and put a check (✓) in the column that identifies its position: beginning, within or end.
지도: 각 대상 단어를 읽으십시오. 문자"x"를 찾아 체크 표시(✓)위치를 식별하는 열에서 시작, 내부 또는 끝.

Target Words	Beginning (First Letter)	Within	End (Last Letter)
1. sixty			
2. oxen			
3. prefix			
4. x-ray			
5. wax			

Directions: Read each sentence and underline the words that begin with the letter "x." Write all the underlined words in alphabetical order on the lines below.
지도: 각 문장을 읽고 문자"x"로 시작하는 단어에 밑줄을 긋습니다. 아래 줄에 밑줄 친 단어를 알파벳 순서로 모두 쓰십시오.

6. Xaria has to go to the hospital for chest x-rays.

7. Xavier enjoys playing the xylophone at concerts.

8. Xianna used the Xerox machine to make photocopies.

9. Xander said, "Xiamen is an island of Southeast China."

10. I have worked for Xola's company for x number of years.

_____   _____   _____

_____   _____   _____

_____   _____   _____

_____

☺ Learn To Read English With Directions In Korean

Classwork

Name: _____ Date: _____ / ____ / _____ Score: _____

Lesson 24.1

Reading Words with the Letter X/x

✓ Lesson Check Point

Directions: Read each target word. Circle the word in the column that has the same "x" sound(s) as the target word.
지도: 각 대상 단어를 읽으십시오. 대상 단어와 동일한 "x" 소리가 있는 열의 단어에 동그라미를 치십시오.

expensive	a. experience
	b. noxious

complexion	a. obnoxious
	b. excellent

Xanadu	a. xylophonist
	b. x-radiation

expect	a. anxious
	b. boxing

Directions: Read each target word. Put a check (✓) under the correct column heading.
지도: 각 대상 단어를 읽으십시오. 올바른 열 제목 아래에 체크(✓)를하십시오.

Target Words	"x" has the /k/ + /s/ sounds as in the word <u>box</u>	"x" has the /z/ sound as in the word <u>xylophone</u>	"x" has the /g/ + /z/ sounds as in the word <u>exhibit</u>	"x" has the /k/ + /sh/ sounds as in the word <u>anxious</u>
1. expect				
2. complexion				
3. Xanadu				
4. expensive				

Unit X Lesson 24.1

Learn To Read English With Directions In Korean

Classwork

Name: _____ Date: ___/___/_____ Score: _____

The Reading Challenge

Lesson 24.2

Reading Multisyllable Words

✓ Lesson Check Point

Directions: Read and divide each target word into syllables. Write each word and place a hyphen (-) between the syllables in the second column. Write the number of syllables in the third column. Use a dictionary or the Internet to check your answers.

지도: 각 대상 단어를 읽고 음절로 나눕니다. 각 단어를 쓰고 두 번째 열의 음절 사이에 하이픈(-)을 넣습니다. 세 번째 열에 음절 수를 쓰십시오. 사전이나 인터넷을 사용하여 답을 확인하십시오.

Target Words	Words Divided into Syllables	Number of Syllables
1. boxer	_____	_____
2. prefix	_____	_____
3. saxophone	_____	_____
4. complexion	_____	_____
5. index	_____	_____
6. textual	_____	_____
7. sixteen	_____	_____
8. perplexing	_____	_____
9. taxicab	_____	_____
10. oxygen	_____	_____

Classwork

Name: _____ Date: ___/___/_____ Score: _____

The Reading Challenge

Lesson 24.2

Reading Multisyllable Words

✓ **Lesson Check Point**

Directions: Read each target word. Circle the word in the row that is divided correctly into syllables. Use a dictionary or the Internet to check your answers.
지도: 각 대상 단어를 읽으십시오. 음절로 올바르게 나누어진 행에 있는 단어에 동그라미를 치십시오. 사전이나 인터넷을 사용하여 답을 확인하십시오.

Model

| oxidized | a. ox-i-dized ⭕ | b. oxi-d-ized | c. o-xi-dized |

1. paradox	a. pa-rad-ox	b. par-ad-ox	c. par-a-dox
2. explorer	a. ex-plor-er	b. exp-lo-rer	c. expl-or-er
3. taxable	a. ta-xa-ble	b. tax-a-ble	c. ta-xab-le
4. existence	a. exi-ste-nce	b. ex-is-tence	c. ex-i-stence
5. hexagon	a. he-xa-gon	b. he-xag-on	c. hex-a-gon
6. exciting	a. ex-cit-ing	b. exc-i-ting	c. exc-it-ing
7. lexical	a. le-xic-al	b. le-xi-cal	c. lex-i-cal
8. expanding	a. ex-pan-ding	b. ex-pand-ing	c. exp-and-ing

Classwork

Name: _____ Date: ___/___/_____ Score: _____

Lesson 24.3

Reading and Writing

Proper and Common Nouns and Adjectives

✓ **Lesson Check Point**

Directions: Read the words in the word box. Put an (X) on the line next to each word that is written incorrectly. Remember that all proper nouns and proper adjectives are capitalized. Use a dictionary or the Internet to check your answers.

지도: 단어 상자에 있는 단어를 읽으십시오. 잘못 쓰여진 각 단어 옆의 줄에 (X)를 표시하십시오. 모든 고유 명사와 고유 형용사는 대문자임을 기억하십시오. 사전이나 인터넷을 사용하여 답을 확인하십시오.

Word Box		
__ xerox Inc.	__ xylems	__ King xerxes I
__ xanthium	__ xenon	__ Xylophone
__ xylene	__ Xiang	__ Xanthic acid
__ X-ray	__ xavier	__ xebec

Directions: Read each unedited sentence and underline the word that is written incorrectly. Write each sentence correctly on the line.

지도: 편집되지 않은 각 문장을 읽고 잘못 쓰여진 단어에 밑줄을긋습 니다. 각 문장을 줄에 올바르게 쓰십시오.

Model
Xia said, "The population of xankandi is 33,000 people."
Xia said, "The population of Xankandi is 33,000 people."

1. Xia is reading about xanthus, the ancient City of Lycia.
_____

2. Mr. and Mrs. Xem visited the Chinese province of xuzhou.
_____

3. My friend, xavier, is scheduled to have an x-ray at six o'clock.
_____

4. My dentist, Dr. Xu, applied a local anesthetic, Xylocaine, to my gums.
_____

Classwork

Name: _____ Date: ___/___/_____ Score: _____

Lesson 25.1

Reading Words with the Letter Y/y

✓ **Lesson Check Point**

Directions: Read each target word. Find the letter "y" and put a check (✓) in the column that identifies its position: beginning, within or end.
지도: 각 대상 단어를 읽으십시오. 문자"y"를 찾아 체크 표시(✓)위치를 식별하는 열에서 시작, 내부 또는 끝.

Target Words	Beginning (First Letter)	Within	End (Last Letter)
1. galaxy			
2. yellow			
3. hyperactive			
4. strawberry			
5. younger			

Directions: Read each sentence and underline the words that begin with the letter "y." Write all the underlined words in alphabetical order on the lines below.
지도: 각 대상 단어를 읽으십시오. 문자"y를 찾아 체크 표시(✓)위치를식별하는 열에서 시작, 내부 또는 끝.

6. Yesterday, I had a relaxing yoga class.

7. Yolanda and Nancy enjoyed my yodeling contest.

8. In Yorktown, I saw a pair of oxen yoked together.

9. The yellow car stopped at the triangular yield sign.

10. Mr. Young lives close to Yellowstone National Park.

_____   _____   _____
_____   _____   _____
_____   _____   _____
            _____

Name: _____ Date: ___/ ___/ _____ Score: _____

Classwork

Lesson 25.1

Reading Words with the Letter Y/y

✓ **Lesson Check Point**

 Directions: Read each target word. Circle the word in the row that has a different "y" sound than the target word.
지도: 각 대상 단어를 읽으십시오. 목표 단어와 다른"y" 소리가 나는 행의 단어에 동그라미를 치십시오.

Target Words				
1. yours	young	candy	year	yield
2. lyric	myself	gymnast	cylinders	symbols
3. Polynesia	sibyl	vinyl	younger	polymer
4. community	energy	baby	penny	pyramid
5. young	money	yours	yes	youth

 Directions: Read the words in the four boxes. Circle two words that have the same "y" sound.
지도: 네 개의 상자에 있는 단어를 읽으십시오. "y"소리가 같은 두 단어에 동그라미를 치십시오.

young	belly
reply	city

cylinder	yesterday
cycles	yahoo

very	apply
your	jelly

happy	shiny
ratify	years

penny	July
syringe	vinyl

plywood	baby
cylinder	identify

Classwork

 Name: _____ Date:___/___/_____ Score:_____

Lesson 25.2

Reading Words with a Vowel before the Letter "y"

✓ **Lesson Check Point**

 Directions: Read each target word. Circle the word in the column that has the same "y" sound as the target word.
지도: 각 대상 단어를 읽으십시오. 목표 단어와 같은 "y" 소리가 나는 열의 단어에 동그라미를 치십시오.

enjoying	a. today
	b. gargoyle

chimney	a. Monday
	b. yielding

Maya	a. they
	b. Kenya

buying	a. Guyana
	b. yield

 Directions: Read each target word. Put a check (✓) under the correct column heading.
지도: 각 대상 단어를 읽으십시오. 올바른 열 제목 아래에 체크(✓)를 하십시오.

Target Words	"y" has the /y/ sound as in the word <u>yes</u>	"oy" has the /oi/ sound as in the word <u>boy</u>	"y" has the /ī/ sound as in the word <u>by</u>	"y" is silent as in the word <u>day</u>
1. enjoying				
2. chimney				
3. Maya				
4. buying				

Classwork

 Name: _____ Date: ___/___/_____ Score: _____

Lesson 25.3

Reading Words with the "cy" Letter Combination

✓ Lesson Check Point

 Directions: Read each target word. Find the "cy" letter combination and put a check (✓) in the column to identify its position in the word: beginning, within or end.
지도: 각 대상 단어를 읽으십시오. "cy" 문자 조합을 찾고 열에 체크(✓)를 넣어 단어에서 시작, 안에 또는 끝의 위치를 식별합니다.

Target Words	Beginning (First 2 Letters)	Within	End (Last 2 Letters)
1. Nancy			
2. bicyclist			
3. cymbal			
4. regency			
5. cytoplasm			

 Directions: Read each target word. Put a check (✓) under the correct column heading.
지도: 각 대상 단어를 읽으십시오. 올바른 열 제목 아래에 체크(✓)를하십시오.

Target Words	"cy" has the /s/ + /ĭ/ sounds as in the word <u>cylinder</u>	"cy" has the /s/ + /ī/ sounds as in the word <u>cycle</u>	"cy" has the /s/ + /ē/ sounds as in the word <u>agency</u>
6. Nancy			
7. bicyclist			
8. cymbal			
9. regency			
10. cytoplasm			

Unit Y
Lesson 25.3

Learn To Read English With Directions In Korean

Classwork

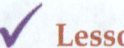 Name: _____ Date:___/___/_____ Score:_____

Lesson 25.4

Reading Words with the Final Letter "y"

✓ **Lesson Check Point**

 Directions: Read each target word. Find the letter "y" and put a check (✓) in the column that identifies its position within the word.
지도: 각 대상 단어를 읽으십시오. 문자"y"를 찾아 체크 표시(✓)단어내에서의 위치를 식별하는 열에서.

Target Words	"y" is at the end of a one syllable word	"y" is at the end of the first syllable	"y" is at the end of a multi-syllable word
1. myself			
2. community			
3. cry			
4. discovery			
5. tycoon			

 Directions: Read each target word. Put a check (✓) under the correct column heading.
지도: 각 대상 단어를 읽으십시오. 올바른 열 제목 아래에 체크(✓)를하십시오.

Target Words	"y" has the /ē/ sound as in the word <u>agency</u>	"y" has the /ī/ sound as in the word <u>flying</u>
6. myself		
7. community		
8. cry		
9. discovery		
10. tycoon		

Classwork

 Name: _____ Date: ___/ ___/ _____ Score: _____

Lesson 25.5

Reading Words with the "yr" Letter Combination

✓ Lesson Check Point

 Directions: Read each target word. Circle the word in the column that has the same "yr" sounds as the target word.
지도: 각 대상 단어를 읽으십시오. 목표 단어와 같은 "yr" 소리가 나는 열의 단어에 동그라미를 치십시오.

| myrrh | a. myrtle |
| | b. myriad |

| Cyrus | a. lyricist |
| | b. gyro |

| myriad | a. lyrical |
| | b. payroll |

| syringe | a. syringa |
| | b. Syria |

 Directions: Read each target word. Put a check (✓) under the correct column heading.
지도: 각 대상 단어를 읽으십시오. 올바른 열 제목 아래에 체크(✓)를 하십시오.

Target Words	"yr" has the /û/ + /r/ sounds as in the word myrtle	"yr" has the /ĭ/ + /r/ sounds as in the word pyramid	"yr" has the /ī/ + /r/ sounds as in the word gyro	"yr" has the /ə/ + /r/ sounds as in the word martyr
1. myrrh				
2. Cyrus				
3. myriad				
4. syringe				

Learn To Read English With Directions In Korean

Classwork

 Name: _____ Date: ___/___/_____ Score: _____

Lesson 25.6

Reading Letter "y" Words with the Schwa Vowel Sound

✓ Lesson Check Point

 Directions: Read each target word. Circle the word in the column that has the same "y" sound as the target word.
지도: 각 대상 단어를 읽으십시오. 대상 단어와 "y" 소리가 같은 열의 단어에 동그라미를 치십시오.

| Polynesian | a. polyvinyl |
| | b. pyramid |

| sibyl | a. mandatory |
| | b. vinyl |

| nicely | a. vacancy |
| | b. polymerize |

| Pennsylvania | a. polymer |
| | b. younger |

 Directions: Read each target word. Put a check (✓) under the correct column heading.
지도: 각 대상 단어를 읽으십시오. 올바른 열 제목 아래에 체크(✓)를 하십시오.

Target Words	"y" has the /ə/ sound as in the word syringe	"y" does not have the /ə/ sound
1. Polynesian		
2. sibyl		
3. nicely		
4. Pennsylvania		

Classwork

Name: _____ Date: ___/___/_____ Score: _____

Lesson 25.7

Reading Words with a Silent Letter "y"

✓ **Lesson Check Point**

 Directions: Read the target words in the word box. Write the words that have a silent letter "y" in the first column. Write the words that do not have a silent letter "y" in the second column.

지도: 단어 상자에 있는 대상 단어를 읽으십시오. 첫 번째 열에 묵음문자 "y"가 있는 단어를 쓰십시오. 두 번째 열에 묵음 문자"y"가 없는 단어를 쓰십시오.

Target Word Box				
prey	mayor	yes	payday	playing
yeast	jeopardy	donkey	midday	yellow
abundantly	yogurt	friendly	safely	always
layer	chewy	youth	prayer	today

Letter "y" is silent

Letter "y" has the /y/ or /ē/ sound

Learn To Read English With Directions In Korean   241   Copyrighted Material

Classwork

Name: _____ Date: ___/___/_____ Score: _____

The Reading Challenge

Lesson 25.8

Reading Multisyllable Words

✓ **Lesson Check Point**

Directions: Read and divide each target word into syllables. Write each word and place a hyphen (-) between the syllables in the second column. Write the number of syllables in the third column. Use a dictionary or the Internet to check your answers.

지도: 각 대상 단어를 읽고 음절로 나눕니다. 각 단어를 쓰고 두 번째 열의 음절 사이에 하이픈(-)을 넣습니다. 세 번째 열에 음절 수를 쓰십시오. 사전이나 인터넷을 사용하여 답을 확인하십시오.

Target Words	Words Divided into Syllables	Number of Syllables
1. yourself	_____	_____
2. Yemenite	_____	_____
3. Yorktown	_____	_____
4. yoga	_____	_____
5. yonder	_____	_____
6. Yankee	_____	_____
7. yardstick	_____	_____
8. yearly	_____	_____
9. yodeling	_____	_____
10. youthfulness	_____	_____

Unit Y Lesson 25.8

Classwork

 Name: _____ Date: ____/____/____ Score: _____

The Reading Challenge

Lesson 25.8

Reading Multisyllable Words

✓ **Lesson Check Point**

 Directions: Read each target word. Circle the word in the row that is divided correctly into syllables. Use a dictionary or the Internet to check your answers.
지도: 각 대상 단어를 읽으십시오. 음절로 올바르게 나누어진 행에 있는 단어에 동그라미를 치십시오. 사전이나 인터넷을 사용하여 답을 확인하십시오.

Model

| yesterday | a. ye-ster-day | b. yest-er-day | c. yes-ter-day ⭕ |

| 1. Yucatán | a. Yuc-a-tán | b. Yu-ca-tán | c. Yu-cat-án |

| 2. yarmulke | a. yar-mul-ke | b. yar-mulk-e | c. yarm-u-lke |

| 3. yodeling | a. yod-e-ling | b. yo-de-ling | c. yo-del-ing |

| 4. youthful | a. youthf-ul | b. youth-ful | c. you-thful |

| 5. Yoruba | a. Yo-ru-ba | b. Yor-u-ba | c. Yo-rub-a |

| 6. Yankee | a. Yank-ee | b. Ya-nk-ee | c. Yan-kee |

| 7. yielding | a. yield-ing | b. yiel-di-ng | c. yieldi-ng |

| 8. younger | a. you-nger | b. youn-ger | c. young-er |

Classwork

Name: _____ Date: ____/___/_____ Score: _____

Lesson 25.9

Reading and Writing

Proper and Common Nouns and Adjectives

✓ **Lesson Check Point**

Directions: Read the words in the word box. Put an (X) on the line next to each word that is written incorrectly. Remember that all proper nouns and proper adjectives are capitalized. Use a dictionary or the Internet to check your answers.

지도: 단어 상자에 있는 단어를 읽으십시오. 잘못 쓰여진 각 단어 옆의 줄에 (X)를 표시하십시오. 모든 고유 명사와 고유 형용사는 대문자임을 기억하십시오. 사전이나 인터넷을 사용하여 답을 확인하십시오.

Word Box					
__	Yemen	__	yokosuka	__	yachting
__	yellow	__	Yankees	__	Yogurt
__	Young	__	yardage	__	yesterday
__	yoruba	__	Yourself	__	yorktown

Directions: Read each unedited sentence and underline the word that is written incorrectly. Write each sentence correctly on the line.

지도: 편집되지 않은 각 문장을 읽고 잘못 쓰여진 단어에 밑줄을 긋습 니다. 각 문장을 줄에 올바르게 쓰십시오.

Model
Is the New York <u>yankees</u> your favorite baseball team?
<u>Is the New York Yankees your favorite baseball team?</u>

1. Yolanda's friend loves to eat yoplait yogurt.
_____

2. All the signs in yorktown are painted yellow.
_____

3. Last year, the young family visited Yosemite National Park.
_____

4. yesterday, Yusef plotted the y-axis and the x-axis on graph paper.
_____

Learn To Read English With Directions In Korean

Classwork

L Name: _____ Date: ___/___/_____ Score: _____

Lesson 26.1

Reading Words with the Letter Z/z

✓ Lesson Check Point

Directions: Read each target word. Find the letter "z" and put a check (✓) in the column that identifies its position: beginning, within or end.
지도: 각 대상 단어를 읽으십시오. 문자"z"를 찾아 체크 표시(✓)위치를 식별하는 열에서 시작, 내부 또는 끝.

Target Words	Beginning (First Letter)	Within	End (Last Letter)
1. blizzard			
2. topaz			
3. Tanzania			
4. zebra			
5. zookeeper			

Directions: Read each sentence and underline the words that begin with the letter "z." Write all the underlined words in alphabetical order on the lines below.
지도: 각 문장을 읽고"z"로 시작하는 단어에 밑줄을 긋습니다. 아래 줄에 밑줄 친 단어를 알파벳 순서로 모두 쓰십시오.

6. Samira zipped up her zebra costume.

7. Danny wants to work at the zoo as a trained zoologist.

8. The two zoom lenses on Zianna's camera are very expensive.

9. In New Zealand, Abdulla wore his shirt with a zigzag design.

10. Valeria is studying the rich cultures of Zambia and Zimbabwe.

_____ _____ _____

_____ _____ _____

_____ _____ _____

_____

L Learn To Read English With Directions In Korean

Classwork

 Name: _____ Date: ___/___/_____ Score: _____

Lesson 26.1

Reading Words with the Letter Z/z

✓ Lesson Check Point

 Directions: Read each target word. Circle the word in the column that has the same "z" sound as the target word.
지도: 각 대상 단어를 읽으십시오. 대상 단어와 "z" 소리가 같은 열의 단어에 동그라미를 치십시오.

crazy	a. matzo
	b. lizard

normalize	a. quartz
	b. dozen

Lutz	a. bar mitzvah
	b. emphasize

verbalize	a. squeezes
	b. quartzite

 Directions: Read each target word. Put a check (✓) under the correct column heading.
지도: 각 대상 단어를 읽으십시오. 올바른 열 제목 아래에 체크(✓)를 하십시오.

Target Words	"z" has the /z/ sound as in the word <u>zipper</u>	"z" has the /s/ sound as in the word <u>quartz</u>
1. crazy		
2. normalize		
3. Lutz		
4. verbalize		

Classwork

Name: _____ Date: ___/___/_____ Score: _____

Lesson 26.2

Reading Words with a Silent Letter "z"

Directions: Read the target words in the word box. Write the words that have a silent letter "z" in the first column. Write the words that do not have a silent letter "z" in the second column.

지도: 단어 상자에 있는 대상 단어를 읽으십시오. 첫 번째 열에 묵음 문자 "z"가 있는 단어를 쓰십시오. 두 번째 열에 묵음 문자"z"가 없는 단어를 쓰십시오.

Target Word Box				
fizzle	sizzler	Brazil	analyze	capitalize
agonize	dozen	dizziness	amazing	gizzard
cadenza	blazing	puzzling	economize	blizzard
sizzles	fuzz	centralize	drizzling	puzzle

Letter "z" is silent

_____
_____
_____
_____
_____
_____
_____
_____
_____

Letter "z" has the /z/ or /s/ sound

_____
_____
_____
_____
_____
_____
_____
_____
_____

Classwork

Name: _____ Date:___/___/_____ Score:_____

The Reading Challenge

Lesson 26.3

Reading Multisyllable Words

✓ **Lesson Check Point**

Directions: Read and divide each target word into syllables. Write each word and place a hyphen (-) between the syllables in the second column. Write the number of syllables in the third column. Use a dictionary or the Internet to check your answers.

지도: 각 대상 단어를 읽고 음절로 나눕니다. 각 단어를 쓰고 두 번째 열의 음절 사이에 하이픈(-)을 넣습니다. 세 번째 열에 음절 수를 쓰십시오. 사전이나 인터넷을 사용하여 답을 확인하십시오.

Target Words	Words Divided into Syllables	Number of Syllables
1. Zaire	_____	_____
2. zealot	_____	_____
3. zodiac	_____	_____
4. zigzag	_____	_____
5. Zulu	_____	_____
6. zeniths	_____	_____
7. zany	_____	_____
8. zinger	_____	_____
9. zestfulness	_____	_____
10. Zambia	_____	_____

Classwork

 Name: _____ Date:___/___/_____ Score: _____

The Reading Challenge

Lesson 26.3

Reading Multisyllable Words

✓ Lesson Check Point

 Directions: Read each target word. Circle the word in the row that is divided correctly into syllables. Use a dictionary or the Internet to check your answers.
지도: 각 대상 단어를 읽으십시오. 음절로 올바르게 나누어진 행에 있는 단어에 동그라미를 치십시오. 사전이나 인터넷을 사용하여 답을 확인하십시오.

Model

zoology	a. zo-ol-o-gy (circled)	b. zoo-lo-gy	c. zool-o-gy

1. Zealand	a. Zea-land	b. Zeal-an-d	c. Zeal-and
2. Zimbabwe	a. Zimb-ab-we	b. Zim-bab-we	c. Zim-ba-bwe
3. zodiac	a. zo-di-a-c	b. zod-ia-c	c. zo-di-ac
4. zoologist	a. zo-ol-o-gist	b. zoo-log-ist	c. zoo-lo-gist
5. zeroing	a. ze-roi-ng	b. zer-o-ing	c. ze-ro-ing
6. zonal	a. zo-nal	b. zon-al	c. zo-n-al
7. Zambia	a. Za-mbi-a	b. Zam-bi-a	c. Zamb-i-a
8. zestful	a. ze-stf-ul	b. ze-stful	c. zest-ful

Learn To Read English With Directions In Korean   249   Copyrighted Material

Classwork

Name: _____ Date: ___/___/_____ Score: _____

Lesson 26.4

Reading and Writing

Proper and Common Nouns and Adjectives

✓ Lesson Check Point

Directions: Read the words in the word box. Put an (X) on the line next to each word that is written incorrectly. Remember that all proper nouns and proper adjectives are capitalized. Use a dictionary or the Internet to check your answers.

지도: 단어 상자에 있는 단어를 읽으십시오. 잘못 쓰여진 각 단어 옆의 줄에 (X)를 표시하십시오. 모든 고유 명사와 고유 형용사는 대문자임을 기억하십시오. 사전이나 인터넷을 사용하여 답을 확인하십시오.

Word Box		
__ Zillion	__ zippers	__ Zealand
__ Zambia	__ Zookeeper	__ Zululand
__ zurich	__ zealous	__ Zoom lens
__ Zeus	__ zanzibar	__ Zoology

Directions: Read each unedited sentence and underline the word that is written incorrectly. Write each sentence correctly on the line.

지도: 편집되지 않은 각 문장을 읽고 잘못 쓰여진 단어에 밑줄을 긋습 니다. 각 문장을 줄에 올바르게 쓰십시오.

Model
The steep path zigzags through the zagros Mountains.
The steep path zigzags through the Zagros Mountains.

1. Zoey lives in the Eastern Time zone.
_____

2. At noon, the Zebras at the Bronx Zoo were sleeping.
_____

3. My school, Zesty Academy, has Zero tolerance for bullying.
_____

4. Mr. Zinger's new movie is a Zillion times better than his first one.
_____

Classwork

 Name: _____ Date:___/___/_____ Score:_____

Appendix 1.0

Introduction of the Letter A/a

✓ **Lesson Check Point**

 Directions: Circle the correct letter "a" pair: uppercase and lowercase letters.
지도: 올바른 문자"a" 쌍에 동그라미를 치십시오: 대문자와 소문자.

Ao   Aa   aE   Au   iA

 Directions: The uppercase letter "A" is in the first column. Look at the four letters in the row and circle the lowercase letter that matches the uppercase letter "A."
지도: 대문자"A"는 첫 번째 열에 있습니다. 행의 네 글자를 보고 대문자 "A"와 일치하는 소문자에 동그라미를 치십시오.

A	o	e	u	a
A	a	c	z	x
A	e	w	a	c
A	o	a	c	u

 Directions: The lowercase letter "a" is in the first column. Look at the four letters in the row and circle the uppercase letter that matches the lowercase letter "a."
지도: 소문자"a"는 첫 번째 열에 있습니다. 행의 네 글자를 보고 소문자 "a"와 일치하는 대문자에 동그라미를 치세요.

a	Z	A	V	W
a	V	C	A	Z
a	D	O	W	A
a	A	H	V	Q

Learn To Read English With Directions In Korean

Classwork

 Name: _____ Date: ___/___/___ Score: _____

Appendix 2.0

Introduction of the Letter B/b

✓ **Lesson Check Point**

 Directions: Circle the correct letter "b" pair: uppercase and lowercase letters.
지도: 올바른 문자"b" 쌍에 동그라미를 치십시오: 대문자와 소문자.

    Bd   Bb   bF   Db   Bk

 Directions: The uppercase letter "B" is in the first column. Look at the four letters in the row and circle the lowercase letter that matches the uppercase letter "B."
지도: 대문자"B"는 첫 번째 열에 있습니다. 행의 네 글자를 보고 대문자 "B"와 일치하는 소문자에 동그라미를 치십시오.

B	b	f	q	d
B	g	b	d	h
B	f	p	d	b
B	h	b	p	k

 Directions: The lowercase letter "b" is in the first column. Look at the four letters in the row and circle the uppercase letter that matches the lowercase letter "b."
지도: 소문자"b"는 첫 번째 열에 있습니다. 행의 네 글자를 보고 소문자 "b"와 일치하는 대문자에 동그라미를 치세요.

b	F	D	B	G
b	Q	P	D	B
b	P	B	F	M
b	H	R	Q	B

Classwork

 Name: _____ Date: ___/___/_____ Score: _____

Appendix 2.0

Letter Recognition B/b

Uppercase and Lowercase Letter

✓ Lesson Check Point

 Directions: Read each target word. Read the words in the row and circle the word that begins with a different letter.
지도: 각 대상 단어를 읽으십시오. 행에 있는 단어를 읽고 다른 문자로시작하는 단어에 동그라미를 치십시오.

Target Words				
1. boy	bin	bean	fat	buns
2. buzz	balloon	house	bandit	blood
3. both	bandage	brick	queen	bang
4. bubbles	drip	bank	bag	break
5. because	puppet	ballot	baggage	black

 Directions: Read the words in the four boxes. Circle two words that start with the uppercase and lowercase letter "b."
지도: 네 개의 상자에 있는 단어를 읽으십시오. 대문자와 소문자"b"로 시작하는 두 단어에 동그라미를 치십시오.

bin	win
tin	Bin

Bit	sit
Hit	bit

Bake	Make
bake	dare

bat	Bat
hat	Sat

Float	oat
Boat	boat

Wet	Best
date	best

Learn To Read English With Directions In Korean   Copyrighted Material

Classwork

 Name: _____ Date: ___/___/_____ Score: _____

Appendix 3.0

Introduction of the Letter C/c

✓ **Lesson Check Point**

 Directions: Circle the correct letter "c" pair: uppercase and lowercase letters.
지도: 올바른 문자 "c" 쌍에 동그라미를 치십시오: 대문자와 소문자.

      Cc   Kc   Co   Oc   cS

 Directions: The uppercase letter "C" is in the first column. Look at the four letters in the row and circle the lowercase letter that matches the uppercase letter "C."
지도: 대문자 "C"는 첫 번째 열에 있습니다. 행의 네 글자를 보고 대문자 "C"와 일치하는 소문자에 동그라미를 치십시오.

C	o	c	u	g
C	v	a	r	c
C	c	g	d	o
C	q	c	p	k

 Directions: The lowercase letter "c" is in the first column. Look at the four letters in the row and circle the uppercase letter that matches the lowercase letter "c."
지도: 소문자 "c"는 첫 번째 열에 있습니다. 행의 네 글자를 보고 소문자 "c"와 일치하는 대문자에 동그라미를 치세요.

c	Q	O	C	G
c	C	T	Q	M
c	D	B	H	C
c	C	K	J	D

Classwork

 Name: _____ Date:___/___/_____ Score:_____

Appendix 3.0

Letter Recognition C/c

Uppercase and Lowercase Letter

✓ Lesson Check Point

 Directions: Read each target word. Read the words in the row and circle the word that begins with a different letter.
지도: 각 대상 단어를 읽으십시오. 행에 있는 단어를 읽고 다른 문자로시작하는 단어에 동그라미를 치십시오.

Target Words				
1. clip	cool	came	poll	color
2. cart	caramel	open	capture	clump
3. cent	cell	queen	choice	chap
4. curtain	chat	center	goat	city
5. church	chocolate	engage	chair	civic

 Directions: Read the words in the four boxes. Circle two words that start with the uppercase and lowercase letter "c."
지도: 네 개의 상자에 있는 단어를 읽으십시오. 대문자와 소문자"c"로 시작하는 두 단어에 동그라미를 치십시오.

book	Camel
Brook	clue

comb	Octopus
Cook	Kite

Cake	keep
Goat	capital

Cat	Queen
cow	open

Grow	cute
Cab	float

come	home
Tom	Candy

Learn To Read English With Directions In Korean

Classwork

 Name: _____ Date: ___/___/_____ Score: _____

Appendix 4.0

Introduction of the Letter D/d

✓ **Lesson Check Point**

Directions: Circle the correct letter "d" pair: uppercase and lowercase letters.
지도: 올바른 문자"d" 쌍에 동그라미를 치십시오: 대문자와 소문자.

      Db   Df   Dd   Bd   Op

Directions: The uppercase letter "D" is in the first column. Look at the four letters in the row and circle the lowercase letter that matches the uppercase letter "D."
지도: 대문자"D"는 첫 번째 열에 있습니다. 행의 네 글자를 보고 대문자 "D"와 일치하는 소문자에 동그라미를 치십시오.

D	p	d	t	b
D	h	y	d	t
D	l	t	b	d
D	t	d	k	f

Directions: The lowercase letter "d" is in the first column. Look at the four letters in the row and circle the uppercase letter that matches the lowercase letter "d."
지도: 소문자"d"는 첫 번째 열에 있습니다. 행의 네 글자를 보고 소문자 "d"와 일치하는 대문자에 동그라미를 치세요.

d	B	Q	D	F
d	K	D	P	B
d	B	T	D	K
d	D	F	B	P

Classwork

 Name: _____ Date: ___/___/_____ Score: _____

Appendix 4.0

Letter Recognition D/d

Uppercase and Lowercase Letter

✓ Lesson Check Point

 Directions: Read each target word. Read the words in the row and circle the word that begins with a different letter.
지도: 각 대상 단어를 읽으십시오. 행에 있는 단어를 읽고 다른 문자로시작하는 단어에 동그라미를 치십시오.

Target Words				
1. dad	day	box	drive	duck
2. deep	pull	drum	dove	dull
3. dwell	doll	dawn	dock	peace
4. dryer	do	dense	queen	dash
5. drink	both	den	down	deer

 Directions: Read the words in the four boxes. Circle two words that start with the uppercase and lowercase letter "d."
지도: 네 개의 상자에 있는 단어를 읽으십시오. 대문자와 소문자 "d"로 시작하는 두 단어에 동그라미를 치십시오.

date	late
open	Draw

Ditch	Queen
dock	boat

Bell	Quite
Deal	doll

Quick	dream
quack	Dawn

Back	dome
belt	Drip

Race	drive
Dog	Quill

Learn To Read English With Directions In Korean   257   Copyrighted Material

Classwork

 Name: _____ Date: ___/___/_____ Score: _____

Appendix 5.0

Introduction of the Letter E/e

✓ **Lesson Check Point**

 Directions: Circle the correct letter "e" pair: uppercase and lowercase letters.
지도: 올바른 문자"e" 쌍에 동그라미를 치십시오: 대문자와 소문자.

    eF   Ex   fE   eE   Ae

 Directions: The uppercase letter "E" is in the first column. Look at the four letters in the row and circle the lowercase letter that matches the uppercase letter "E."
지도: 대문자"E"는 첫 번째 열에 있습니다. 행의 네 글자를 보고 대문자 "E"와 일치하는 소문자에 동그라미를 치십시오.

E	r	e	f	a
E	c	a	w	e
E	e	c	x	r
E	z	s	e	a

 Directions: The lowercase letter "e" is in the first column. Look at the four letters in the row and circle the uppercase letter that matches the lowercase letter "e."
지도: 소문자"e"는 첫 번째 열에 있습니다. 행의 네 글자를 보고 소문자 "e"와 일치하는 대문자에 동그라미를 치세요.

e	D	E	R	F
e	G	H	T	E
e	E	F	V	D
e	F	E	S	X

Classwork

 Name: _____ Date:___/___/_____ Score:_____

Appendix 6.0

Introduction of the Letter F/f

✓ **Lesson Check Point**

 Directions: Circle the correct letter "f" pair: uppercase and lowercase letters.
지도: 올바른 문자"f" 쌍에 동그라미를 치십시오: 대문자와 소문자.

    fE   Fh   fF   Ef   Tf

 Directions: The uppercase letter "F" is in the first column. Look at the four letters in the row and circle the lowercase letter that matches the uppercase letter "F."
지도: 대문자"F"는 첫 번째 열에 있습니다. 행의 네 글자를 보고 대문자 "F"와 일치하는 소문자에 동그라미를 치십시오.

F	l	t	k	f
F	j	l	f	m
F	t	f	b	h
F	f	l	t	h

 Directions: The lowercase letter "f" is in the first column. Look at the four letters in the row and circle the uppercase letter that matches the lowercase letter "f."
지도: 소문자"f"는 첫 번째 열에 있습니다. 행의 네 글자를 보고 소문자 "f"와 일치하는 대문자에 동그라미를 치세요.

f	F	E	K	H
f	L	F	J	E
f	E	K	H	F
f	H	F	D	B

Classwork

Name: _____ Date: ___/___/_____ Score: _____

Appendix 6.0

Letter Recognition F/f

Uppercase and Lowercase Letter

✓ **Lesson Check Point**

Directions: Read each target word. Read the words in the row and circle the word that begins with a different letter.

지도: 각 대상 단어를 읽으십시오. 행에 있는 단어를 읽고 다른 문자로시작하는 단어에 동그라미를 치십시오.

Target Words				
1. face	force	fault	house	form
2. fire	pizza	fizz	friend	flow
3. fork	frisk	quiet	fourth	fall
4. flirt	love	from	fast	fur
5. full	fright	flash	firm	boys

Directions: Read the words in the four boxes. Circle two words that start with the uppercase and lowercase letter "f."

지도: 네 개의 상자에 있는 단어를 읽으십시오. 대문자와 소문자"f"로 시작하는 두 단어에 동그라미를 치십시오.

Field	flake
Years	take

both	Fig
fond	Hours

fame	teach
Fist	Laugh

book	Drip
fight	Few

Flank	tea
Pup	fair

happens	fee
Dreams	Float

Learn To Read English With Directions In Korean

Classwork

 Name: _____ Date: ___/___/_____ Score: _____

Appendix 7.0

Introduction of the Letter G/g

✓ **Lesson Check Point**

 Directions: Circle the correct letter "g" pair: uppercase and lowercase letters.
지도: 올바른 문자"g" 쌍에 동그라미를 치십시오: 대문자와 소문자.

    yG   Gj   gJ   Gg   gO

 Directions: The uppercase letter "G" is in the first column. Look at the four letters in the row and circle the lowercase letter that matches the uppercase letter "G."
지도: 대문자"G"는 첫 번째 열에 있습니다. 행의 네 글자를 보고 대문자 "G"와 일치하는 소문자에 동그라미를 치십시오.

G	p	q	y	g
G	j	y	g	p
G	g	j	y	q
G	j	g	q	y

 Directions: The lowercase letter "g" is in the first column. Look at the four letters in the row and circle the uppercase letter that matches the lowercase letter "g."
지도: 소문자"g"는 첫 번째 열에 있습니다. 행의 네 글자를 보고 소문자 "g"와 일치하는 대문자에 동그라미를 치세요.

g	Q	O	J	G
g	U	G	O	J
g	Q	K	C	G
g	G	Q	P	O

Learn To Read English With Directions In Korean

Classwork

 Name: _____ Date: ___/___/_____ Score: _____

Appendix 7.0

Letter Recognition G/g

Uppercase and Lowercase Letter

✓ **Lesson Check Point**

 Directions: Read each target word. Read the words in the row and circle the word that begins with a different letter.

지도: 각 대상 단어를 읽으십시오. 행에 있는 단어를 읽고 다른 문자로 시작하는 단어에 동그라미를 치십시오.

Target Words				
1. gel	guest	garb	jeep	gown
2. grant	pet	goal	guard	gulp
3. game	grief	grant	queen	go
4. goat	glove	ball	glaze	grown
5. gold	jump	glide	gray	ghost

 Directions: Read the words in the four boxes. Circle two words that start with the uppercase and lowercase letter "g."

지도: 네 개의 상자에 있는 단어를 읽으십시오. 대문자와 소문자 "g"로 시작하는 두 단어에 동그라미를 치십시오.

gold	open		ground	Down		Once	June
Queen	Greece		Gulf	jump		Graph	game

Ooze	Gone		year	Grub		Glee	gram
greed	jeep		Dock	glare		joke	Day

Classwork

 Name: _____ Date:___/___/_____ Score:_____

Appendix 8.0

Introduction of the Letter H/h

✓ **Lesson Check Point**

 Directions: Circle the correct letter "h" pair: uppercase and lowercase letters.
지도: 올바른 문자"h" 쌍에 동그라미를 치십시오: 대문자와 소문자.

    Hf   hH   Ht   hB   Hb

 Directions: The uppercase letter "H" is in the first column. Look at the four letters in the row and circle the lowercase letter that matches the uppercase letter "H."
지도: 대문자"H"는 첫 번째 열에 있습니다. 행의 네 글자를 보고 대문자 "H"와 일치하는 소문자에 동그라미를 치십시오.

H	h	f	t	b
H	m	h	f	t
H	l	k	h	f
H	b	t	d	h

 Directions: The lowercase letter "h" is in the first column. Look at the four letters in the row and circle the uppercase letter that matches the lowercase letter "h."
지도: 소문자"h"는 첫 번째 열에 있습니다. 행의 네 글자를 보고 소문자 "h"와 일치하는 대문자에 동그라미를 치세요.

h	T	F	U	H
h	H	J	F	M
h	E	M	C	H
h	D	H	B	T

Classwork

 Name: _____ Date: ___/___/_____ Score: _____

Appendix 8.0

Letter Recognition H/h

Uppercase and Lowercase Letter

✓ Lesson Check Point

 Directions: Read each target word. Read the words in the row and circle the word that begins with a different letter.
지도: 각 대상 단어를 읽으십시오. 행에 있는 단어를 읽고 다른 문자로시작하는 단어에 동그라미를 치십시오.

Target Words				
1. home	hat	land	heart	hill
2. head	horse	heat	hulk	boat
3. hatch	heel	down	harm	here
4. heir	hold	high	host	love
5. hint	half	hitch	team	hemp

 Directions: Read the words in the four boxes. Circle two words that start with the uppercase and lowercase letter "h."
지도: 네 개의 상자에 있는 단어를 읽으십시오. 대문자와 소문자 "h"로 시작하는 두 단어에 동그라미를 치십시오.

tune	love		Hole	bless		flame	Hint
help	Hold		pole	hiss		blink	hence

hook	Heel		Hit	kind		dress	hope
trees	peel		hood	look		Here	from

Learn To Read English With Directions In Korean

Classwork

 Name: _____ Date:___/___/_____ Score:_____

Appendix 9.0

Introduction of the Letter I/i

✓ **Lesson Check Point**

 Directions: Circle the correct letter "i" pair: uppercase and lowercase letters.
지도: 올바른 문자"i" 쌍에 동그라미를 치십시오: 대문자와 소문자.

    Ji   Ti   Ii   jI   Il

 Directions: The uppercase letter "I" is in the first column. Look at the four letters in the row and circle the lowercase letter that matches the uppercase letter "I."
지도: 대문자"I"는 첫 번째 열에 있습니다. 행의 네 글자를 보고 대문자 "I"와 일치하는 소문자에 동그라미를 치십시오.

I	j	i	t	u
I	q	g	j	i
I	i	t	g	l
I	l	t	i	h

 Directions: The lowercase letter "i" is in the first column. Look at the four letters in the row and circle the uppercase letter that matches the lowercase letter "i."
지도: 소문자"i"는 첫 번째 열에 있습니다. 행의 네 글자를 보고 소문자 "i"와 일치하는 대문자에 동그라미를 치세요.

i	I	T	J	L
i	K	G	H	I
i	Y	L	I	T
i	J	I	Y	K

Classwork

 Name: _____ Date: ___/___/_____ Score: _____

Appendix 10.0

Introduction of the Letter J/j

✓ **Lesson Check Point**

 Directions: Circle the correct letter "j" pair: uppercase and lowercase letters.
지도: 올바른 문자"j" 쌍에 동그라미를 치십시오: 대문자와 소문자.

    Gj   Ji   jJ   Jl   Pj

 Directions: The uppercase letter "J" is in the first column. Look at the four letters in the row and circle the lowercase letter that matches the uppercase letter "J."
지도: 대문자"J"는 첫 번째 열에 있습니다. 행의 네 글자를 보고 대문자 "J"와 일치하는 소문자에 동그라미를 치십시오.

J	p	j	n	q
J	j	q	y	k
J	b	c	j	v
J	y	h	c	j

 Directions: The lowercase letter "j" is in the first column. Look at the four letters in the row and circle the uppercase letter that matches the lowercase letter "j."
지도: 소문자"j"는 첫 번째 열에 있습니다. 행의 네 글자를 보고 소문자 "j"와 일치하는 대문자에 동그라미를 치세요.

j	B	Q	J	G
j	G	V	F	J
j	J	U	C	O
j	Q	H	J	T

Classwork

 Name: _____ Date:___/___/_____ Score:_____

Appendix 10.0

Letter Recognition J/j

Uppercase and Lowercase Letter

✓ **Lesson Check Point**

 Directions: Read each target word. Read the words in the row and circle the word that begins with a different letter.
지도: 각 대상 단어를 읽으십시오. 행에 있는 단어를 읽고 다른 문자로 시작하는 단어에 동그라미를 치십시오.

Target Words				
1. jaw	just	house	Jim	jumbo
2. jolt	bunny	jelly	juice	joy
3. junk	job	jam	yearly	jump
4. jet	giggles	joke	June	joint
5. just	jigsaw	puppy	journal	Jack

 Directions: Read the words in the four boxes. Circle two words that start with the uppercase and lowercase letter "j."
지도: 네 개의 상자에 있는 단어를 읽으십시오. 대문자와 소문자"j"로 시작하는 두 단어에 동그라미를 치십시오.

quest	journey
yarn	Join

Jacket	boat
gold	just

pie	you
juicy	Jelly

Jumbo	jail
good	yes

junk	great
Job	queen

youth	Jungle
jealous	guest

Classwork

 Name: _____ Date: ___/___/_____ Score: _____

Appendix 11.0

Introduction of the Letter K/k

✓ **Lesson Check Point**

 Directions: Circle the correct letter "k" pair: uppercase and lowercase letters.
지도: 올바른 문자"k" 쌍에 동그라미를 치십시오: 대문자와 소문자.

    Bk   Kk   kL   Mk   Kl

 Directions: The uppercase letter "K" is in the first column. Look at the four letters in the row and circle the lowercase letter that matches the uppercase letter "K."
지도: 지도: 대문자"K"는 첫 번째 열에 있습니다. 행의 네 글자를보고대문자 "K"와 일치하는 소문자에 동그라미를 치십시오.

K	p	h	k	q
K	k	f	b	l
K	f	b	d	k
K	h	k	p	l

 Directions: The lowercase letter "k" is in the first column. Look at the four letters in the row and circle the uppercase letter that matches the lowercase letter "k."
지도: 소문자"k"는 첫 번째 열에 있습니다. 행의 네 글자를 보고소문자 "k"와 일치하는 대문자에 동그라미를 치세요.

k	B	K	N	L
k	K	P	L	B
k	B	X	K	C
k	P	G	L	K

Classwork

 Name: _____ Date: ___/___/_____ Score: _____

Appendix 11.0

Letter Recognition K/k

Uppercase and Lowercase Letter

✓ **Lesson Check Point**

 Directions: Read each target word. Read the words in the row and circle the word that begins with a different letter.
지도: 각 대상 단어를 읽으십시오. 행에 있는 단어를 읽고 다른 문자로시작하는 단어에 동그라미를 치십시오.

Target Words				
1. keep	kale	kedge	heal	knoll
2. kick	laugh	knot	kid	ketch
3. knight	karts	home	kept	kick
4. know	kill	bald	kind	keel
5. keys	down	knock	keg	knob

 Directions: Read the words in the four boxes. Circle two words that start with the uppercase and lowercase letter "k."
지도: 네 개의 상자에 있는 단어를 읽으십시오. 대문자와 소문자"k"로 시작하는 두 단어에 동그라미를 치십시오.

light	house
Kale	keep

From	Keen
Right	kick

key	blue
low	Kept

Knock	Bold
kid	laugh

Rose	kind
Knit	bay

know	Karts
West	team

Learn To Read English With Directions In Korean

Classwork

 Name: _____ Date: ___/___/_____ Score: _____

Appendix 12.0

Introduction of the Letter L/l

✓ Lesson Check Point

 Directions: Circle the correct letter "l" pair: uppercase and lowercase letters.
지도: 올바른 문자"l" 쌍에 동그라미를 치십시오: 대문자와 소문자.

    Lb   Kl   lL   Lh   lJ

 Directions: The uppercase letter "L" is in the first column. Look at the four letters in the row and circle the lowercase letter that matches the uppercase letter "L."
지도: 대문자"L"는 첫 번째 열에 있습니다. 행의 네 글자를 보고대문자 "L"와 일치하는 소문자에 동그라미를 치십시오.

L	h	l	f	b
L	l	k	y	p
L	f	b	l	d
L	h	b	k	l

 Directions: The lowercase letter "l" is in the first column. Look at the four letters in the row and circle the uppercase letter that matches the lowercase letter "l."
지도: 소문자"l"는 첫 번째 열에 있습니다. 행의 네 글자를 보고소문자 "l"와 일치하는 대문자에 동그라미를 치세요.

l	B	K	L	D
l	H	F	K	L
l	L	H	C	P
l	D	L	V	H

Classwork

 Name: _____ Date:___/___/_____ Score:_____

Appendix 12.0

Letter Recognition L/l

Uppercase and Lowercase Letter

✓ Lesson Check Point

 Directions: Read each target word. Read the words in the row and circle the word that begins with a different letter.
지도: 각 대상 단어를 읽으십시오. 행에 있는 단어를 읽고 다른 문자로시작하는 단어에 동그라미를 치십시오.

Target Words				
1. love	lace	home	low	lent
2. load	tree	laugh	lid	loaf
3. last	lip	lease	lapse	mail
4. learn	hope	lark	least	lungs
5. large	limbs	life	lamps	boats

 Directions: Read the words in the four boxes. Circle two words that start with the uppercase and lowercase letter "l."
지도: 네 개의 상자에 있는 단어를 읽으십시오. 대문자와 소문자 "l"로 시작하는 두 단어에 동그라미를 치십시오.

teach	found
lake	Leave

branch	League
touch	loud

leech	Trees
dreams	Lamb

Lounge	leash
Bold	keeps

Young	Lean
lame	drawn

lime	Friends
Lawn	deep

Learn To Read English With Directions In Korean

Classwork

 Name: _____ Date: ___/___/_____ Score: _____

Appendix 13.0

Introduction of the Letter M/m

✓ Lesson Check Point

 Directions: Circle the correct letter "m" pair: uppercase and lowercase letters.
지도: 올바른 문자"m" 쌍에 동그라미를 치십시오: 대문자와 소문자.

    Mn   Nm   Um   Mm   Mw

 Directions: The uppercase letter "M" is in the first column. Look at the four letters in the row and circle the lowercase letter that matches the uppercase letter "M."
지도: 대문자"M"는 첫 번째 열에 있습니다. 행의 네 글자를 보고 대문자 "M"와 일치하는 소문자에 동그라미를 치십시오.

M	m	n	v	w
M	v	m	w	s
M	n	x	p	m
M	m	v	n	j

 Directions: The lowercase letter "m" is in the first column. Look at the four letters in the row and circle the uppercase letter that matches the lowercase letter "m."
지도: 소문자"m"는 첫 번째 열에 있습니다. 행의 네 글자를 보고 소문자 "m"와 일치하는 대문자에 동그라미를 치세요.

m	N	V	Z	M
m	K	M	N	U
m	W	V	M	X
m	N	M	V	W

Classwork

Name: _____ Date:___/___/_____ Score:_____

Appendix 13.0

Letter Recognition M/m

Uppercase and Lowercase Letter

✓ Lesson Check Point

Directions: Read each target word. Read the words in the row and circle the word that begins with a different letter.
지도: 각 대상 단어를 읽으십시오. 행에 있는 단어를 읽고 다른 문자로시작하는 단어에 동그라미를 치십시오.

Target Words				
1. maid	nose	mud	mock	mince
2. moon	make	mixed	used	mouth
3. mint	went	moist	map	musk
4. meal	meat	need	mole	Maine
5. must	mix	mail	moan	under

Directions: Read the words in the four boxes. Circle two words that start with the uppercase and lowercase letter "m."
지도: 네 개의 상자에 있는 단어를 읽으십시오. 대문자와 소문자"m"로 시작하는 두 단어에 동그라미를 치십시오.

none	Made
wind	mood

nod	vase
Miss	mean

night	Mouse
might	wage

mold	Much
Whose	Noun

mild	noise
watch	Mane

mumps	voice
Moat	nail

Classwork

 Name: _____ Date: ___/ ___/ _____ Score: _____

Appendix 14.0

Introduction of the Letter N/n

✓ Lesson Check Point

 Directions: Circle the correct letter "n" pair: uppercase and lowercase letters.
지도: 올바른 문자"n" 쌍에 동그라미를 치십시오: 대문자와 소문자.

    nM   nN   wN   Nu   Wn

 Directions: The uppercase letter "N" is in the first column. Look at the four letters in the row and circle the lowercase letter that matches the uppercase letter "N."
지도: 대문자"N"는 첫 번째 열에 있습니다. 행의 네 글자를 보고 대문자 "N"와 일치하는 소문자에 동그라미를 치십시오.

N	w	m	n	v
N	n	v	w	x
N	m	b	n	w
N	v	n	c	x

 Directions: The lowercase letter "n" is in the first column. Look at the four letters in the row and circle the uppercase letter that matches the lowercase letter "n."
지도: 소문자"n"는 첫 번째 열에 있습니다. 행의 네 글자를 보고 소문자 "n"와 일치하는 대문자에 동그라미를 치세요.

n	S	M	N	X
n	C	V	M	N
n	N	M	Z	V
n	M	N	X	W

Classwork

 Name: _____ Date:___/___/_____ Score:_____

Appendix 14.0

Letter Recognition N/n

Uppercase and Lowercase Letter

✓ **Lesson Check Point**

 Directions: Read each target word. Read the words in the row and circle the word that begins with a different letter.
지도: 각 대상 단어를 읽으십시오. 행에 있는 단어를 읽고 다른 문자로시작하는 단어에 동그라미를 치십시오.

Target Words				
1. neck	nine	news	milk	next
2. noon	used	neat	notch	niche
3. name	nice	note	wrong	nip
4. numb	none	new	nod	male
5. notice	nerve	unto	nuke	Nile

 Directions: Read the words in the four boxes. Circle two words that start with the uppercase and lowercase letter "n."
지도: 네 개의 상자에 있는 단어를 읽으십시오. 대문자와 소문자"n"로 시작하는 두 단어에 동그라미를 치십시오.

Mail	van
Nile	nail

Noise	under
wine	noon

flag	Nine
miss	nice

Noun	note
word	Mouth

night	mind
Next	set

news	win
united	Nod

Learn To Read English With Directions In Korean

Classwork

 Name: _____ Date: ___/___/_____ Score: _____

Appendix 15.0

Introduction of the Letter O/o

✓ **Lesson Check Point**

 Directions: Circle the correct letter "o" pair: uppercase and lowercase letters.
지도: 올바른 문자"o" 쌍에 동그라미를 치십시오: 대문자와 소문자.

    Oc   oO   Uo   pO   Qo

 Directions: The uppercase letter "O" is in the first column. Look at the four letters in the row and circle the lowercase letter that matches the uppercase letter "O."
지도: 대문자"O"는 첫 번째 열에 있습니다. 행의 네 글자를 보고 대문자 "O"와 일치하는 소문자에 동그라미를 치십시오.

O	s	p	g	o
O	c	o	b	j
O	q	d	c	o
O	o	g	q	h

 Directions: The lowercase letter "o" is in the first column. Look at the four letters in the row and circle the uppercase letter that matches the lowercase letter "o."
지도: 소문자"o"는 첫 번째 열에 있습니다. 행의 네 글자를 보고 소문자 "o"와 일치하는 대문자에 동그라미를 치세요.

o	Q	C	G	O
o	O	D	U	R
o	C	B	O	D
o	G	O	C	E

Classwork

 Name: _____ Date: ___/___/_____ Score: _____

Appendix 16.0

Introduction of the Letter P/p

✓ **Lesson Check Point**

 Directions: Circle the correct letter "p" pair: uppercase and lowercase letters.
지도: 올바른 문자"p" 쌍에 동그라미를 치십시오: 대문자와 소문자.

    Pp   Bp   Dp   Pg   Fp

 Directions: The uppercase letter "P" is in the first column. Look at the four letters in the row and circle the lowercase letter that matches the uppercase letter "P."
지도: 대문자"P"는 첫 번째 열에 있습니다. 행의 네 글자를 보고 대문자 "P"와 일치하는 소문자에 동그라미를 치십시오.

P	p	q	b	d
P	b	f	p	q
P	h	p	b	f
P	q	d	s	p

 Directions: The lowercase letter "p" is in the first column. Look at the four letters in the row and circle the uppercase letter that matches the lowercase letter "p."
지도: 소문자"p"는 첫 번째 열에 있습니다. 행의 네 글자를 보고 소문자 "p"와 일치하는 대문자에 동그라미를 치세요.。

p	Q	P	B	F
p	H	B	D	P
p	F	P	S	D
p	P	F	D	B

Classwork

Name: _____ Date: ___/___/_____ Score: _____

Appendix 16.0

Letter Recognition P/p

Uppercase and Lowercase Letter

✓ Lesson Check Point

Directions: Read each target word. Read the words in the row and circle the word that begins with a different letter.
지도: 각 대상 단어를 읽으십시오. 행에 있는 단어를 읽고 다른 문자로시작하는 단어에 동그라미를 치십시오.

Target Words				
1. pitch	pack	grow	pound	purse
2. plots	bind	plush	proud	plight
3. peace	plate	page	quest	prowl
4. pale	good	plant	poor	pull
5. punch	prude	quick	pike	pool

Directions: Read the words in the four boxes. Circle two words that start with the uppercase and lowercase letter "p."
지도: 네 개의 상자에 있는 단어를 읽으십시오. 대문자와 소문자"p"로 시작하는 두 단어에 동그라미를 치십시오.

Praise	quaint
youth	phase

point	Prince
quart	group

grew	purse
Prime	quiet

Pink	quick
place	jam

jump	quite
Paid	peace

young	peach
guess	Port

Learn To Read English With Directions In Korean   278   Copyrighted Material

Classwork

 Name: _____ Date: ___/___/_____   Score: _____

Appendix 17.0

Introduction of the Letter Q/q

✓ **Lesson Check Point**

 Directions: Circle the correct letter "q" pair: uppercase and lowercase letters.
지도: 올바른 문자 "q" 쌍에 동그라미를 치십시오: 대문자와 소문자.

    Qd   Gq   Oq   qQ   Qp

 Directions: The uppercase letter "Q" is in the first column. Look at the four letters in the row and circle the lowercase letter that matches the uppercase letter "Q."
지도: 대문자 "Q"는 첫 번째 열에 있습니다. 행의 네 글자를 보고 대문자 "Q"와 일치하는 소문자에 동그라미를 치십시오.

Q	g	h	p	q
Q	q	j	y	b
Q	p	q	b	d
Q	y	p	q	b

 Directions: The lowercase letter "q" is in the first column. Look at the four letters in the row and circle the uppercase letter that matches the lowercase letter "q."
지도: 소문자 "q"는 첫 번째 열에 있습니다. 행의 네 글자를 보고 소문자 "q"와 일치하는 대문자에 동그라미를 치세요.

q	D	O	Q	P
q	Q	A	D	O
q	O	C	G	Q
q	G	Q	C	O

Classwork

 Name: _____ Date: ___/___/_____ Score: _____

Appendix 17.0

Letter Recognition Q/q

Uppercase and Lowercase Letter

✓ **Lesson Check Point**

Directions: Read each target word. Read the words in the row and circle the word that begins with a different letter.

지도: 각 대상 단어를 읽으십시오. 행에 있는 단어를 읽고 다른 문자로시작하는 단어에 동그라미를 치십시오.

Target Words				
1. quack	quaint	quick	please	quiz
2. quilt	guess	quip	quire	quote
3. quirt	quirk	young	quit	quartz
4. quench	quite	quiet	jump	quince
5. quake	quota	quail	quest	guest

Directions: Read the words in the four boxes. Circle two words that start with the uppercase and lowercase letter "q."

지도: 네 개의 상자에 있는 단어를 읽으십시오. 대문자와 소문자"q"로 시작하는 두 단어에 동그라미를 치십시오.

pajamas	Qualm
quality	Orchid

jacket	peanut
quarrel	Quarter

joint	quicken
oxygen	Quartz

quest	jumper
Quiver	yours

quote	Quotient
picture	Ocean

quick	painter
young	Quebec

Learn To Read English With Directions In Korean   280   Copyrighted Material

Classwork

 Name: _____ Date: ___/___/_____ Score: _____

Appendix 18.0

Introduction of the Letter R/r

✓ Lesson Check Point

 Directions: Circle the correct letter "r" pair: uppercase and lowercase letters.
지도: 올바른 문자"r" 쌍에 동그라미를 치십시오: 대문자와 소문자.

    Rz   rR   jR   rE   Fr

 Directions: The uppercase letter "R" is in the first column. Look at the four letters in the row and circle the lowercase letter that matches the uppercase letter "R."
지도: 대문자"R"는 첫 번째 열에 있습니다. 행의 네 글자를 보고 대문자 "R"와 일치하는 소문자에 동그라미를 치십시오.

R	x	r	v	u
R	r	x	z	c
R	b	h	c	r
R	n	z	r	s

 Directions: The lowercase letter "r" is in the first column. Look at the four letters in the row and circle the uppercase letter that matches the lowercase letter "r."
지도: 소문자"r"는 첫 번째 열에 있습니다. 행의 네 글자를 보고 소문자 "r"와 일치하는 대문자에 동그라미를 치세요.

r	Y	U	R	Z
r	R	H	C	M
r	U	N	F	R
r	M	R	D	O

Learn To Read English With Directions In Korean   Copyrighted Material

Classwork

Name: _____ Date: ___/___/_____ Score: _____

Appendix 18.0

Letter Recognition R/r

Uppercase and Lowercase Letter

✓ Lesson Check Point

Directions: Read each target word. Read the words in the row and circle the word that begins with a different letter.
지도: 각 대상 단어를 읽으십시오. 행에 있는 단어를 읽고 다른 문자로시 작하는 단어에 동그라미를 치십시오.

Target Words				
1. race	roach	reel	match	rains
2. rode	nurse	range	roam	rule
3. rinse	ranch	mouse	robe	reed
4. raise	rend	rock	rank	cease
5. ripping	cards	read	rack	rope

Directions: Read the words in the four boxes. Circle two words that start with the uppercase and lowercase letter "r."
지도: 네 개의 상자에 있는 단어를 읽으십시오. 대문자와 소문자 ""로 시작하는 두 단어에 동그라미를 치십시오.

rate	moose
Piece	Rice

rob	Rave
nose	mother

Part	Roar
mouse	rhythm

Pat	maple
roost	Rat

team	Price
rope	Rich

dream	Room
ramp	neck

Learn To Read English With Directions In Korean

Classwork

 Name: _____ Date:___/___/_____ Score:_____

Appendix 19.0

Introduction of the Letter S/s

✓ Lesson Check Point

 Directions: Circle the correct letter "s" pair: uppercase and lowercase letters.
지도: 올바른 문자"s" 쌍에 동그라미를 치십시오: 대문자와 소문자.

    sA   sB   Zs   Cs   sS

 Directions: The uppercase letter "S" is in the first column. Look at the four letters in the row and circle the lowercase letter that matches the uppercase letter "S."
지도: 대문자"S"는 첫 번째 열에 있습니다. 행의 네 글자를 보고 대문자 "S"와 일치하는 소문자에 동그라미를 치십시오.

S	c	o	d	s
S	s	c	u	o
S	o	a	s	c
S	u	s	c	o

 Directions: The lowercase letter "s" is in the first column. Look at the four letters in the row and circle the uppercase letter that matches the lowercase letter "s."
지도: 소문자"s"는 첫 번째 열에 있습니다. 행의 네 글자를 보고 소문자 "s"와 일치하는 대문자에 동그라미를 치세요.

s	G	S	O	C
s	Q	C	U	S
s	S	U	O	C
s	Z	Q	S	V

Learn To Read English With Directions In Korean

Classwork

Name: _____ Date: ___/___/_____ Score: _____

Appendix 19.0

Letter Recognition S/s

Uppercase and Lowercase Letter

✓ Lesson Check Point

Directions: Read each target word. Read the words in the row and circle the word that begins with a different letter.
지도: 각 대상 단어를 읽으십시오. 행에 있는 단어를 읽고 다른 문자로시 작하는 단어에 동그라미를 치십시오.

Target Words				
1. smart	soft	chart	smith	shop
2. sail	opens	saw	skit	soil
3. skill	smooth	shoot	seat	van
4. source	soup	side	zero	sight
5. sky	snooze	cake	short	smell

Directions: Read the words in the four boxes. Circle two words that start with the uppercase and lowercase letter "s."
지도: 네 개의 상자에 있는 단어를 읽으십시오. 대문자와 소문자""로 시작하는 두 단어에 동그라미를 치십시오.

zero	Six
shore	cone

Shield	cup
sink	zoo

shame	Said
zap	clean

Cross	slurp
Shine	win

none	child
soap	Snail

camp	song
zebra	Shake

Classwork

Name: _____ Date: ___/___/_____ Score: _____

Appendix 20.0

Introduction of the Letter T/t

✓ **Lesson Check Point**

 Directions: Circle the correct letter "t" pair: uppercase and lowercase letters.
지도: 올바른 문자 "t" 쌍에 동그라미를 치십시오: 대문자와 소문자.

| Tf | tE | Tt | tF | iT |

 Directions: The uppercase letter "T" is in the first column. Look at the four letters in the row and circle the lowercase letter that matches the uppercase letter "T."
지도: 대문자 "T"는 첫 번째 열에 있습니다. 행의 네 글자를 보고 대문자 "T"와 일치하는 소문자에 동그라미를 치십시오.

T	t	h	f	d
T	b	f	t	h
T	l	t	b	f
T	h	d	b	t

 Directions: The lowercase letter "t" is in the first column. Look at the four letters in the row and circle the uppercase letter that matches the lowercase letter "t."
지도: 소문자 "t"는 첫 번째 열에 있습니다. 행의 네 글자를 보고 소문자 "t"와 일치하는 대문자에 동그라미를 치세요.

t	F	T	H	E
t	T	B	E	F
t	H	B	T	Y
t	R	F	S	T

Classwork

 Name: _____ Date: ___/___/_____ Score: _____

Appendix 20.0

Letter Recognition T/t

Uppercase and Lowercase Letter

✓ **Lesson Check Point**

 Directions: Read each target word. Read the words in the row and circle the word that begins with a different letter.
지도: 각 대상 단어를 읽으십시오. 행에 있는 단어를 읽고 다른 문자로시작하는 단어에 동그라미를 치십시오.

Target Words				
1. twin	that	day	trust	talk
2. tooth	tight	team	top	face
3. tempt	key	time	trash	tweed
4. torch	though	their	temp	live
5. treat	thick	twice	herd	thief

 Directions: Read the words in the four boxes. Circle two words that start with the uppercase and lowercase letter "t."
지도: 네 개의 상자에 있는 단어를 읽으십시오. 대문자와 소문자 "t"로 시작하는 두 단어에 동그라미를 치십시오.

Floor	Trade
tear	draw

horses	toil
lunch	Track

tease	keep
Toll	load

Text	Pie
troop	Joy

Egg	lone
theme	Trip

taste	pants
beach	Think

Classwork

 Name: _____   Date: ___/___/_____   Score: _____

Appendix 21.0

Introduction of the Letter U/u

✓ **Lesson Check Point**

 Directions: Circle the correct letter "u" pair: uppercase and lowercase letters.
지도: 올바른 문자"u" 쌍에 동그라미를 치십시오: 대문자와 소문자.

    uU   Yu   Gu   Uv   Au

 Directions: The uppercase letter "U" is in the first column. Look at the four letters in the row and circle the lowercase letter that matches the uppercase letter "U."
지도: 대문자"U"는 첫 번째 열에 있습니다. 행의 네 글자를 보고 대문자 "U"와 일치하는 소문자에 동그라미를 치십시오.

U	u	v	c	y
U	h	x	u	z
U	j	b	v	u
U	s	u	g	a

 Directions: The lowercase letter "u" is in the first column. Look at the four letters in the row and circle the uppercase letter that matches the lowercase letter "u."
지도: 소문자"u"는 첫 번째 열에 있습니다. 행의 네 글자를 보고 소문자 "u"와 일치하는 대문자에 동그라미를 치세요.

u	Y	T	U	Z
u	U	B	N	Y
u	C	Q	U	D
u	J	V	G	U

Classwork

 Name: _____ Date: ____/____/_____ Score: _____

Appendix 22.0

Introduction of the Letter V/v

✓ **Lesson Check Point**

 Directions: Circle the correct letter "v" pair: uppercase and lowercase letters.
지도: 올바른 문자"v" 쌍에 동그라미를 치십시오: 대문자와 소문자.

| vW | Vu | Cv | Vv | Wv |

 Directions: The uppercase letter "V" is in the first column. Look at the four letters in the row and circle the lowercase letter that matches the uppercase letter "V."
지도: 대문자"V"는 첫 번째 열에 있습니다. 행의 네 글자를 보고 대문자 "V"와 일치하는 소문자에 동그라미를 치십시오.

V	w	v	x	y
V	y	w	n	v
V	v	x	y	u
V	x	z	v	w

 Directions: The lowercase letter "v" is in the first column. Look at the four letters in the row and circle the uppercase letter that matches the lowercase letter "v."
지도: 소문자"v"는 첫 번째 열에 있습니다. 행의 네 글자를 보고 소문자 "v"와 일치하는 대문자에 동그라미를 치세요.

v	X	Z	V	Y
v	Y	W	X	V
v	V	Y	N	M
v	W	V	X	C

Classwork

Name: _____ Date:___/___/_____ Score:_____

Appendix 22.0

Letter Recognition V/v

Uppercase and Lowercase Letter

✓ Lesson Check Point

Directions: Read each target word. Read the words in the row and circle the word that begins with a different letter.
지도: 각 대상 단어를 읽으십시오. 행에 있는 단어를 읽고 다른 문자로시작하는 단어에 동그라미를 치십시오.

Target Words				
1. voice	volt	wool	vase	verse
2. verb	vest	vow	vogue	used
3. vain	west	veil	vault	vine
4. view	void	mouse	versed	vile
5. vote	vex	voiced	wig	vein

Directions: Read the words in the four boxes. Circle two words that start with the uppercase and lowercase letter "v."
지도: 네 개의 상자에 있는 단어를 읽으십시오. 대문자와 소문자 "v"로 시작하는 두 단어에 동그라미를 치십시오.

skill	vouch
Vamp	Wrote

vague	Van
rose	name

whiz	valve
mail	Vice

Vent	cove
Weep	verge

vane	Very
must	goat

Visit	card
vet	West

Learn To Read English With Directions In Korean   289   Copyrighted Material

Classwork

 Name: _____ Date: ___/___/_____ Score: _____

Appendix 23.0

Introduction of the Letter W/w

✓ Lesson Check Point

 Directions: Circle the correct letter "w" pair: uppercase and lowercase letters.
지도: 올바른 문자"w" 쌍에 동그라미를 치십시오: 대문자와 소문자.

    wU   Ww   Xw   Vw   Wv

 Directions: The uppercase letter "W" is in the first column. Look at the four letters in the row and circle the lowercase letter that matches the uppercase letter "W."
지도: 대문자"W"는 첫 번째 열에 있습니다. 행의 네 글자를 보고 대문자 "W"와 일치하는 소문자에 동그라미를 치십시오.

W	x	w	v	z
W	v	z	w	y
W	w	y	v	m
W	n	v	y	w

 Directions: The lowercase letter "w" is in the first column. Look at the four letters in the row and circle the uppercase letter that matches the lowercase letter "w."
지도: 소문자"w"는 첫 번째 열에 있습니다. 행의 네 글자를 보고 소문자 "w"와 일치하는 대문자에 동그라미를 치세요.

w	V	W	Y	M
w	X	Y	V	W
w	W	V	X	M
w	Y	F	W	X

Classwork

Name: _____ Date: ___/___/_____ Score: _____

Appendix 23.0

Letter Recognition W/w

Uppercase and Lowercase Letter

✓ **Lesson Check Point**

Directions: Read each target word. Read the words in the row and circle the word that begins with a different letter.
지도: 각 대상 단어를 읽으십시오. 행에 있는 단어를 읽고 다른 문자로시작하는 단어에 동그라미를 치십시오.

Target Words				
1. wind	west	vacuum	whole	waste
2. wrote	night	wink	wolf	wish
3. which	wrap	whom	were	vessel
4. wept	whale	card	whose	wide
5. wash	wrench	watch	word	zebra

Directions: Read the words in the four boxes. Circle two words that start with the uppercase and lowercase letter "w."
지도: 네 개의 상자에 있는 단어를 읽으십시오. 대문자와 소문자 "w"로 시작하는 두 단어에 동그라미를 치십시오.

crow	Work
visitor	wave

wheat	nerve
zoom	Wax

Village	cars
wild	Wheel

will	x-rays
Would	Nile

Worth	when
violet	Never

corn	ways
Wine	vintage

Learn To Read English With Directions In Korean   291   Copyrighted Material

Classwork

 Name: _____ Date: ___/___/_____ Score: _____

Appendix 24.0

Introduction of the Letter X/x

✓ **Lesson Check Point**

 Directions: Circle the correct letter "x" pair: uppercase and lowercase letters.
지도: 올바른 문자"x" 쌍에 동그라미를 치십시오: 대문자와 소문자.

    Xw   xY   xX   Sx   Kx

 Directions: The uppercase letter "X" is in the first column. Look at the four letters in the row and circle the lowercase letter that matches the uppercase letter "X."
지도: 대문자"X"는 첫 번째 열에 있습니다. 행의 네 글자를 보고 대문자 "X"와 일치하는 소문자에 동그라미를 치십시오.

X	k	x	y	z
X	v	w	x	m
X	x	z	e	s
X	v	z	h	x

 Directions: The lowercase letter "x" is in the first column. Look at the four letters in the row and circle the uppercase letter that matches the lowercase letter "x."
지도: 소문자"x"는 첫 번째 열에 있습니다. 행의 네 글자를 보고 소문자 "x"와 일치하는 대문자에 동그라미를 치세요.

x	K	X	Z	M
x	W	K	V	X
x	X	M	K	Y
x	V	Y	X	Z

Classwork

Name: _____   Date: ____/____/_____   Score: _____

Appendix 24.0

Letter Recognition X/x

Uppercase and Lowercase Letter

✓ **Lesson Check Point**

Directions: Read each target word. Read the words in the row and circle the word that does not contain a letter "x."
지도: 각 대상 단어를 읽으십시오. 행에 있는 단어를 읽고 문자"x"가 포함되지 않은 단어에 동그라미를 치십시오.

Target Words				
1. fix	wax	excite	sing	flax
2. box	taxes	expo	foxes	cold
3. flex	ox	night	taxi	exalt
4. exam	toxin	axle	sixty	loving
5. text	vex	young	next	coax

Directions: Read the words in the four boxes. Circle two words that start with the uppercase and lowercase letter "x."
지도: 네 개의 상자에 있는 단어를 읽으십시오. 대문자와 소문자"x"로 시작하는 두 단어에 동그라미를 치십시오.

vogue	xylems		youth	voiced		kept	Xanthous
Xanthine	kid		xanthone	Xenograft		one	x-axis

xylem	voiced		Xyster	know		Xylene	xylose
Xerox	keys		yes	xylan		moose	view

Learn To Read English With Directions In Korean   293   Copyrighted Material

Classwork

 Name: _____ Date: ___/___/_____ Score: _____

Appendix 25.0

Introduction of the Letter Y/y

✓ **Lesson Check Point**

 Directions: Circle the correct letter "y" pair: uppercase and lowercase letters.
지도: 올바른 문자"y" 쌍에 동그라미를 치십시오: 대문자와 소문자.

    Yx   yY   Yz   Ky   Vy

 Directions: The uppercase letter "Y" is in the first column. Look at the four letters in the row and circle the lowercase letter that matches the uppercase letter "Y."
지도: 대문자"Y"는 첫 번째 열에 있습니다. 행의 네 글자를 보고 대문자 "Y"와 일치하는 소문자에 동그라미를 치십시오.

Y	v	y	b	x
Y	x	z	y	u
Y	y	x	z	w
Y	x	z	v	y

 Directions: The lowercase letter "y" is in the first column. Look at the four letters in the row and circle the uppercase letter that matches the lowercase letter "y."
지도: 소문자"y"는 첫 번째 열에 있습니다. 행의 네 글자를 보고 소문자 "y"와 일치하는 대문자에 동그라미를 치세요.

y	V	X	Z	Y
y	Y	V	X	Z
y	W	Y	X	M
y	U	M	Y	X

Classwork

 Name: _____ Date: ___/___/_____ Score: _____

Appendix 25.0

Letter Recognition Y/y

Uppercase and Lowercase Letter

✓ **Lesson Check Point**

 Directions: Read each target word. Read the words in the row and circle the word that begins with a different letter.
지도: 각 대상 단어를 읽으십시오. 행에 있는 단어를 읽고 다른 문자로시작하는 단어에 동그라미를 치십시오.

Target Words				
1. yield	grown	yogurt	yam	yeast
2. yacht	jeep	yolk	yucca	yawn
3. yuppie	yodel	young	quick	your
4. yellow	yelp	please	yummy	yoga
5. yourself	yank	yes	yo-yo	game

 Directions: Read the words in the four boxes. Circle two words that start with the uppercase and lowercase letter "y."
지도: 네 개의 상자에 있는 단어를 읽으십시오. 대문자와 소문자"y"로 시작하는 두 단어에 동그라미를 치십시오.

gum	jump
yelp	Youth

Yarn	quill
paint	yells

jet	You
globe	yaw

jog	yak
Year	grace

Yet	yams
judge	glow

yawn	June
Yeast	peach

Learn To Read English With Directions In Korean   295   Copyrighted Material

Classwork

 Name: _____ Date:___/___/_____ Score:_____

Appendix 26.0

Introduction of the Letter Z/z

✓ **Lesson Check Point**

 Directions: Circle the correct letter "z" pair: uppercase and lowercase letters.
지도: 올바른 문자"z" 쌍에 동그라미를 치십시오: 대문자와 소문자.

zZ　　　　Nz　　　　Zn　　　　zM　　　　zA

 Directions: The uppercase letter "Z" is in the first column. Look at the four letters in the row and circle the lowercase letter that matches the uppercase letter "Z."
지도: 대문자"Z"는 첫 번째 열에 있습니다. 행의 네 글자를 보고대문자 "Z"와 일치하는 소문자에 동그라미를 치십시오.

Z	n	x	z	t
Z	v	z	x	w
Z	m	w	s	z
Z	z	v	w	n

 Directions: The lowercase letter "z" is in the first column. Look at the four letters in the row and circle the uppercase letter that matches the lowercase letter "z."
지도: 소문자"z"는 첫 번째 열에 있습니다. 행의 네 글자를 보고소문자 "z"와 일치하는 대문자에 동그라미를 치세요.

z	B	V	Z	N
z	W	Z	X	U
z	Z	S	W	V
z	A	N	X	Z

Classwork

 Name: _____   Date: ___/ ___/ _____   Score: _____

Appendix 26.0

Letter Recognition Z/z

Uppercase and Lowercase Letter

✓ **Lesson Check Point**

 Directions: Read each target word. Read the words in the row and circle the word that begins with a different letter.
지도: 각 대상 단어를 읽으십시오. 행에 있는 단어를 읽고 다른 문자로시작하는 단어에 동그라미를 치십시오.

Target Words				
1. zebu	zap	zebra	cage	zoo
2. zones	seals	zany	zeal	zest
3. zip	zing	zero	zinc	flesh
4. Zhan	zoom	moon	ziti	zonal
5. zest	sung	zone	zoos	zebra

 Directions: Read the words in the four boxes. Circle two words that start with the uppercase and lowercase letter "z."
지도: 네 개의 상자에 있는 단어를 읽으십시오. 대문자와 소문자"z"로 시작하는 두 단어에 동그라미를 치십시오.

cents	Zeta
zing	sea

mix	zap
Zip	sick

Zoom	zit
index	wind

zinc	remix
Zipper	cents

nice	Plant
ziti	Zone

rest	Zoo
eggs	zoom

Classwork

**Your Next Step:
Learn To Read English Vowels With Directions In Korean**

www.ingramcontent.com/pod-product-compliance
Lightning Source LLC
Chambersburg PA
CBHW080800300426
44114CB00020B/2775